HOMEWORK

Research on Teaching Monograph Series

HOMEWORK

Harris Cooper

UNIVERSITY OF MISSOURI—COLUMBIA

Longman
New York & London

Homework

Longman Inc., 95 Church Street, White Plains, N.Y. 10601

Associated companies:
Longman Group Ltd., London
Longman Cheshire Pty., Melbourne
Longman Paul Pty., Auckland
Copp Clark Pitman, Toronto
Pitman Publishing Inc., New York

Executive editor: Raymond T. O'Connell
Production editor: Helen B. Ambrosio
Text art: Hal Keith
Production supervisor: Judith Stern

"The Scientific Guidelines for Integrative Research Reviews," Harris M. Cooper.
Review of Educational Research, 52(2), Summer 1982.

Homework, *Timothy Keith. Kappa Delta Pi © 1986. Reprinted with permission.*

"Homework—And Why," David A. England and Joannis K. Flatley. Fastback
#218, 1985.

Library of Congress Cataloging-in-Publication Data
Cooper, Harris M.
  Homework.

  (Research on teaching monograph series)
  Bibliography: p.
  Includes index.
  1. Homework. 2. Educational literature—United
States. I. Title. II. Series.
LB1048.C66 1990   371.3′028′12   88-9255

ISBN 0-8013-0208-0
ISBN 0-8013-0207-2 (pbk.)

88 89 90 91 92 93 9 8 7 6 5 4 3 2 1

For Seth and Emily, my homework

Contents

PART IV VARIATIONS IN THE HOMEWORK PROCESS

PART V IMPLICATIONS FOR PRACTICE AND RESEARCH

Foreword

Homework has been a popular topic among education critics and would-be school reformers in recent years. Comparisons of American schooling practices with those of Europe or Japan frequently conclude that American students do not do enough homework, and calls for more homework commonly appear in the literature of the back-to-basics movement and the school improvement movement, as well as in the school reform guidelines issued by various commissions and governmental agencies. Seldom do the writers of these documents cite any research in support of their policy recommendations, let alone review the research base in detail. In effect, they take it for granted that the purposes of homework are clear, that its effectiveness is well established, and that teachers will know what homework to assign and how to ensure that the work is appropriately checked and followed up.

The reality is much different. As Harris Cooper shows in this comprehensive review, only a modest body of scholarly work on the topic of homework has been completed to date, and the knowledge base that it has produced, although useful, does not support the unqualified enthusiasm for homework that typifies current policy advocacy. As with so many other educational policy issues, it appears that we need less heat and more light on the topic.

Cooper's comprehensive analysis and synthesis of the scholarly literature on homework in this volume have several features worth noting. First, this study is methodologically sophisticated. Cooper has been an important contributor to our knowledge of the logic and procedures to follow when conducting scholarly reviews of research literature, and in this volume he provides a model of the sophisticated application of those guidelines. He combines clarity of definition of terms and rules for inclusion or exclusion of evidence, a historical purview to provide context, and detailed analysis of individual studies with the latest in meta-analysis and related statistical techniques for drawing conclusions from weighted combinations of data sets.

Second, the material is interesting and informative. Readers who were under the impression that the currently popular thinking about homework has always been the conventional wisdom will be surprised to find that views about the purposes and value of homework have been sharply different in different historical eras, and have even included the view that homework is counterproductive and should be avoided. Readers will also find their own views of homework becoming more differentiated in response to Cooper's analyses, which indicate, for example, that homework is more likely to contribute to a gain in student achievement at some grade levels than at others, or that homework should be construed as a tool for individualizing instruction, not only as a tool for accomplishing common goals with the class as a whole.

Finally, although the review shows that the database on homework is limited and that more research is needed (in particular, on what kinds of homework to assign and how to manage checking and follow-up procedures), it also indicates that the existing research base does support a variety of conclusions about how much and what kinds of homework assignments should be made, for what purposes, and to what kinds of students. After reviewing the evidence for these conclusions, Cooper pulls them together in a final chapter in the form of policy guidelines for school districts, individual schools, and individual teachers. Educators can act on these guidelines with the confidence that they are supported by empirical research findings, not just theoretical rationales.

In sum, this is a state-of-the-art piece of work, both as a model of conceptual and methodological sophistication in reviewing scholarly literature and as a critical review and synthesis of the extant literature on homework. It will be the definitive source on the topic for years to come. I want to commend Professor Cooper for his achievement and to recommend his book to readers interested both in sophisticated thinking and in research-based information about the role of homework in our schools.

Jere E. Brophy
Michigan State University

Preface

How much time should children spend doing homework?
Should elementary school children do any homework at all?
Do high achievers or low achievers benefit most from homework?
What role should parents play in the homework process?
Does homework improve students' attitudes, or does it lead to burnout?

Homework is a source of controversy. Educational policymakers, teachers, parents, and students argue over the questions posed above, and many others. Sometimes the debate embodies broad philosophical disagreements about the schooling process. Sometimes the difference of opinion is very specific and concrete. Sometimes teachers, parents, and students simply disagree over how young people ought to spend their non-school time. Because it sits at the interface of the school and the home, homework affects and is affected by both environments.

One way to help untangle the debates surrounding homework is to look at the empirical research. Systematic examination of homework began nearly 75 years ago, yet the 100 or so studies that have been conducted are more frequently used to fuel debates than to resolve them. In this book, I gather, summarize, and integrate the empirical evidence concerning the effects both of homework per se and of specific homework procedures.

The book is written with three goals in mind. First, I hope my conclusions help school administrators and teachers develop homework policies that benefit students. Three chapters are especially relevant for this purpose. In Chapter 1 the reader will find an introduction to the issues surrounding homework. Most readers will discover that the homework process is more complex than they had originally thought. In Chapter 10 a nontechnical summary of homework research is presented. This chapter can be read and understood without reference to the material in Chapters 2 through 9. Chapter 11 examines some existing homework policy guidelines. The policies are evaluated in light of the findings of the review. My own recommendations, based on the research integration, are also offered.

Second, I hope the review helps future homework researchers identify areas that are most in need of investigation. Researchers will be especially interested in Chapters 5 through 9, which present detailed summaries of past research examining the effects of homework and variations in the homework process. Chapter 12 presents my recommendations concerning fruitful avenues for the next generation of homework research.

Finally, I hope the procedures I used to integrate the research prove instructive to others who are interested in making sense of social science literatures. I have tried to apply state-of-the-art techniques for gathering and integrating the homework research. Chapters 3 and 4 describe what I did, and Chapter 2 summarizes past reviews of the homework literature.

ACKNOWLEDGMENTS

A project of this kind always reflects the labor of numerous individuals. Cathy Luebbering typed endless drafts of the manuscript, created the graphics, and helped with document retrieval. Alan Strathman spent many hours in the University of Missouri library tracking down twice the number of books and articles referred to here. Robert Rosenthal helped the author with the calculation of effect sizes. Larry Hedges checked the statistical analysis procedures. James Guinn, Pamela Miller, and Alan Strathman helped with the preliminary categorization of studies. Brad Bushman served as a second coder for purposes of checking coding reliability. Jere Brophy critically reviewed the entire manuscript. Peter Hall made critical comments on the homework process and my conception of it. Gail Hinkel edited the manuscript. I am greatly indebted to these people for putting substance in and taking mistakes out of this book. If there are still mistakes, the mistakes are mine.

Primary financial support for the project was provided by the National Science Foundation Directorate for Science and Engineering Education under Grant No. MDR-8550343. The Center for Research in Social Behavior at the University of Missouri also provided support during the researching and writing of this book. However, the opinions, findings, conclusions, and recommendations expressed in this book are mine and do not necessarily reflect the views of the National Science Foundation or the Center.

HOMEWORK

Part I

Introduction

1

Defining and Refining the Notion of Homework

The completion of a homework assignment involves the complex interaction of more influences than any other part of the schooling process. Teachers begin and end the process in the classroom. They can structure and monitor assignments in a multitude of ways. Individual student differences play a major role because, more than classroom-bound activities, homework allows more personal discretion about whether, when, and how to complete the assignment. Parents and siblings often participate in assignments, sometimes voluntarily, sometimes by design. The home environment influences the process by creating an ambiance conducive to or inhibitive of study. Students often work on home assignments together, so there is a role for peers too. And finally, the broader community plays a role by providing other leisure activities that compete for the student's time.

Perhaps this multiplicity of influences explains the diversity of opinion about whether homework is an effective learning device. At any moment during the past half-century, the educational literature has contained contemporaneous arguments for and against the practice. But at different times the proponents and opponents of homework have alternately held sway (see Foyle, 1984, for an extended review of shifting viewpoints throughout the twentieth century).

ATTITUDES TOWARD HOMEWORK DURING THE PAST HALF-CENTURY

Early in the twentieth century, homework was believed to be an important means for disciplining children's minds (Brink, 1937). The mind was viewed

3

as a muscle. Memorization—most often of concrete material like multiplication tables, names, and dates—not only led to knowledge acquisition but was also good mental exercise. Because memorization could easily be accomplished at home, homework was a key schooling strategy.

By the 1940s a reaction against homework set in. Developing problemsolving ability, as opposed to learning through drill, became a central task of education. The use of homework as punishment or to enhance memorization skills was questioned. There was greater emphasis on developing student initiative and interest in learning. In addition, the life adjustment movement viewed home study as an intrusion on students' time to pursue other private, at-home activities (LaConte, 1981).

The trend toward less homework was reversed in the late 1950s, after the Russians launched the Sputnik satellite. Americans became concerned that a lack of rigor in the educational system was leaving children unprepared to face a complex technological future and to compete against our ideological adversaries. Sputnik precipitated a greater emphasis on knowledge of subject matter, and homework was viewed as a means for accelerating the pace of knowledge acquisition.

By the mid-1960s the cycle again reversed itself. Homework came to be seen as one sign of excessive pressure on students to achieve. Contemporary learning theories were again cited in questioning the value of most approaches to homework. And yet again, the possible detrimental emotional consequences of too much homework were brought to the fore. For example, Wildman (1968) wrote: "Whenever homework crowds out social experience, outdoor recreation, and creative activities, and whenever it usurps time devoted to sleep, it is not meeting the basic needs of children and adolescents" (p. 203).

CONTEMPORARY ATTITUDES TOWARD HOMEWORK

Today, views of homework have again shifted toward a more positive assessment. In the wake of declining achievement-test scores, increasing concern for traditional values, and the general alarm sounded by *A Nation at Risk: The Imperative for Educational Reform* (National Commission on Excellence in Education, 1983), public perception of the value of homework is undergoing its third renaissance in the past 50 years.

The seventeenth annual Gallup poll of attitudes toward the public schools (Gallup, 1985) revealed that 40% of adults sampled believed that elementary school children should be assigned more homework, while 38% felt that present levels were adequate. For high school students, 47% felt more homework was in order, while 31% disagreed. The percentage difference between those endorsing more homework and those not endorsing more homework was smaller among parents of children attending public schools, but dramatically larger among parents of children in private school (53% of elementary school parents wanted more homework, while 22% were against more homework; for high school parents, the percentages were 60% versus 19%, respectively). Parents whose children were receiving average or below-average grades were more likely to endorse more homework, as were nonwhite parents and residents of inner cities.

Several large school districts have conducted polls of their students, teachers, and parents. Some of these document the increasingly favorable attitude toward homework. For instance, the Los Angeles County School District annually conducts a survey of its staff and parents. More than 3,000 teachers and 9,000 parents, selected using random and stratified sampling procedures, participated in the 1984 and 1985 surveys (LAUSD, 1984, 1985). In 1984, 85% of teachers approved of upgraded standards for homework. In 1985, the figure rose to 89%. In 1984, about 2.7% of parents used the opportunity to make open-ended comments to recommend that the amount of homework should be increased. In 1985, 7% of parents made an unsolicited call for more homework.

In its annual survey, Edmonton Public Schools has been asking children in elementary grades (K–6) the question "Does homework help you learn?" In 1985, 81% of the children answered "yes," compared with 78% in 1981 (Edmonton Public Schools, 1985).

OVERVIEW OF THE PRESENT REVIEW

The role of research in forming, or informing, the attitudes of teachers, parents, and policymakers toward homework has been minimal. The lack of effect can be attributed to two sources. First, because of the number and complexity of influences on the effectiveness of homework, no simple, general finding that proves or disproves the utility of homework has been forthcoming. Instead, variations in the context of homework studies have often led to divergent results. Second, because research on homework is difficult and costly, few studies of high quality have been conducted. Good research involves the random assignment of homework and no-homework manipulations (or variations on the homework theme) to ongoing classrooms for extended periods of time with appropriate follow-up assessments of effectiveness. This type of research requires overcoming logistic and perhaps even ethical barriers so difficult that it has rarely, if ever, been attempted.

Despite these shortcomings, research on homework has often been cited to support one viewpoint or another. Furthermore, even though research is sparse, it is ample enough that persons hoping to substantiate a point of view can find a few studies to support whatever position they desire. And perhaps most regrettably, research has not helped define the role of homework in schooling, or helped even out the oscillations in public attitudes.

This book presents a comprehensive review of research concerning the effectiveness of homework. An attempt was made to collect all research conducted in the past 50 years that examined the effects of homework or that compared variations in homework assignments, processes, and contexts. Furthermore, the project was undertaken with no strong predisposition regarding homework's overall effectiveness. Instead, the goal of the research synthesis was to gather, summarize, and integrate the relevant research guided by only one bias—that the review would favor the results of studies with the soundest methodology. I hoped that this integration might (a) help clarify conceptually the issues surrounding homework and its effectiveness, (b) identify issues about which research-based conclusions can be drawn, (c) make policy recommendations based on what is and is not known about homework, and (d) suggest issues that future researchers might profitably pursue.

The book is divided into several parts. Part I, the introduction, contains two chapters. In Chapter 1, (a) a general definition of homework is presented, along with suggestions concerning important distinctions in homework assignments, (b) the possible effects of homework, both positive and negative, are outlined, and (c) an attempt is made to develop a temporal model of the homework process—including classroom, home, student, and subject matter variables. Chapter 2 includes a review of the conclusions of past attempts to synthesize the homework literature.

Part II describes how the literature review was carried out. The two chapters contain information on the literature-searching strategy, the methodological distinctions among studies that were examined as possible influences on study results, and procedures and conventions employed when statistical techniques were used to synthesize the results of studies.

Part III examines research on the effects of homework per se. Chapters 5 and 6 describe studies in which students doing homework were compared with students doing no homework or with students doing supervised study. Chapter 7 reviews reseach that examined the relation between academic outcomes and the amount of time a student spends on homework.

Part IV looks at how variations in assignments might influence the effects of homework. In Chapter 8, the content of homework and responsiveness to student individual differences are examined for their effect on the impact of homework. Chapter 9 looks at research on home and community factors and classroom follow-up. Parts III and IV both provide detailed descriptions of individual studies and summaries of the studies' results.

Part V assesses the implications of this review's findings for practice and future research. Chapter 10 is a nontechnical but exhaustive summary of the research contained in Parts III and IV. Chapter 11 addresses the policy implications of the review, and Chapter 12 makes suggestions about improving future homework research.

This book is written so that audiences with different purposes can focus on different chapters and still have their questions answered. For instance, a teacher or principal can get a broad overview of the homework research and its implications for the classroom by focusing on this introductory chapter and on the chapters in Part V that summarize the results of the review and relate them to homework policies. A reader interested in conducting a replication of this review or in learning how to apply recent advances in reviewing methodology would benefit most from Chapter 2's review of past reviews and the procedures described in Part II. Those hoping to contribute to the primary homework literature will want to attend especially to Parts III and IV, as well as to the final chapter on how to improve research. Needless to say, the most complete understanding of both research results and methods will be obtained from carefully reading the entire book.

DEFINITION OF HOMEWORK

For the purposes of this review, homework is defined as tasks assigned to students by school teachers that are meant to be carried out during non-school hours. Students may complete homework assignments during study hall, library time, or even during subsequent classes. However, this definition explicitly excludes (a) in-school guided study, (b) home study courses delivered through the mail, television, or on audio- or videocassette, and (c) extracurricular activities, such as sports teams and clubs.

Distinctions in Homework Assignments

Homework can be classified according to (a) its amount, (b) its purpose, (c) the skill area utilized, (d) the degree of individualization, (e) the degree of choice permitted the student, (f) the completion deadline, and (g) its social context. Although numerous categorizations of homework have been offered, these classifications describe the major distinctions proposed by most writers and researchers. Table 1.1 summarizes the distinctions in homework.

The *amount* of homework refers simply to the frequency with which homework is assigned or the length of particular assignments. Differences in frequency and length can be dramatic, though they are often expressed in relative terms (i.e., often versus rarely, long versus short).

The *purposes* of a homework assignment can be divided into instructional and noninstructional objectives. Lee and Pruitt (1979) identified four instructional goals of homework. The most common purpose of homework is practice or review. Practice assignments are meant to reinforce the learning of material already presented in class and to help students master specific skills. Examples of practice assignments include answering the study questions in a textbook or completing math exercises.

TABLE 1.1. Distinctions in Homework Assignments

Classifications	*Within Classifications*
Amount	Frequency
	Length
Purpose	Instructional
	Practice
	Preparation
	Extension
	Integration
	Noninstructional
	Parent-child communication
	Fulfilling directives
	Punishment
	Community relations
Skill area utilized	Writing
	Reading
	Memory or retention
Degree of individualization	Geared to individual student
	Geared to groups of students
Degree of student choice	Compulsory
	With task options
	Voluntary
Completion deadline	Long-term
	Short-term
Social context	Independent
	Assisted
	Parent, sibling, other
	Student group

Preparation assignments introduce material to be presented in subsequent lessons. These assignments might involve advance reading, observation of events, or simply thought-questions. Their aim is to help students obtain the maximum benefit when the new material is covered in class by providing background information or experiences.

Quite often the difference between practice and preparation homework is not in the content of the assignment but in its temporal relation to the material being covered in class—the same material presented before class discussion is preparation, while after class discussion it is practice or review. Some homework assignments can have both practice and preparation objectives by introducing new material along with old. This technique has been called a distributed or spiral strategy—as opposed to a massed strategy, in which an assignment relates to only one topic.

Lee and Pruitt's third instructional goal for homework is called extension. Extension homework attempts to have the student transfer previously learned skills to new situations. This often involves the application of abstract principles in circumstances not covered in class. For example, students might learn about the factors that led to the French Revolution and be asked to apply them to other revolutions. The primary difference between practice homework and extension homework is the degree of abstract thinking required. However, both practice homework and extension homework can serve a diagnostic function for the teacher, helping identify areas where student learning may be incomplete.

Finally, homework can serve the purpose of integration—or creativity, as Lee and Pruitt called it. Integrative homework requires the student to apply many separately learned skills and concepts to produce a single product. Examples might include book reports, science projects, or creative writing.

There are other purposes of homework in addition to enhancing instruction. For example, Epstein (1983) identified seven purposes, including (a) establishing communication between parent and child, (b) fulfilling directives from school administrators, and (c) punishing students. To this might be added the public relations objective of simply informing parents about what is going on in school.

In sum, then, homework assignments rarely reflect a single purpose. Instead, most assignments have elements of several different purposes. Some of these relate to instruction, while others may meet the purposes of the teacher, the school administration, or even the school district.

In addition to differences in purpose, homework can call for the *exercise of different skills*. Students may be asked to read, to submit written products, or to perform practice drill to enhance memory or retention of material. Written products are often required as evidence that the assignment was completed. Drill activities involve mechanical, routine exercises—for example, practicing multiplication tables or rehearsing a public speech.

Homework can vary also in the *degree of individualization*, which refers to whether assignments are tailored to meet the needs of each student or whether a single assignment is presented to groups of students or to the class as a whole.

The *degree of choice* afforded a student, which refers to whether the homework assignment is compulsory or voluntary, is another variation. Within compulsory homework assignments, students can be given different degrees of discretion concerning which or how many parts of the assignment to complete.

Related to the degree of choice is the fact that *completion deadlines* for homework assignments can vary. Some assignments are short-term and meant to be completed overnight or for the next class meeting. Other assignments are long-term, with students given perhaps a week or several weeks to complete the task.

Finally, homework assignments can vary according to the *social context* in which they are carried out. Some assignments are meant to be completed by the individual student independent of other people. Assisted homework explicitly calls for the involvement of another person, typically a parent but perhaps a sibling or friend. Still other assignments involve groups of students working cooperatively to produce a single product.

THE EFFECTS OF HOMEWORK

The list of potential effects of home study is long. As might be expected, educators and researchers have suggested both positive and negative consequences. The positive effects of homework can be grouped into four categories: (a) immediate academic effects, (b) long-term academic effects, (c) nonacademic effects, and (d) parental involvement effects.

The immediate effects of homework on academic achievement and learning is the most frequent rationale for continuing homework assignment. Proponents of homework argue that it increases the amount of time students spend on academic tasks. As such, the benefits of increased instructional time uncovered in the time-on-task literature (see Denham & Lieberman, 1980) should accrue to children engaged in home study. Regardless of the theoretical rationale, among the suggested positive academic effects of homework are (a) better retention of factual knowledge, (b) increased understanding of material, (c) better critical thinking, concept formation, and information-processing skills, and (d) enrichment of the core curriculum. Obviously, all these benefits will not accompany any single homework assignment, but assignments can be tailored to promote one or more of these outcomes.

The long-term academic consequences of homework are not necessarily enhancements to achievement in particular academic domains, but rather the establishment of general practices that facilitate learning. Homework is therefore expected to (a) encourage children to learn during their leisure time, (b) improve children's attitudes toward school, and (c) improve children's study habits and skills. Two theoretical notions might underlie these contentions. First, homework blurs the distinction between learning time and leisure time and thus connotes that the two should not be viewed as discrete activities. Second, homework removes learning from the classroom, where teachers closely monitor students' activities, and places it in the home, where the external justifications for on-task academic behavior are less obvious. The relative lack of external constraints at home "causing" students to work on school assignments should lead students to focus on the intrinsic value of the tasks themselves. (See Deci & Ryan, 1985, for a general review of the literature on the relationship between intrinsic and extrinsic justifications and attitudes toward tasks). Each of these mechanisms should indirectly affect achievement in all academic areas.

Homework has also been offered as a means for developing personal attributes in children that extend beyond academic pursuits. Because homework generally requires students to complete tasks with less supervision and under less severe time constraints than is the case in school, home study is said to promote greater self-discipline and self-direction, better time organization, more inquisitiveness, and more independent problem-solving. These skills and attributes apply to the nonacademic spheres of life as well as to the academic spheres.

Finally, homework may have positive effects for the parents of school-children. By having students bring work home for parents to see, and perhaps by requesting that parents take part in the process, teachers can use homework to increase parents' appreciation of and involvement in schooling. Parental involvement may have positive effects on children as well. Students become aware of the connection between home and school, and parents can demonstrate an interest in the academic progress of their children.

Some of the negative effects that have been attributed to home study directly contradict the suggested positive effects. For instance, although some have argued that homework can improve students' attitudes toward school, others counter that attitudes may be negatively influenced. They appeal to what is called a "satiation effect" as the underlying causal mechanism—specifically, that the potential of any activity to prove rewarding is limited. By increasing the time spent on school learning, children may become overexposed to academic tasks. Homework may also lead to general physical and emotional fatigue. Thus, homework may undermine good attitudes and strong achievement motivation.

Another argument used against homework is that it denies access to leisure-time and community activities. Proponents of this effect point out that doing homework is not the only circumstance under which after-school learning takes place. Many leisure-time activities teach important academic and life skills. The key is to find the proper balance of leisure and learning.

Involving parents in the schooling process can have negative consequences. Sometimes parents pressure students to complete homework assignments or to do them with unrealistic rigor. Also, parents may create confusion if they are unfamiliar with the material that is sent home for study or if their approach to learning differs from that taught in school.

Parental involvement in homework can sometimes go beyond simple tutoring or assistance. This raises the more general possibility that homework might promote cheating or an overreliance on others for help with assignments. Although a lack of supervision can enhance self-direction and self-discipline, it may also lead some students to copy assignments or to receive inappropriate help from others.

Finally, some opponents of homework have argued that home study increases differences between high-achieving and low-achieving students, especially when the achievement difference is related to economic variables. They suggest that high achievers from well-to-do homes will have greater parental support for home study, including more appropriate parental assistance, and that these students are more likely to have quiet, well-lit

TABLE 1.2. Positive and Negative Effects of Homework

Positive Effects

Immediate achievement and learning
    Better retention of factual knowledge
    Increased understanding
    Better critical thinking, concept formation, information-processing
    Curriculum enrichment
Long-term academic
    Encourage learning during leisure time
    Improved attitude toward school
    Better study habits and skills
Nonacademic
    Greater self-direction
    Greater self-discipline
    Better time organization
    More inquisitiveness
    More independent problem-solving
Greater parental appreciation of and involvement in schooling

Negative Effects

Satiation
    Loss of interest in academic material
    Physical and emotional fatigue
Denial of access to leisure-time and community activities
Parental interference
    Pressure to complete assignments and perform well
    Confusion of instructional techniques
Cheating
    Copying from other students
    Help beyond tutoring
Increased differences between high and low achievers

places in which to do assignments and better resources to help them complete assignments successfully. Thus, homework may increase time-on-task for better students from better homes, but at the same time, for disadvantaged children, create frustrating situations that are detrimental to learning. In such cases, homework may contribute to a social ill, rather than help remedy it.

Table 1.2 presents a list of the positive and negative effects that have been attributed to home study. Although the list of potential negative effects of homework appears to be shorter than the list of positive effects, a number of detrimental outcomes could be listed by arguing that home study actually impedes the immediate and long-term academic and nonacademic effects mentioned above as positive effects. However, having made that point, there is little reason to list these reversed effects individually.

FACTORS AFFECTING THE INFLUENCE OF HOMEWORK

With a few exceptions, the positive and negative consequences of homework represent potentially independent outcomes. For instance, it is possible for homework to improve study habits at the same time that it denies access to other leisure-time activities. It is also possible for some types of assignments to produce positive effects while other assignments produce negative ones. In fact, in light of the host of ways homework assignments can be construed and carried out, complex patterns of effects can be expected. Therefore, before organizing the research literature, it is necessary to propose a model containing the factors that are likely to influence the effects of homework.

Coulter (1979) was the first researcher to present a temporal model of the homework process. He proposed that the process could be divided into three phases. In the initial classroom phase, teachers acted to motivate, structure, and facilitate the completion of homework assignments. These efforts, along with students' personal characteristics, determined whether students chose to do the homework assignment or to engage in other activities. During the home-community phase, several factors that affect performance—including pupil abilities, the home learning environment, tutoring resources, and community resources—combined to influence the students' actual performance on the home study task. Finally, during classroom follow-up the teacher's feedback on homework, testing of homework-related performance, and relating of homework assignments to other classwork were posited as affecting test results, attitudes, and ultimately school achievement.

Keith (1982) performed a formal path analysis that included the amount of time spent on homework as a predictor of high school grades. His model contained none of the initial classroom or classroom follow-up variables contained in Coulter's analysis, undoubtedly because information on these variables was not included in the longitudinal study that provided Keith's database. Instead, Keith's model proposed that a student's race and family background (i.e., parents' education and father's occupation) were exogenous variables affecting the student's ability and field of study (i.e., academic versus vocational). Time spent on homework was seen as a function of all four prior variables. Grades in high school was the final variable in the model.

Table 1.3 presents a modified and expanded temporal model of the homework process. Like Coulter's model, this model does not propose specific directional hypotheses relating the components to one another. Attempting to specify paths at this stage in the study of homework would probably be premature and would certainly require such complexity that the heuristic value of the exercise would be lost. Also like Coulter, the model retains the notion that the homework process can be divided into

TABLE 1.3. A Process Model of Factors Influencing the Effectiveness of Homework

Exogenous Factors	Assignment Characteristics	Initial Classroom Factors	Home-Community Factors	Classroom Follow-Up	Outcomes or Effects

Student characteristics
Ability
Motivation
Study habits
Subject matter
Grade level
	Amount
	Purpose
	Skill area utilized
	Degree of individualization
	Degree of student choice
	Completion deadlines
	Social context
		Provision of materials
		Facilitators
		Suggested approaches
		Links to curriculum
		Other rationales
			Competitors for student time
			Home environment
			  Space
			  Light
			  Quiet
			  Materials
			Others' involvement
			  Parents
			  Siblings
			  Other students
				Feedback
				  Written comments
				  Grading
				  Incentives
				Testing of related content
				Use in class discussion
					Assignment completion
					Assignment performance
					Positive effects
					  Immediate academic
					  Long-term academic
					  Nonacademic
					  Parental
					Negative effects
					  Satiation
					  Denial of leisure time
					  Parental interference
					  Cheating
					  Increased student differences

two classroom phases with a home-community phase between. Borrowing from Keith, student ability and other individual-difference variables are viewed as exogenous to the homework process. However, the student characteristics of race and family background are not among these. Indeed, they are not included anywhere in the model. This is because race and family background are typically used in research as proxy variables meant to assess indirectly cultural differences in students' home environments. In the present theoretical model, differences in home environments are directly represented under home-community factors. The subject matter of the homework assignment and the grade level or age of the student are also included as exogenous factors.

Neither earlier model included a set of influences relating to the characteristics of the assignment. The present model contains such a set, distinguishing assignments according to amount, purpose, skill area, degree of choice and individualization, completion deadlines, and the social context in which homework is to be performed. The distinctions subsumed by these categories were covered as distinctions in homework assignments and are summarized in Table 1.1.

Finally, Table 1.3 includes a broad delineation of the outcomes or effects of homework as the final step in the process. These are reproduced from Table 1.2. The categories listed in Table 1.3 and expanded on in Tables 1.1 and 1.2 will be used in the literature review to distinguish among the various definitions, distinctions in assignments, and contexts employed in primary research.

2

Review of Past Reviewers' Conclusions

The present synthesis is only the latest in a long series of reviews of the effects of homework. In this chapter, previously published reviews of the empirical literature are summarized, along with some unpublished reviews that are cited frequently. This review of reviews focuses narrowly on the questions that guided this synthesis. Reviews of public opinion surveys regarding homework (e.g., Friesen, 1978) or of school district policies (e.g., Pennsylvania Department of Education, 1984) are not included. Short reviews of reviews, typically written for teachers and administrators, also are not covered (e.g., Jongsma, 1985; Otto, 1985; Strother, 1984). Finally, several of the research reviews that contained discussions of definitions, survey results, and policy guidelines are discussed elsewhere in this book.

GOLDSTEIN (1960)

Goldstein posed two different questions about the value of homework: (a) does it contribute immediately and directly to achievement and (b) does it contribute to academic proficiency through a long-term effect on study skills and attitudes? He noted that the first contribution could be gauged fairly easily by properly designed experiments. The second contribution was more difficult to assess because controlled experiments would have to follow-up on students years after the manipulation of homework policies.

Goldstein's review focused on 17 homework studies published during the 30 years prior to 1959. These were gleaned from entries on home study listed in *Education Index*, most of which were anecdotal or polemical—

they primarily documented the generally negative attitude toward homework held by the public and educators during the 1940s and 1950s. Of the 17 empirical studies, none was conducted in grades 1 through 4, seven related to grades 5 and 6, eight (including four of the previous seven studies) related to grades 7 through 9, and six studies concerned grades 10 through 12.

Goldstein's description of the individual studies was punctuated by two recurring observations. First, he bemoaned the generally low quality of the experimental designs in most studies and the lack of detail in the published descriptions. Few studies employed random assignment to homework and no-homework treatments. Most employed student matching (sometimes carefully controlled, sometimes not), pretest-posttest designs without a control group, or correlational data. Second, Goldstein found numerous cases in which researchers interpreted data that were favorable toward homework in a negative fashion. He believed that "fair assessment of the value of homework has been hampered by a tendency for authors of experimental research to frame their conclusions in terms that favor preconceived notions about homework and for subsequent authors to cite these unfavorable conclusions rather than the actual research findings" (p. 222).

With regard to the question of homework's immediate and direct effects on achievement, the major conclusion of Goldstein's review was:

> Statements that homework contributes little or nothing to immediate academic achievement are not warranted by the experimental findings. On the contrary, the data in most studies suggest that regular homework favors higher academic achievement, and a few of the best-designed experiments show this quite clearly (p. 221).

The general assessment was qualified by the provisos that (a) since no research had been conducted on students in the early primary grades, no conclusions about homework's effects during these years could be made and (b) there was some indication that the effect of homework might be influenced by grade level, subject matter, and student individual differences (though what these might be were not specified).

Goldstein found only one study that addressed his second question concerning the long-term effect of homework on attitudes and study skills. This study indicated that a no-homework policy in elementary school had an adverse effect on performance in high school. More generally, a few studies suggested "that children feel more secure and better oriented in the classroom when they are doing regular homework" (p. 222).

FRIESEN (1979)

Friesen summarized the results of 24 studies on homework's effects conducted between 1923 and 1976. He noted that most studies compared homework with no homework, especially studies conducted prior to 1950. This review mainly consisted of noninterpretive descriptions of each study.

After pointing out that past reviewers differed in their interpretation of the literature, Friesen concluded that "the results of the studies do not provide a clear-cut endorsement for either the homework or the no-homework groups" (p. 15). Drawing from the finding of one study, he suggested that teachers are best equipped to decide whether homework will contribute to their students' achievement.

AUSTIN (1979)

Austin's review focused exclusively on the effect of homework on mathematics achievement. In addition to procedural problems that compromised the validity of several studies, Austin pointed out that the results of studies conducted before 1950 may be of questionable utility because of changes in school-age populations. Furthermore, he noted that some studies contained multiple dependent variables, often employing attitude measures as well as measures of mathematics achievement. Therefore, instead of using the study as the unit of analysis, Austin examined each comparison separately.

If studies were combined without regard to the year in which they were performed, 16 comparisons showed significant results favoring the homework group, 13 comparisons showed no differences, and no comparison favored the no-homework group. If only post-1950 studies were considered, 7 comparisons—5 from one study—favored homework, and 4 comparisons showed no difference.

Austin drew nine conclusions based on the research conducted after 1950:

1. Homework is preferable to no homework for grades 4 through 10 (there was little research focusing on other grades).
2. The effects of homework may be cumulative.
3. Parent involvement may improve the effectiveness of homework, but also may have no effect.
4. Drill homework may not be of much value.
5. Homework appears to improve computational skills.
6. The effect of homework on problem-solving skills is unclear, with one study favoring homework and two studies finding no difference between homework groups and no-homework groups.
7. Few data on the effects of the length of homework assignments were available.
8. No study found a relationship between homework and attitude toward mathematics.
9. Comments on homework papers can improve achievement, but not all homework needs to be graded.

COULTER (1979)

Coulter began his review by pointing out that during the late 1960s and early 1970s the emphasis in educational research on classroom processes led to a neglect of the role of home study in learning. He suggested that one reason classroom research demonstrated only weak relations between teacher or student behavior and educational outcomes may have been that much formal learning occurs outside the classroom, especially at the secondary grades.

Coulter classified homework research into three broad categories and reviewed each category separately. The first type of study investigated the effects of homework on achievement. He concluded that studies conducted during the 1930s generally supported the view that regularly assigned homework enhanced school achievement. However, similar to Goldstein, Coulter suggested that these studies had been misinterpreted and, coupled with a perception that disadvantaged students were being further penalized by homework, this led to a shift away from required homework and toward more in-school study. Since the 1930s, Coulter observed, researchers had been less interested in the quantity or presence versus absence of homework, and more interested in the relation between particular kinds of homework and their effects on the achievement of particular types of students. He wrote, "Common sense suggests that some students will profit from additional time on certain tasks. The real questions relate to which students, which tasks, which sequences and which structures" (p. 25).

The second group of studies reviewed by Coulter dealt with the introduction and structuring of homework assignments. He interpreted five studies as suggesting that achievement might be enhanced by homework if the assignment is meant to provide a base for new in-class instruction. Learning might also be facilitated if assignments on a given topic were interspersed with other topics and were spaced over time. This was especially true for low- and middle-ability students.

Four studies investigating the effect of homework feedback comprised Coulter's third category of research. None of the studies demonstrated that providing comments or grading homework increased achievement. Coulter suggested that there may have been no effect because (a) the studies did not monitor the quality of comments as opposed to their quantity or (b) the criterion tests were not logically related to the treatment—that is, general achievement, as opposed to performance on future homework assignments, was measured.

Coulter concluded his review by suggesting that the conceptualization and implementation of homework research had been too narrow. He argued that distinctions in the process of how homework is carried out, ranging from teacher introduction of assignments to parental involvement, home environment, and back again to teacher reaction, needed to be considered when the effect of homework was the focus of research.

HARDING (1979)

Harding concluded that research had not yet adequately evaluated the effectiveness of homework. Past studies had serious methodological flaws. Most looked at homework versus no homework, and a few studies indicated that some types of homework were more effective than others. Grade level and subject matter also seemed to influence homework's effect, though the majority of studies had been done in one subject area—mathematics. Harding found 17 studies favoring homework and 20 studies showing that "homework is not an effective way to promote academic achievement" (p. 37).

KNORR (1981)

Knorr's review covered 29 studies conducted before 1960 (the 17 included in Goldstein [1960], plus 12 others) and 26 studies conducted after 1960. Knorr concluded that the additional 12 pre-1960 studies generally supported a more positive relation between homework and achievement than the studies reviewed by Goldstein. However, Knorr judged homework research conducted in the twentieth century to be generally inconclusive and suggested that "we may be spending our energies on trying to answer one or two questions that are so broad and that encompass a set of factors so complex as to make the questions unanswerable" (p. 45). Instead, she suggested that assessments of whether homework meets the objectives of local school districts should be tested at the local level.

MARSHALL (1983)

Marshall's review was the first to estimate the size of the homework effect. In homework studies, an effect size is a way to quantitatively describe the influence of the treatment. Marshall used the d-index to express effect sizes. The d-index gauges how many standard deviation (SD) units separate two group means. For instance, suppose a homework group outperforms a no-homework group by .3 SD units. This means the average student doing homework had a score that placed him or her three-tenths of a standard deviation above the average student in the distribution of no-homework group scores. Fuller treatments of how effect sizes are calculated and interpreted can be found in Chapters 4 and 10.

Marshall focused on 38 experimental studies of mathematics achievement and found that homework had positive effects on problem-solving ability and concept learning, but a negative effect on computation skills. The latter conclusion is opposite that of Austin (1979). Although 90% of problem-solving comparisons (a +.3 SD unit effect) and 78% of concept-learning comparisons favored homework (a +.2 SD unit effect), when the type of achievement was computational skill, 64% of comparisons favored no homework (a −.1 SD unit effect). Also, an analysis of grade level indicated that homework may have a stronger effect on junior and senior high school students than on younger students.

PASCHAL, WEINSTEIN, AND WALBERG (1984)

Paschal and colleagues also conducted a quantitative synthesis of homework research. Their review began by noting that only 16.4% of children's potential educative hours are spent in school, while 2.5 times this amount of time is spent watching television.

The database of the meta-analysis was 15 studies conducted after 1966. The 15 studies contained 81 comparisons involving achievement, motivational, or attitudinal effects of homework. Paschal and colleagues found that 69 of the 81 comparisons, or 85%, favored the homework experimental group when different features of homework were compared. In terms of an overall effect size, the mean of the treated group was .36 standard deviations above that of the untreated group (the comparisons were weighted so that individual studies contributed equally to the overall effect). Such a result would occur by chance less than once in 10,000 times.

The meta-anaylsis also examined the influence of 54 methodological, conceptual, and practical factors on the effect of homework. Many of these were found to influence the relation of homework or different homework strategies and the dependent variables. For instance, the influence of homework was strongest for fourth- and fifth-graders, a finding that directly contradicts results of Marshall's meta-analysis. Homework was also more efficacious when reading and social science outcomes were at issue than it was for math. Homework that was graded or received comments from the teacher had larger effects than homework with no feedback. This finding conflicts with Coulter's (1979) interpretation of the research. Traditional homework assignments surpassed nontraditional homework, and daily assignments were superior to less frequently assigned homework. Finally, numerous other factors, most involving the design of the research, also emerged as potential influences on the outcome of a homework study.

Paschal and colleagues concluded that the "evidence showed a moderately large average effect of assigned homework that is commented on or graded" (p. 104). However, they cautioned that much of the homework literature is opinionated and polemical and contains few methodologically adequate studies.

KEITH (1986, 1987)

In two reviews aimed primarily at teachers, school administrators, and school psychologists, Keith presented a highly favorable assessment of homework's effectiveness. Although his review covered all types of research, it focused primarily on the results of recent, large-sample, cross-sectional studies.

Keith concluded that homework enhances student achievement from elementary school through high school, that this effect appears across a variety of subject areas and levels of student ability, and that homework may be especially effective for students from low-income families. He also found that homework can help develop positive motivational and concentration skills that generalize to nonschool settings.

With regard to various homework strategies, Keith found no evidence favoring practice homework or preparation homework when they were compared with one another, but suggested that each may be most effective under different circumstances. He did find evidence favoring individualized assignments for certain students and systematic homework that is integrated into classroom instruction. Keith also reported that research indicated that parent involvement in homework had positive effects, as did all forms of teacher feedback (i.e., grading, comments, and reinforcement for completion).

Keith concluded by stating that homework is a cost-effective intervention. With the appropriate focus on quality and feedback, "homework's effect on learning will be even greater than that shown in research, where quality of assignments is rarely controlled" (Keith, 1987, p. 22).

ENCYCLOPEDIA OF EDUCATIONAL RESEARCH

Each of the five editions of the *Encyclopedia of Educational Research* has contained a brief review of the homework literature. The conclusions of these assessments vary considerably. Most negative was the assessment of Otto (1941, 1950) that appeared in the first two editions. Otto wrote:

> Researches at the elementary school level show: (a) there is a very small relationship between the amount of time spent in home study and pupil progress; (b) homework is not significantly related to achievement as measured by teachers' marks or standardized tests; (c) homework at the elementary school level has a slight positive relationship to success in high school; (d) voluntary homework has about as many values as compulsory homework; (e) the benefits of assigned homework are too small to counterbalance the disadvantages, especially for pupils in poor homes; (f) compulsory homework does not result in significantly improved academic accomplishments to justify the retention of the achievement argument as the chief justification for home-study assignments (Otto, 1950, p. 380).

This assessment is often cited as the most negative interpretation of homework research.

Strang's (1960) review placed little faith in outcomes of homework studies. She contended that even the best evidence was inconclusive because so many variables influenced scholastic achievement, because research reports contained too little information on the background of the students studied, and because the kind of homework under discussion was often poorly defined. However, based on the limited investigations, surveys, and descriptions, she did suggest that homework should allow more student initiative and choice, should be individualized, and should receive approval from the teacher when successfully completed.

Holtzman (1969) eschewed drawing any general conclusions about the effectiveness of homework. Instead, he simply claimed that "the home environment, interest and educational background of parents, nature of the assignment, and follow through by the teacher are but a few of the important factors which determine the success or failure of home study" (p. 1389).

Finally, Rickards (1982) concluded that although most recommendations about how to make homework effective make a good deal of sense, there is virtually no experimental evidence to support any recommendations. He called for well-designed and well-executed experimental research that studies different types of homework in different contexts.

NATIONAL EDUCATION ASSOCIATION

Throughout the years, the National Education Association (NEA) has published a series of booklets entitled "What Research Says to Teachers." Homework has been the topic of a booklet in the series that has been revised four times.

Strang (1955, 1968, 1975) wrote the first three editions of the booklet entitled *Homework*. The latter two were heavily influenced by Goldstein's (1960) review. Strang (1968) concluded that "the findings of the best research indicate that systematically assigned homework contributes to academic achievement to a variable degree for able learners; to some extent for the average; and to a more marked degree for the slow learner" (p. 29).

LaConte (1981) prepared the most recent edition of the *Homework* booklet. First, he noted that most research had focused on high school mathematics and indicated that under certain circumstances homework did improve test scores. However, he cautioned that there was no conclusive evidence that homework is very effective. This was especially true for practice-type homework and less true for preparation homework. LaConte also concluded that the research indicated that "homework for young children is not only inappropriate, but may well be counterproductive" (p. 17). Research supported the practice of increasing the amount of home study with increasing student age and ability.

Finally, in an NEA monograph outside the series, Epps (1966) found that homework research led to few definitive conclusions, because of both a lack of research and poor research design.

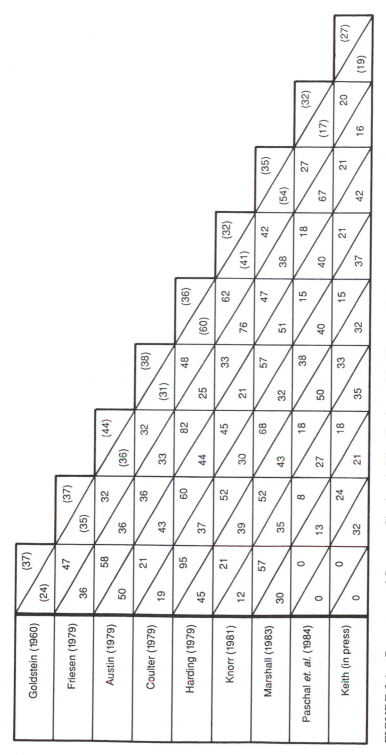

FIGURE 2.1. Percentages of Common Citations in Nine Reviews of the Homework Research. *Note.* Entries above the diagonal in each box are the percentages of citations in the review listed in the column that also appear in the review listed in the row. Entries below the diagonal are the reverse. Entries in a review's own column and row (given in parentheses) are averages.

TABLE 2.1. Summary of Conclusions of Previous Reviews

Author (year)	General Conclusion	Factors Influencing Homework Effect	Observations on Research
Goldstein (1960)	Regular homework favors higher achievement.	Grade level. Subject matter. Student differences.	Low quality. Lack of detail in reports. Author conclusions differ from results. No research on grades 1–4.
Friesen (1979)	No clear-cut endorsement of homework or no homework.	Teachers are best equipped to decide about homework.	
Austin (1979)	Math homework is preferable to no homework for grades 4–10 and may be cumulative; no effect on attitudes.	Parent involvement. Activity. Skill area (e.g., improves computational skills).	Procedural problems. Pre-1950 studies may be of questionable utility.
Coulter (1979)	Homework can be effective under certain conditions; grading or comment studies found no effect.	Student differences. Tasks. Sequences. Structures. Home environment.	Too narrowly conceptualized and implemented.
Harding (1979)	Homework has not yet been effectively evaluated; studies were evenly divided in direction of effect.	Grade level. Subject matter.	Serious methodological flaws. Looked only at homework vs. no homework.
Knorr (1981)	Inconclusive.	Complex set of factors.	Questions asked are too broad. Effects should be tested at local level.

Source	Conclusion	Factors	
Marshall (1983)	Math homework effect depends on skill area.	Skill area (e.g., positive effect on problem-solving, concept-learning; negative effect on computation).	Generally poor protection against threats to validity.
Paschal et al. (1984)	Homework is generally effective.	Grade level. Subject matter. Grading or comments. Frequency.	Research design factors influence outcomes of studies.
Keith (1986, 1987)	Homework is generally effective.	Quality of assignments. Appropriateness for the student.	Most done at high school level.

Encyclopedia of Educational Research

Otto (1941, 1950)	Little relation between home study and pupil progress; positive effect too small to counterbalance negative effects.
Strang (1960)	Even best evidence remains inconclusive.
Holtzman (1969)	No general conclusion; many factors influence effect.
Rickards (1982)	No evidence to support any recommendations.

National Education Association

Epps (1966)	No definitive conclusion; lack of and inadequate research.
Strang (1955, 1968, 1975)	Systematically assigned homework contributes to achievement, but magnitude of effect depends on student ability.
LaConte (1981)	No conclusive evidence that homework is effective; effect depends on grade level and type.

SUMMARY

The conclusions of past reviewers of homework research (Table 2.1) show extraordinary variability. Interpretations of the overall literature range from an assessment that homework is generally harmful, to conclusions that it is generally helpful. Even in regard to specific areas of application, such as within different subject areas, grades, or student ability levels, the reviews often directly contradict one another.

The inconsistency cannot be attributed to changes in the underlying literature over time. The most recent reviews, many of which appeared within a year or two of one another, demonstrate as much diversity in conclusions compared with one another as they do compared with earlier reviews. Figure 2.1 displays the amount of overlap in citations to empirical research between the nine major reviews. Because each review shares about 40% of its references with other reviews, some of the discrepancy in conclusions may be due to authors' reviewing different segments of the literature. The most comprehensive review appears to be Harding's (1979), which contained about 60% of the citations found in other reviews, while 36% of its citations were cited elsewhere.

A common thread running through all the previous reviews is a general condemnation of the quality and quantity of experimental research on homework. The inconsistency in conclusions can probably be attributed to this lack of high-quality information.

Putting aside the conflicting overall interpretations, the past reviewers have performed the important service of laying out the issues that must be taken into account when the effects of homework are assessed. Reviewers have clearly delineated the positive and negative effects of homework that ought to serve as dependent variables in future primary studies of the area. Also, the reviews suggest a comprehensive catalog of contextual factors that might influence the effectiveness of home study. These are contributions to future research that should be put to service. They were used earlier in developing a conceptual framework for viewing the homework process, and they formed the basis of the distinctions in research that are examined in the present review.

Part II

Reviewing Methods

3

Formulating the Problem and Searching the Literature

Until recently, the methods reviewers used when they integrated research literature rarely came under close inspection. The use of critical, objective criteria to evaluate reviews was a significant by-product of the reintroduction of methods for the quantitative synthesis of results across studies (e.g., Glass, McGaw, & Smith, 1981). The popularity of these meta-analytic techniques helped social scientists realize that statistical results could be integrated in a more open and systematic fashion. Greater rigor was soon expected in all phases of integrative research review.

This chapter delineates the procedures employed in conducting this review of the homework literature. Much like the methods section of a primary research study, this chapter provides the reader with enough detail on the methods of review so that (a) critical judgments can be made about the validity of the review's conclusions and (b) reviewers attempting to replicate the conclusions stand a reasonable chance of doing so. This chapter and the next should also be instructive for readers interested in applying some of the recent developments in review methodology to other areas in the social sciences.

In a recent monograph (Cooper, 1984), I described a conceptualization of the integrative review as a research project. I suggested that "locating and integrating separate research projects involves inferences as central to the validity of knowledge as the inferences involved in primary data interpretation" and that "research reviewers must be required to use the same rigorous methodology that is required of primary researchers" (p. 10). In the service of these goals, I offered a scheme for evaluating review methodologies. The scheme divided the reviewing process into five stages, each of which encompassed a unique question, function, set of procedures,

TABLE 3.1. The Integrative Review Conceptualized as a Research Project

Stage Characteristics	Stage of Research				
	Problem Formulation	*Data Collection*	*Data Evaluation*	*Analysis and Interpretation*	*Public Presentation*
Research question asked	What evidence should be included in the review?	What procedures should be used to find relevant evidence?	What retrieved evidence should be included in the review?	What procedures should be used to make inferences about the literature as a whole?	What information should be included in the review report?
Primary function in review	Constructing definitions that distinguish relevant from irrelevant studies.	Determining which sources of potentially relevant studies to examine.	Applying criteria to separate "valid" from "invalid" studies.	Synthesizing valid retrieved studies.	Applying editorial criteria to separate important from unimportant information.
Procedural differences that create variation in review conclusions	1. Differences in included operational definitions. 2. Differences in operational detail.	Differences in the research contained in sources of information.	1. Differences in quality criteria. 2. Differences in the influence of nonquality criteria.	Differences in rules of inference.	Differences in guidelines for editorial judgment.

Sources of potential invalidity in review conclusions					
	1. Narrow concepts might make review conclusions less definitive and robust. 2. Superficial operational detail might obscure interacting variables.	1. Accessed studies might be qualitatively different from the target population of studies. 2. People sampled in accessible studies might be different from target population of people.	1. Nonquality factors might cause improper weighting of study information. 2. Omissions in study reports might make conclusions unreliable.	1. Rules for distinguishing patterns from noise might be inappropriate. 2. Review-based evidence might be used to infer causality.	1. Omission of review procedures might make conclusions irreproducible. 2. Omission of review findings and study procedures might make conclusions obsolete.

Source. From "Scientific guidelines for conducting integrative research reviews" by H.M. Cooper, *Review of Educational Research*, 1982, 52, 291–302.

and potential threats to the validity of the review's conclusions. Table 3.1 outlines the five stages. In describing the procedures used to review the homework literature, the conceptualization depicted in Figure 3.1 will be used as an organizing device.

THE PROBLEM FORMULATION STAGE

The first stage of any research project involves the formulation of the problem. During problem formulation, the most important decisions concern what constructs will be of interest and how broadly or narrowly they will be defined. The latter decision has implications for the kinds of empirical operations that are considered relevant to the question under consideration. In this review, for example, a decision had to be made about whether home study courses like those offered through the mail, on tape, or on television were to be included in the definition of homework. One reviewer might consider these activities to be homework, whereas another reviewer might not (as was the case here).

Another important decision during problem formulation concerns how much detail to retain on the methodological and conceptual distinctions that appear in the research literature. The distinctions that reviewers choose to retain in how a concept is defined or how studies are conducted delimit the search for variables that might alter the process under study. For instance, two distinctions that may be related to the effects of homework are grade level and subject matter. Should the reviewer consider the possibility that the effect of homework may differ for students at various grade levels and for students studying different subjects? Of course, these are clear choices of variables that might moderate the effects of homework, so they should be included in any good review as a distinction in how homework has been studied. But what about a variable such as the area of the country in which a study was conducted? At some point, every reviewer draws a line concerning the review's level of operational detail. Because these lines are drawn in different places, reviews of the same topic can reach different conclusions.

There are two threats to validity that arise during problem formulation. First, reviewers who focus only on a few operational definitions leave open more rival interpretations of their data. If the results of studies provide consistent findings and if homework is allowed to be defined in many different ways, then we can be more confident that the homework treatment is causing the result. This is the principle of multiple operationism (Webb et al., 1981). Also, because narrow conceptualizations provide little information about how many different contexts or populations a finding applies to, they potentially restrict the external validity of conclusions.

Second, reviewers who focus on too few operational details within their conceptualizations run the risk of missing important influences on the generality of their results. If a reviewer of the homework literature neglects to assess whether grade level influences the effects of homework, and if grade level is in fact an influence, the conclusions of the review may be misleading.

The key to good reviewing, then, is (a) to define concepts broadly, but not so broadly that they lose meaning, and (b) to examine considerable operational detail, but not so much as to muddle the presentation or fill the review with findings that are significant by chance alone. Both these goals can be accomplished by carefully grounding a concept in the theories and research that precede the review.

FORMULATING THE PROBLEM OF HOMEWORK

Chapter 1 explained how homework was defined in this review and identified variables that were examined as potential influences on the homework effect. Homework was defined as tasks assigned by teachers that are meant to be carried out during nonschool hours. Implicit in this definition was the notion that only homework related to academic learning was of interest. A type of homework that this definition excludes would be homework assignments given by therapists to aid in the recovery of clients with psychological disturbances. Also explicitly excluded from the definition, although related to academics, were (a) in-school guided study, (b) home study courses delivered through the mail or on audio- or video-cassette, and (c) extracurricular activities, such as sports teams and clubs. Other activities, most notably tutoring, fall at the perimeter. However, the decision was made to exclude tutoring studies because they are so numerous that they deserve separate and full treatment. Finally, no interest was taken in studies concerning programmed instruction, textbook comparisons, or larger schooling interventions of which homework was one of several inseparable parts. In general, then, it might be said that a traditional, "classroom teacher" definition of homework was employed to define the limits of the concept and its relevant research operations.

The schooling-related outcomes used in this review to assess the effects of homework were broadly defined. These included any of the possible effects listed in Table 1.2 or any others found in the empirical literature that would fit within the broad classes of positive and negative outcomes. However, although the list of effects of homework that educators have offered is long, the actual outcomes examined in research were extremely limited.

The distinctions in homework and in the homework process that might influence its effects were also outlined in Chapter 1 and presented in Tables 1.1 and 1.3. Of course, because most studies of homework did not describe their methods in detail, it is impossible to categorize them on each potential distinction. Furthermore, within sets of studies examining the same homework question, it is often difficult to find variation on many of the potential mediators of effect. Thus, as with the outcome measures, the theoretical model of the homework process far outstrips the complexity of the associated research.

Finally, two population-related restrictions were placed on the studies covered by this review. First, only studies on English-speaking students or students in English-speaking cultures were used. Operationally, this meant that a few studies conducted in Mexico and Latin America were excluded. The studies included were all conducted in the United States, Canada, Great Britain, and Australia. It was believed that including the few studies in Spanish-speaking countries could lead readers to consider the results of the review to be of greater generality than might be warranted. Because of the paucity of studies, conclusions about the effects of homework in non-English-speaking countries, at this point, need strong grounding in sound, logical arguments and should not be simple inferences from accumulated data.

Second, studies of homework at the college level were excluded. The college population and the college classroom seemed sufficiently distinct from primary and secondary schools that the notion of home study required an entirely different conceptualization for this setting. Certainly, the effects of homework and the temporal process model presented in Chapter 1 would have to be significantly revised to be made relevant to college students. Therefore, studies included in this review were restricted to those conducted using students through the high school years.

THE DATA COLLECTION STAGE

The second stage of research involves the procedures that are used to gather data. The decisions a reviewer makes during data collection will determine the population of elements that will be the referent of the review.

In integrative research reviewing, the identification of populations is complicated by the fact that the review involves two goals. First, the reviewer wants the research synthesis to reflect accurately the methods and findings employed in past studies. Either through exhaustive coverage of the literature or through representative sampling, an attempt is made to ensure that studies employing particular methods or obtaining particular results are not systematically excluded from the review. Second, the reviewer hopes that the studies included will allow inferences to be made about the individuals (or other units) and settings that are the focus of the topic area. Although steps can be taken to see that research methods and outcomes are adequately represented in a review, reviewers can include in their results only the kinds of people and places that have been sampled in primary research. If no study has examined the effects of homework on first-graders or in physics classes, there is little the reviewer can do other than to draw inferences from closely related studies.

The first threat to the validity of a review that accompanies data gathering is that the review may not include—indeed, probably will not include—all studies pertinent to the topic of interest. Reviewers attempt to minimize this threat by using multiple techniques for gathering past research. In a 1986 paper, I outlined 15 different ways that reviewers go about locating research that is relevant to their syntheses (Cooper, 1986a). Each of these techniques has a different "filtering system" and is therefore likely to contain bias in the sample of studies it will produce. Some, if not all, of this bias can be removed from the resulting review by employing multiple search strategies that complement one another or contain different filters.

The second threat to data-gathering validity is that the individuals and settings in the retrieved studies may not represent all individuals and settings in the target population. The reviewer cannot be faulted for this, *if* the retrieval procedures were exhaustive. However, reviewers must take care to qualify their results by stating explicitly what types of people and settings are missing.

The Search of the Homework Literature

In preparation for this review, an attempt was made to search the educational literature exhaustively for studies on the effects of homework. To accomplish this, eight searching strategies were employed.

First, several computerized database searches were conducted. The databases included were the Educational Resources Information Center (ERIC), the U.S. Government Printing Office Monthly Catalog, the National Technical Information Service, and the Psychological Abstracts (PsychInfo). In all cases the keyword used to retrieve documents was "homework" or the word "home" adjacent to the word "work." Also in all cases, both the titles of articles and the descriptors attached to articles by the database services were scanned.

ERIC and PsychInfo were by far the most productive sources of references. These databases cover the educational and psychological literatures published beginning with the year 1966 for ERIC and 1967 for PsychInfo. The search of ERIC, ending in November 1986, included 346 citations. PsychInfo, through January 1986, included 249 citations. The government databases added 48 more citations. In addition to the searches conducted specifically for this review, other researchers interested in homework provided three more on-line searches using different but related keyword strategies.

Each search was printed off-line, including authors, titles, sources, and the full abstract. Every abstract was read and judged for its relevance to the task at hand. Documents were examined in full if there was even a *remote* chance that they contained a description of a study of the effects of homework or an interesting position, theory, or conceptualization of the homework issue.

Of the available sources, the computerized databases have the least restrictive criteria for inclusion of citations. However, there are two reasons for not relying exclusively on the computer. First, the keyword descriptor system is far from foolproof. It is likely that the systems themselves contain documents of great relevance to a homework literature search that do not contain the word "homework" in the title or descriptor list. Second, computerized databases will not contain the oldest and newest research. Most databases go back only to the mid-1960s. In addition, there is a time lag between when a manuscript becomes public and when it is entered into the computerized system, so the most recent works will not be included.

To overcome these weaknesses of the computer, five other strategies were employed. The first involved examining the reference lists included in past reviews of the homework literature. Each of the reviews discussed in Chapter 2 (see Table 2.1) was used as a potential source of documents not retrieved by the computer. Second, the references cited in primary research reports were examined. Both these strategies are excellent means for counteracting the computer's shortcomings of omitting older research and research relevant to, but not primarily directed at, the study of homework.

In order to retrieve the newest documents, letters were sent to 13 researchers who had made recent contributions to the homework literature. Of the 13 requests, three led to the retrieval of studies not found through other means. Also, 25 requests for information were sent to the deans of the schools of education ranked as the most productive educational research institutions (see Eash, 1983). The deans were asked to bring this homework project to the attention of their faculties and asked that relevant documents be sent. Twelve responses were forthcoming, and seven of these included manuscripts, reprints, or suggestions about where additional research might be found. Finally, research convention programs of the American Educational Research Association were examined for possible papers or symposiums that included presentations on homework.

None of the strategies described so far is efficient for locating what is often called the "fugitive literature," which consists of reports that never become a part of the traditional channels through which scientists communicate about their research. Because of its nature, a substantial fugitive literature might exist on a topic such as homework. In order to find these reports, two search strategies were employed. First, letters of inquiry were sent to the 53 state agencies that deal primarily with education, as listed in the National Directory of State Agencies (1984–85). Some 36 agencies responded, and 5 of these included reports of statewide assessments in which homework was included as a variable. Second, 110 requests were sent to the directors of research and evaluation in selected North American school districts. Half the districts responded, and 11 of these provided research reports, though not all were relevant to the question of the effects of homework.

Retrieval of documents was carried out in four ways: (a) use of the facilities of the University of Missouri Elmer Ellis Library, (b) interlibrary loan requests, (c) purchase of dissertations from University Microfilms, and (d) requests to the authors of documents. Ultimately, well over 200 full-length documents were examined. Only six documents were unobtainable, and based on the titles, only one of these had a high likelihood of containing relevant data.

An Overview of the Homework Search Results

A large percentage of the documents uncovered by the literature search were irrelevant to an examination of the effects of homework. Some of these documents were excluded because the type of homework or homework-related activities they described did not fit within the definition used here. This was especially true of homework articles found in the psychological literature, where the term "homework" is used to describe a phase of therapeutic treatment or a job-training device. Other reports were of tangential interest because they examined public attitudes toward homework. Still others did not examine homework's effects but were useful as background information. These involved descriptions and suggestions about homework policies, conceptualizations of the homework process, and examinations of homework's positive and negative effects. These documents are referred to throughout this book.

Table 3.2 summarizes the reports found in this search that described research examining the schooling-related effects of homework or variations in homework assignments. The parentheses contain the number of research reports on each topic. A single report might be included in the table more than once if it contained information on more than one topic. More detailed analyses of the literature on each topic are contained in the chapters that follow. For now it will suffice to get a broad overview of the

TABLE 3.2. Aspects of Homework Examined in Past Research

Homework versus no homework (28)
Homework versus supervised study (14)
Time spent on or amount of homework (39)
Instructional purpose (i.e., practice, preparation, extension, creative) (9)
Skill area (i.e., reading versus writing) (2)
Degree of choice (i.e., compulsory versus voluntary) (3)
Degree of individualization (4)
Degree of parent involvement (8)
Presence versus absence of instructional feedback and grading (6)
Presence versus absence of affective evaluative comments and incentives (4)

Note. The number in parentheses is the number of studies that have examined each topic. Some reports contained information on more than one topic.

general nature of the literature and how it relates to the process model of homework described in Chaper 1.

The literature search produced homework studies concerning 10 distinct, but broad, hypotheses. Two of these related to the general efficacy of homework as an instructional strategy. Stated as questions, these are:

1. Do students who are assigned homework have higher achievement or better attitudes than students who are not assigned homework?
2. Do students who are assigned homework have higher achievement or better attitudes than students who are required to do in-school studying?

Five of the hypotheses dealt with whether the following characteristics of the homework assignment influenced its effect on student achievement and attitudes:

1. The amount of homework assigned or the time students spend on homework
2. Its instructional purpose
3. The skill areas utilized
4. The degree of individualization
5. The degree of student choice.

One hypothesis concerned a home-community factor—whether the presence or absence of parental supervision influenced homework's effects. Finally, the last two conceptual hypotheses, related to classroom follow-up, examined whether the effects of homework were influenced by (a) the presence versus absence of instructional feedback or grading and (b) different types of affective evaluative feedback (e.g., praise and criticism) or incentives provided by the teacher.

Within studies investigating each of the broad hypotheses, some researchers also examined exogenous factors (e.g., student characteristics, subject area, grade level) that might moderate the effect of homework or a particular homework strategy. It is also possible to examine the effects of some of these moderators through between-study comparisons.

When we compare the hypotheses motivating research with the factors listed in Table 1.3, it appears that most of the process variables proposed as influencing the effect of homework have been the focus of at least some empirical study. Those factors missing from past research involve initial classroom and home-community factors (for which only parent involvement has been studied). Also, as will be evident shortly, it is rarely the case that *all* of the possible variations in homework within each factor have been studied. For some factors, the amount of research is scant and/or the utility of the studies that have been performed is questionable.

SUMMARY

For this review, the concept of homework was defined in a traditional classroom sense, focusing on assignments made by teachers that are meant to be completed during nonschool hours. The outcomes of homework were broadly defined to include any schooling-related effects. Also broadly defined were variables that could influence the effects of homework. These include any of the variables described in the process model of homework presented in Chapter 1.

Two restrictions were placed on the populations of students that would be included in the review. First, non-English-speaking students or classrooms were excluded from study, primarily because of a lack of data relevant to them. Second, the effects of homework on learning by postsecondary students were not included. An understanding of the homework process in college settings would require development of a process model significantly different from that presented in Chapter 1.

Eight literature-searching strategies were used to locate research relevant to the effects of homework. Central to the search was the use of computerized databases. To compensate for shortcomings of the databases, the reference lists of past review articles and primary research reports were examined, and requests for information were sent to active researchers in the homework area and to deans of schools of education. Recent convention programs of the American Educational Research Association were also examined. Finally, in order to locate the fugitive literature, inquiries were sent to state education agencies and to the directors of research and evaluation units of school districts.

The literature search yielded over 100 empirical research reports that dealt with 10 aspects of homework. Two of these involved the general effectiveness of homework (compared to no-treatment controls or to in-school supervised study controls). Five dealt with various characteristics of the homework assignment, one with home or community factors (i.e., parental involvement), and two with classroom follow-up. These 10 questions will be used to organize the presentation of the results of the review.

4

Evaluating and Synthesizing the Literature

Once a literature search has been conducted and its findings have been judged for conceptual relevance, each research project is carefully scrutinized with regard to its methodological procedures and surrounding context. Then the process of synthesizing the results of studies begins. The reviewer attempts to formulate conclusions that are descriptive of the literature as a whole. These two phases of reviewing can be called, respectively, data evaluation and data analysis.

THE DATA EVALUATION STAGE

During data evaluation, the reviewer makes critical judgments about the quality of individual studies. Decisions are made about how much credence should be given to the findings of each study when an overall statement about the literature is constructed. This weighting decision is typically based on a host of assessments concerning the adequacy of a study's methodology. Also during data evaluation, the reviewer makes choices about what aspects of the context that surrounds the study (e.g., its age, location, characteristics of the treatment) should be examined as potential influences on the study's outcomes.

Decisions about the quality of studies can vary considerably from one reviewer to another. Although most reviewers place great value on internal validity, they disagree on the importance of external, statistical, and measurement validity (see Cooper, 1986b). Furthermore, reviewers disagree about the informational utility of flawed studies. Some reviewers believe that flawed studies may still contain some valuable information, while others believe that data from flawed studies cannot be trusted. Therefore, there are many different approaches to data evaluation.

What is agreed on is that nonmethodological criteria should not be used to assess the credibility of studies. For example, studies should not be devalued because their findings contradict the beliefs of the reviewer, because they were performed by researchers at less prestigious universities, or because the researcher happened to be of one gender or the other. To the extent that evaluative judgments are influenced by factors unrelated to methodological quality, the validity of a review's conclusions will be compromised.

The validity of a review will also be influenced by the completeness of the primary research report. For instance, if a reviewer believes that the ability level of students is related to the effects of homework, the validity of the review will be lessened if few primary reports contain information on the intellectual functioning of the students in the studies. Wider confidence intervals must be placed around the review conclusions if a reviewer must omit numerous studies from such an analysis because of missing data.

Evaluating Homework Research Reports

The procedure employed in this review for evaluating the methodology of studies has been called the "methods description approach." For a discussion of why I prefer this procedure over others, the reader is referred to an earlier study of mine (Cooper, 1984). In this approach, studies are *not* excluded a priori because of flawed methodology. Instead, each study is coded using a set of objective descriptions of its procedures. The coded procedures are presumed to bear on the ability of researchers and reviewers to draw strong inferences from the study's results. The coded aspects of methodology are then empirically related to the studies' outcomes to determine if the methods have an effect. If they do, the results of studies using the most rigorous procedures are given greater weight.

In this review, only one characteristic of studies was employed to weight results on an a priori basis. Studies were divided into two groups, according to whether they were conducted before or after the year 1962. All inferences about homework are based on studies conducted in the past 25 years. Studies conducted prior to 1962 are described for historical and comparative purposes. Educational, familial, and social patterns of behavior have changed enough in the last quarter-century that data from earlier studies is likely to have questionable relevance to decisions made about homework today.

Coding Studies According to Methodology

Codings for studies examining (a) the effects of homework compared with the effects of no homework and (b) the relation between the amount of time a student spent on homework and the student's achievement are described below. The procedures were not all coded for each of the 10 aspects of homework that have received research attention (see Chapter 3). The decision whether to use them was based on the nature of the sample of studies. Also, other codings were sometimes used to describe studies that had other aspects of homework as their focus.

How Students were Assigned to Treatments. Although this determination seems straightforward, the homework versus no homework literature contained some surprisingly vague areas. Thus, three different "levels" of random assignment could be identified. First, and most desirable, were instances in which students were randomly assigned to classrooms or to homework conditions within classrooms just prior to institution of the treatment.

The next type of random assignment included studies in which students were "computer assigned" to classrooms at the beginning of a school semester. This procedure frequently appeared in studies conducted in high schools. The homework treatment was applied at the classroom level some time after the semester began. Researchers claim that this type of assignment to classrooms generates near-random groups of students. However, the flaw in this procedure is that because some students may be in remedial sections or be taking special subjects that prohibit their being assigned to one of the classes, a particular type of student may be overrepresented in one class. Also, because the assignment occurs some time before the treatment is administered, different processes within the classrooms before the study began may have altered the nature of the students.

The third type of random assignment occurred when treatments were randomly assigned to classrooms but students were not. For purposes of this review, this procedure was considered random assignment only if the number of assigned classrooms exceeded 14. If fewer than 14 classes were involved, the study was called a nonequivalent control group design. This category was also used to describe studies in which the homework treatment was not randomly assigned to intact classrooms. Obviously, this fourth type of design is open to many threats to internal validity (see Cook & Campbell, 1979).

Studies involving the amount of time a student spent on homework were all categorized as correlational. These studies involved no direct assignment of students to homework conditions, but instead simply measured differences in homework procedures that occurred naturally.

Other Procedures for Producing Student Equivalence. Studies were found that employed three other techniques for attempting to ensure student equivalence in treated and untreated conditions. These sometimes appear in conjunction with one another as well as in conjunction with random assignment.

The first procedure involved the counterbalancing of treatments. A study was coded for counterbalancing when each group of students appeared in each condition of the homework treatment. Counterbalancing was usually accomplished by having students switch conditions at the end of a particular unit of study.

The second procedure was a priori matching. This typically involved pairing students in intact classrooms—sometimes within the same classroom, sometimes between classes—before the experiment began on attributes relevant to the outcome measure. Students without matches were excluded from the data analysis. Different homework treatments were then assigned to the groups of students. Matching sometimes also occurred before students were randomly assigned to conditions.

The third procedure for producing student equivalence was the use of analysis of covariance or a related procedure. Here student attributes were included in statistical analysis to control for differences on a post hoc basis.

Repeated Measurements. Homework versus no homework studies could be distinguished by whether or not they contained measurements taken at multiple intervals and analyzed their data accordingly. Studies were not coded as including repeated measures if different measures were taken at the same time or if the same measure was taken at several times but the temporal factor was not retained in the data analysis.

Sample Size. Studies were described according to how many schools, classrooms, and students were involved.

Standardization of Outcome Measures. With regard to achievement, three distinctions were made in outcome measures. These included whether the measure involved classroom tests, classroom grades, or a standardized achievement test. Obviously, the same study could contain more than one of these measures.

The Teacher as Experimenter. In experimental research it is often advisable that those who administer a treatment be unaware of the condition they are administering. If awareness is present it can subtly influence aspects of the administration that are unrelated to the treatment (Rosenthal, 1964). For instance, if a teacher believes homework is effective and he or she is teaching both a homework class and no-homework class, the belief might subtly affect the pacing or enthusiasm of in-class instruction so as to positively influence the homework class, even though these treatment differences are unrelated to homework.

In most types of homework studies, it is impossible to keep teachers blind to students' treatment conditions. However, there might be cause for special concern about biased results if the person conducting the experiment is also the person teaching the classes in the study (as opposed to teachers asked by the experimenter to take part in the study). In such cases, the experimenter-teacher will not only have strong beliefs about the veracity of the hypothesis, but also have a personal stake in the outcome of the research. For this reason, a coding was made for whether or not the experimenter conducting the study also served as the teacher of the classes involved.

Sampling Procedures. Studies of the amount of time students spent on homework were distinguished according to how participants were chosen, because these studies often involved large samples. Three types of sampling procedures were coded. Random sampling was coded for all studies using strict random or stratified random sampling procedures. Convenience sampling was coded for studies that chose participants based on their availability. The third type of sampling involved instances in which all members of the relevant population were included in the study. This occurred, for instance, when a statewide assessment of achievement was related to student self-reports about homework and all students in the state participated.

Respondent. Studies of time spent on homework also could be distinguished according to who provided the measure of time. In most instances the students themselves gave self-reports of time spent on homework. In some instances, however, parents described their children's behavior, or teachers described the frequency of assignments.

Unit of Analysis. Each study was coded as to whether the student or the classroom was the unit of data analysis. Which unit is more appropriate depends on the level at which the treatment is administered—that is, if students within the same classroom receive different homework conditions, then the student would be the appropriate unit of analysis, but if the treatment is administered to whole classes, then the class unit should be used. As will be evident shortly, the mistake of using the student as the unit of analysis when treatments were administered to classrooms is widespread in the homework literature.

Coding Other Study Characteristics

In addition to the methodological procedures of a study, several other study characteristics were coded because past research or theorizing suggested that they might be related to a study's outcome. Again, not all codings were used for each of the 10 aspects of homework, and some codings were added for particular aspects.

Type of Document. One study characteristic related to the type of research report. Nine categories were used to distinguish the research reports: dissertation, master's thesis, class paper, journal article, ERIC document, state report, book, book chapter, and school board report.

Year in which the Research Was Conducted. As discussed above, this coding was used to identify studies that would be examined only for their historical importance. In many instances, the year of the study was estimated by the year in which the research report became available.

Location. The nation or state in which each study was conducted was coded for homework versus no homework studies. For studies of time spent on homework, whether the sample was national, statewide, multiple district, or single district in scope was also recorded.

Grade Level. Although grade level was coded as a continuous variable, for purposes of examining differences in study outcomes the grades were usually grouped into elementary school (through fifth grade), junior high school (sixth through ninth grade), and high school (tenth through twelfth grade).

Family Socioeconomic Status. The socioeconomic status (SES) of the students' families was coded as low, middle, or high. However, family SES was not reported often enough to include it in any of the analyses, except when students from different economic backgrounds were compared within the same study.

Racial Background. Racial background was also rarely reported.

Ability. As with family SES, the ability level of the students could be examined as a characteristic only when it was used as a variable for distinguishing students within the same study.

Subject Matter. Twelve different distinctions were made in the type of subject matter. Four related to math: (a) a math category in which the specific skill area was not identified, (b) computation, (c) concepts, and (d) problem-solving. Three categories concerned language and literacy: (a) reading comprehension, (b) language and vocabulary, and (c) spelling. The other subjects were (a) social studies, (b) history, and (c) science. One category was used to encompass studies that reported results across multiple subjects, and a final category was used for all remaining subjects (e.g., health, foreign language).

In some of the analyses described below, subject matter categories were collapsed because of the small numbers of specific cases.

Treatment Duration. The number of weeks a treatment lasted was recorded for homework versus no homework comparisons. Treatment duration differed from the overall length of a study if counterbalancing was used.

Number of Homework Assignments Per Week. This number, when reported, could range from 1 to 5.

Statistical Results

Finally, a number of statistical results were retrieved from each research report. These typically included the mean and standard deviation of the different homework treatment groups, the correlation between time spent on homework and achievement, or the associated inferential statistics. A fuller description of the statistics and how they were treated will be postponed until the section on data analysis.

The Reliability of Codings

There is always a chance—indeed, a strong likelihood—that some study characteristics will be inaccurately coded. This can occur because of ambiguities in research reports, unclear coding definitions, or coder error. In order to minimize the number of coding errors, nearly all studies were coded independently by two persons. Codings were then compared, and any discrepancies were resolved through reference to the original document.

Assessments were made of the reliability of the initial independent codings for the homework versus no homework studies and for studies of time spent on homework. These are reported in Table 4.1. The table includes both Cohen's kappa measure of reliability (Frick & Simmel, 1978) and the percent agreement. Although the intercoder reliabilities are quite high, it should also be kept in mind that they relate to agreement before discrepancies were examined and resolved. Thus, the effective reliabilities are certainly higher. It is also true that there are still some errors

TABLE 4.1. Reliability of Codings for Aspects of Homework Research

Coding Category	Homework Versus No Homework		Time Spent on Homework	
	Kappa[a]	% Agreement	Kappa[a]	% Agreement
Type of document	1.00	100	1.00	100
Assignment procedure	0.87	93	All correlational	
Counterbalancing	0.84	92	NA	NA
Matching	1.00	100	NA	NA
Repeated measures	0.84	92	NA	NA
No. schools/classes/students	NA	93/100/100	NA	92/100/100
Standardization	1.00	100	1.00	100
Teacher as experimenter	0.75	80	NA	NA
Sampling procedure	NA	NA	1.00	100
Location	NA	100	0.86	92
Grade level	NA	100	NA	100
Subject matter	1.00	100	NA	100
Treatment duration	1.00	100	NA	NA
Assignments per week	0.71	79	1.00	100
Respondent	All students		1.00	100

[a] Cohen's kappa measure of reliability (see Frick & Simmel, 1978).
Note. NA = not applicable.

in the data set, but it is unlikely that any remaining errors would dramatically change any of this review's conclusions were they to be corrected.

DATA ANALYSIS AND INTERPRETATION

During analysis and interpretation, the results of the individual research reports are synthesized into a unified statement. The process requires that the reviewer search for commonalities and discrepancies in findings relating to the same hypotheses, that some scheme be adopted for integrating findings that are commensurate, and that efforts be made to resolve or explain differences in findings. Interpretation demands that the reviewer distinguish systematic data patterns from "noise" or chance fluctuation. To carry out this task, the research synthesizer must apply some rules of inference. Interpretation also involves placing the findings in a broader context so as to give them meaning (see Cooper, 1986c).

Reviewers can come to different conclusions about a literature because they employ different techniques to interpret the findings. Traditionally, the integration of studies has been carried out through an informal, unobservable process of mental algebra, the rules of which are rarely known, even to the reviewer. More recently, the formal statistical procedures applied to primary research data have been extended to the task of integrating quantitative results across studies (see Hedges & Olkin, 1985; Rosenthal, 1984). These procedures, called meta-analysis, include techniques for (a) combining the probabilities associated with independent inferential statistics, (b) generating average estimates of magnitude of treatments, called effect sizes, and (c) analyzing the differences in effect sizes to determine whether they are systematically related to other features of the studies. Cooper and Rosenthal (1980) demonstrated that reviewers using meta-analysis interpret a literature differently from reviewers using the traditional, narrative technique.

The major threat to the validity of a review's conclusion during the analysis and interpretation stage is that the rules of inference may be illogical or irrelevant to the data at hand. In traditional review, it is difficult to gauge the appropriateness of inference rules because they are not very often made explicit. For quantitative reviews, the suppositions of the statistical tests are generally known and *some* statistical biases can be removed. Regardless of the strategy used, the possibility always exists that the reviewer has used an invalid rule when making inferences from the literature.

Data Analysis of Homework Studies

The data analysis strategies used to synthesize the homework studies were arrived at through a series of decisions. First, it was deemed most appropriate to perform separate syntheses for each of the 10 aspects of homework that have been researched. The two sets of studies that examined homework per se (versus no-treatment controls and versus in-school study), the five sets that examined characteristics of the homework assignment (amount, instructional purpose, skill area, individualization, and student choice), the one set that dealt with a home-community factor (parent involvement), and the two sets that dealt with classroom follow-up (instructional and affective feedback) were all viewed as examining conceptually distinct areas of concern. Synthesizing studies across these areas would produce results with unclear conceptual and empirical referents.

Second, for research in all areas, an attempt was made to determine (a) the direction of effect for each comparison of homework treatments, (b) the statistical significance level associated with each comparison, and (c) an estimate of the magnitude of the homework treatment's effect.

Finally, for each of the 10 areas a separate decision was made concerning whether its research was amenable to the application of quantitative synthesis procedures. This decision was based on (a) the number of studies in the area and (b) the similarity in methods used in the studies. Using these criteria, four research questions were deemed suitable candidates for meta-analysis. These involved (a) comparisons of homework versus no homework, (b) comparisons of homework versus in-class supervised study, (c) studies relating the time students spent on homework to achievement, and (d) studies of whether homework meant for practice and/or for review was more effective than homework addressing only same-day class lessons (i.e., an instructional purpose). The other areas of research either had too few studies or the studies were too heterogeneous in construction or conceptualization to warrant using meta-analysis.

Measuring Homework Treatment Effects

Eight of the 10 areas of research lent themselves to the calculation of a d-index to estimate the magnitude of the treatment differences (Cohen, 1977). The d-index is an appropriate measure of effect when the difference between two group means is being compared.

The d-index expresses the difference between two treatments in terms of standard deviation units. The formula for the d-index is:

$$d = \frac{M1 - M2}{SD}$$

where M1 and M2 are the means of the groups, and SD is an estimate of the groups' standard deviation. Thus, a d-index of .5 signifies that the two group means are separated by one-half standard deviation. Assume, for instance, that M1 is the mean achievement for a group of students doing homework and M2 is the mean for a no-homework group. A d-index equal to .5 would indicate that the average student in the homework group had an achievement score equal to that of students who were half a standard deviation above the control group mean.

A statistic related to the d-index—and one that many people find intuitively more meaningful—is called U3 (Cohen, 1977). U3 tells the percentage of people in the group with the lower mean that was exceeded by 50% of the people in the higher-mean group. If the d-index for a homework versus no-homework comparison is .5, U3 is 69.1%. This indicates that the average student in the homework group had an achievement score higher than 69.1% of the students in the no-homework condition. In many instances, the effect of homework treatments will be expressed in terms of the d-index and U3 both.

Although the basic formula for the d-index is straightforward, in practice many decisions have to be made about how it is to be calculated. First, a rule must be adopted for how the standard deviation used in the denominators will be estimated. One rule is to use the standard deviation of the control group. Another rule is to assume that the standard deviation of both groups would be equal if all members of the underlying populations could be measured. Then, the average of the treatment and control group standard deviations gives the best estimate of the population value. This second strategy was used here, primarily for reasons described below.

Second, procedures must be adopted for estimating the d-index when the means and/or standard deviations of the treatment groups are not reported. One such method involves the following manipulation of the t-test:

$$d = \frac{2t}{\sqrt{df\ error}}$$

where t equals the value of the t-test and df error equals the degrees of freedom for error associated with the comparison. This formula estimates the d-index, assuming that the standard deviations of the two groups are equal. Because this formula was used so often in generating effect sizes in the homework literature, the average of the standard deviations was used in all cases. If F-tests with one degree of freedom in the numerator are reported, the d-index can be calculated by substituting $\sqrt{F}$ for t in the above formula.

In a few cases (for example, when F-tests with multiple degrees of freedom in the numerator were reported), other quantitative manipulations or assumptions about data had to be made to generate an effect size. These were rare, and the same procedure was not often used more than once.

There are always instances in which a research report does not contain enough data to obtain even a rough estimate of the study's effect size. In these instances, it is sometimes advisable to contact authors and request the needed data. This procedure was not used for this review because (a) the actual number of instances in which estimates could not be derived was small, (b) most instances that did occur involved research conducted more than a decade ago, and (c) even when researchers receive such requests they frequently ignore them. It is unlikely that the conclusions of this review would change greatly if these data were available.

Finally, a decision must be made about whether the standard deviation estimate in the d-index should be reduced by the removal of variance due to factors other than the homework treatment. For example, suppose a study compared a homework treatment and a no-homework treatment. In analyzing the data, a two-factor analysis of variance was performed in which not only variance due to treatment but also variance due to student ability and the interaction between treatment and ability was examined. The F-test for treatment taken from this analysis is based on an error term from which the two additional factors have been removed. Thus, an estimated d-index would likely be larger than one based on a simple t-test of the difference between the homework and no-homework groups. Put differently, the estimate of the standard deviation in the d-index is based on an average of four groups (say, two treatments by two levels of ability) rather than on an average of two more heterogeneous groups (two treatments).

In this review, the d-indexes were expressed using a standard deviation unreduced by other factors. One reason for this decision was that different studies used various additional factors and different numbers of factors when treatments were analyzed in complex designs. Some studies used pretests as additional factors; others used intelligence, achievement, gender, personality variables, treatment variations, or some combination of these. There was thus rarely enough homogeneity in analytic designs to claim that d-indexes based on reduced standard deviations actually referred to the same target populations.

Second, the use of the unreduced standard deviation gives the d-index a clear referent. It refers to the effect of the homework treatment on the outcome measure with all other influences on the outcome treated as error or as unexplained variance. In fact, we know the sources of some of this error—for example, other things besides homework influence achievement. However, by ignoring these sources in estimating the d-index we arrive at an estimate of homework's effect that is independent of any other effects, as both main effects or in interaction with homework. Of course, the interactive effects of homework with other aspects of the student and school setting will be given ample consideration, but will not be used to alter the estimate of a homework treatment's simple effect.

One implication of using the unreduced standard deviation is that the estimate of homework's effect is calculated to its most conservative, smallest possible value. This needs to be kept in mind when the effect of the homework treatment is interpreted.

Finally, for two areas of homework research—those involving (a) the relation between time spent on homework and achievement and (b) parent involvement—both the treatment and outcome variables were continuous measurements. Therefore, the Pearson product-moment correlation co-efficient, or r-index, was used as the measure of effect. This measure and its interpretation are familiar to social scientists. The r-index can be converted to a d-index using the following formula:

$$d = \frac{2r}{\sqrt{1 - r^2}}$$

This formula will be used in the substantive interpretation of homework treatment effects to compare effects across areas.

As with the d-indexes, attempts were made to retrieve r-indexes that were unreduced by other factors—that is, to work with zero-order rather than semi-partial correlations.

Synthesizing Homework Treatment Effects

Two meta-analytic techniques were used to synthesize studies in the four research areas where quantitative integration was deemed appropriate. These were (a) the estimation of an average effect size and 95% confidence interval and (b) a homogeneity analysis to determine whether the effect sizes were drawn from the same population. Both procedures are described in detail in Hedges and Olkin (1985).

One problem that arises in estimating average effects and analyzing the variance among effects involves deciding what constitutes an independent test of the hypothesis. Sometimes a single research report may contain multiple tests of the same hypothesis. This occurs because (a) different populations of respondents were sampled and their data were reported separately, (b) multiple measures of the same construct were collected and each measure was analyzed separately, or (c) more than one study was reported in a single research report. In these instances the reviewer must decide whether each statistical test, each sample, study, or research report, is to be considered an independent test of the hypothesis.

As I suggested elsewhere (Cooper, 1984), a shifting unit will be used in this review. This strategy places independence somewhere between the sample and statistical test levels. First, each statistical test is coded as if it were an independent event. For example, if a single study comparing homework versus no homework contains two measures of achievement, say a standardized measure and a class test, separately for fifth- and sixth-graders, a total of four effect sizes would be coded. All codings for the four effects might be identical, except for the entries under "standardization," "grade level," and "number of students," which might be different for the two grades. However, for the estimate of homework's overall effect, the two achievement measures would be averaged within each grade so that the study contributed only two effect sizes. For an analysis in which the effects of homework are compared for different measures of achievement, this study would contribute all four effects.

In essence, the shifting unit approach assumes that independence ought to lie at the sample, or study unit level. However, so as not to lose the considerable information available when possible influences on an effect size are examined within the same sample, it "compromises" this independence. The object is to retain as much data as possible without violating too greatly the assumption of independent observations that underlies the validity of the quantitative synthesis techniques.

Estimates of average effect sizes were calculated by weighting each d-index or r-index by the number of participants on which the estimate was based. In the above example the two effect sizes contributed by the homework versus no homework study to the overall estimate of effect (one at each grade level averaged over two achievement measures) would each be weighted by the number of students in its sample. Average effect sizes were calculated across all results within an area of research and also for subgroups of results within areas, if the homogeneity analyses described below indicated that these would be informative.

Combined probabilities were not calculated for each hypothesis. Instead, 95% confidence intervals were estimated for the average effect sizes. A confidence interval establishes a range of values within which the true effect size is expected to fall. When a 95% confidence interval is specified, it means that the probability is .95 and that the true effect size lies between the two values. If a d-index or r-index confidence interval does not contain a value of zero, then a statistically significant ($p < .05$) treatment effect exists.

Homogeneity analyses compare the amount of variance exhibited by a set of effect sizes with the variance expected if only sampling error is operating. If the exhibited variance is significantly greater than sampling error, the meta-analysis tests whether characteristics of the comparisons are associated with, or explain, the "excess" variance. For example, if the homework versus no-homework effect sizes exhibit more variance than is expected by sampling error, a test might be made to see whether homework effects differed for various grade levels and thus explain some of the excess variance.

Hedges and Olkin (1985) described how the homogeneity analysis can be carried out using the General Linear Model program of the Statistical Analysis System computer package (SAS, 1985). A weighting of the effect sizes serves as the dependent variable, and the comparison characteristics serve as the "independent" variables. The sums of squares due to the tested influences are treated as chi-square statistics.

Hedges and Olkin (1985) also suggest that, when effect sizes are heterogeneous, the meta-analyst enter sets of possible influencing variables in the regression equations in a hierarchical fashion. In practice, however, sets of methodological or other characteristics of studies tend to be highly intercorrelated. When they are entered into the same prediction equations, it is often difficult to interpret their individual contributions. Therefore, in the homework meta-analyses described below, potential influences on effect sizes were examined individually. Then the correlations between significant influences were examined post hoc to determine if the interpretation of results needed to be modified by the confounding of features in research designs.

SUMMARY

In this review, a methods description approach was used to examine the effects of methodology on study outcomes. The methods factors examined included student assignment procedures, other procedures for producing student equivalence, use of repeated measurements, sample sizes, standardization of outcome measures, teachers as experimenters, sampling procedures, respondent types, and units of analyses. In addition to these methodological factors, numerous other characteristics of studies were examined for their influence on homework's effect. These included the document type, year the research was conducted, location of the study, grade level, family economic status, racial background and ability level of students, subject matter, and several aspects of the homework treatment.

Estimates of the reliability of codings across two coders were quite high, ranging from $k = .75$ to $k = 1.00$. Effective reliability was even higher, because the discrepancies between coders were resolved through reference to the original documents.

The data resulting from the literature search and coding of studies were analyzed separately for each of the 10 areas of research described in Chapter 3. For each study, an attempt was made to generate a d-index or r-index measure of the treatment effect. The d-index measures the difference between two group means in terms of common standard deviation units.

Two meta-analytic techniques were used to synthesize the results across studies: (a) the estimation of an average effect size and 95% confidence interval and (b) a homogeneity analysis to determine if effect sizes within a research area were drawn from the same population. These procedures were adopted from Hedges and Olkin (1985).

Part III

Homework Versus Alternative Treatments

5

Homework Versus No-Treatment

The assessment of a treatment's effectiveness is always a relative matter. The initial response to the question "Is homework effective?" must be: "Compared with what?" The studies reviewed in this chapter compared students doing homework with control students who received no homework or any other treatment meant to compensate for the lack of home study. The researchers intended that all students would be treated identically during school hours. However, some of the students were given additional academic work to complete during nonschool hours, while others were not.

EARLY STUDIES COMPARING HOMEWORK AND NO-TREATMENT

Studies in the 1930s

Because the comparison of homework to no treatment seems so basic to an assessment of homework's effects, it is not surprising to discover that these types of studies have a long history. In fact, one of the most active decades for homework versus no-treatment comparisons was the 1930s. Several characteristics of the six studies conducted during the 1930s are summarized in Table 5.1. All six used student achievement as the measure of homework's effect. None of the studies employed random assignment of students to treatments, but every study employed at least one other technique meant to produce equivalence of students in the two comparison groups.

TABLE 5.1. Studies Comparing Homework and No Homework Conducted during the 1930s

Characteristics	Carmichael	Montgomery	Steiner	Teahan	Vincent	Foran & Weber
Year	1933	1933	1934	1935	1937	1939
Type of document	Master's thesis	Master's thesis	Journal article	Journal article	Journal article	Journal article
Location of study	Calif.	W.V.	Pa.	N.J.	N.Y.	NA
Research design	One group pretest-posttest	NEC with counterbalancing	NEC	NEC	NEC	NEC with counterbalancing
Student equivalence procedure	None	Matching	Matching	Matching	Matching	None
Grade level	5–8	7–9	7	6–8	5–6	7
Subject matter	Eight subjects	Math, English	Math, English	Math	Math, English, geography	Math
No. schools/classes/students	1/8/230	1/6/60	1/2/39	1/12/NA	1/3/NA	7/7/292
Treatment duration	3 years	1 semester	18 weeks	23 weeks	20 weeks	1 semester
Assignments per week	5	5	5	3	NA	NA
Experimenter as teacher	No	NA	No	No	NA	No
Unit tests or grades	None	None	None	None	None	None
Comprehensive tests	Standardized	Standardized	Standardized	Standardized	Teacher	Standardized

Note. NEC = nonequivalent control group; NA = not available.

Each study contained a comprehensive measure of achievement, and in five of the six instances this measure was a standardized test. The grade levels of students involved in the studies were surprisingly narrow, ranging from fifth grade to ninth grade. The duration of the treatment before the effect of homework was assessed was about one semester in five of the studies, and three years in the sixth study. The studies varied considerably in their sample size. Two studies had more than 200 participants, two studies had fewer than 60 participants, and two did not report the number of students involved but did report the number of classrooms as 3 and 12. Only one of the studies employed formal statistical procedures to test the differences between the homework and no-homework treatments.

The study by Carmichael (1933) is unique. Rather than reporting on a treatment instituted at the request of the researcher, this study examined the effects of a district-wide change in homework policy. The study compared the achievement of students in the El Segundo, California, school district before and after a policy prohibiting homework was instituted. The pre- and posttreatment intervals were three years. The outcome measure was the Stanford Achievement Test.

All six of the studies assessed the effects of homework on achievement in mathematics. Four of the six comparisons favored the homework group, one favored the no-treatment group, and one found different effects for different skill areas. In the latter study, Carmichael (1933) found generally positive effects for homework on math reasoning, but negative effects on computation. Two other studies examined separate math subskills. Steiner (1934) found positive effects for homework on both the reasoning and the computation subscales of the Stanford Achievement Test, with a slightly larger effect of homework on reasoning. However, the fundamentals and problems subtests of the Unit Scales of Attainment Achievement Test showed a more positive effect for homework on fundamentals than on problems. Likewise, Foran and Weber (1939) found positive effects for homework on both problem-solving and computation, but a larger effect on computation.

In sum, these early studies were generally positive in their assessment of homework's effect on math achievement, but found small and generally inconsistent results when homework's effects on math subskills were calculated.

Four studies looked at homework's effect on achievement in English. Two of the studies reported overall findings without attention to potential differences among English subskills. Vincent (1937) found a negative effect for English homework on comprehensive examinations prepared by teachers. Montgomery (1933) also obtained an overall result favoring no homework when the Stanford Achievement Test was used as the outcome measure. However, Montgomery did find positive effects for homework on seventh- and eighth-graders, although these were overshadowed by a large negative effect for ninth-graders.

Two additional studies examined different English subskills. Carmichael (1933) found positive effects for homework on spelling, language usage, and literature; a negative effect for word meaning; and no difference for paragraph meaning. Steiner (1934) found positive effects for homework on punctuation and grammar usage, a negative effect on capitalization, and one positive and one negative effect on two measures of language usage.

Taken together, the studies conducted in the 1930s revealed no indication of a positive effect of homework on English achievement, but there was some indication that the effect of homework might vary for different English subareas.

Finally, two studies examined homework's effects on subjects other than math and English. Vincent (1937) found positive effects for homework on geography achievement in the fifth grade but negative effects in the sixth grade. Carmichael (1933) found positive effects for homework on history/civics.

Studies Conducted between 1940 and 1962

From 1940 through 1962, only five additional comparisons of homework versus no homework were reported. These studies are outlined in Table 5.2. As with the 1930s studies, none of these studies employed random assignment, and all used achievement as the outcome measure. All but one used some means other than random assignment to produce equivalent groups of students. These studies tended to be shorter in duration than the 1930s studies, and they accordingly employed unit tests as well as more encompassing measures to assess homework's effect. Students in these studies were somewhat older than those in the earlier studies, with grade levels ranging from ninth grade through the end of high school. These studies also generally involved small numbers of students, ranging from 22 to 58 participants.

Three of the studies tested homework's effect on math achievement. Hines (1957) gave 17 different unit and comprehensive tests, both teacher-developed and standardized, to students doing and not doing homework in geometry. All the comparisons favored the homework condition, but none reached statistical significance. The average d-index was +.61, meaning that the average student doing homework had an average test score over one-half a standard deviation above the average student doing no homework.

Schroeder (1960) gave algebra students four unit tests from the textbook, four teacher-developed quarterly examinations, and one final examination. Two of the unit tests, all the quarterlies, and the final exam favored homework, but only one comparison reached statistical significance. The average effect across the nine tests was d = +.13.

Anderson (1946) also reported a positive effect for homework on math

TABLE 5.2. Studies Comparing Homework and No Homework Conducted between 1940 and 1962

Characteristics	Anderson	Schneider	Schain	Hines	Schroeder
Year	1946	1953	1954	1957	1960
Type of document	Journal article	Journal article	Journal article	Journal article	Master's thesis
Location of study	Okla.	N.Y.	NA	Fla.	Minn.
Research design	NEC	NEC	NEC with counterbalancing	NEC	NEC
Student equivalence procedure	Matching	None	Matching	Matching	Matching
Grade level	8	High school	High school	High school	9
Subject matter	Math, English, Social Studies	Economics	History	Geometry	Algebra
No. schools/classes/students	1/2/58	1/2/51	1/1/22	1/2/32	1/2/40
Treatment duration	5 units	½ term	2 weeks	1 year	1 year
Assignments per week	NA	NA	5	2–3	5
Experimenter as teacher	No	NA	Yes	No	Yes
Unit tests or grades	Teacher	Teacher	Teacher	Teacher	Textbook
Comprehensive tests	No	No	Teacher	Teacher, Standardized	Teacher

Note. NEC = nonequivalent control group; NA = not available.

achievement. However, the only numerical results presented were combined scores for three subjects: math, English, and social studies. The effect of homework across all three subject areas was extremely large, with d equaling +1.39.

It appears that this second set of early studies produced results similar to those of the studies conducted in the 1930s with regard to achievement in mathematics. Without examining possible differences in subskills, the effect of homework on achievement was found to be generally positive.

In addition to the mathematics studies, Schneider (1953) looked at the effect of homework on teacher-developed tests in two economics classes, and Schain (1954) examined homework in history classes. Schneider reported a nonsignificant difference favoring no homework, and Schain reported results favoring homework but did not test for significance.

Finally, two of the early studies comparing homework and no homework looked at whether the effect was moderated by the ability of the student. Montgomery (1933) found a positive effect for homework on English among lower-I.Q. students but negative effects for average and bright students. In math, homework had a large positive effect for brighter students, a negative effect for average students, and a small positive effect for slower students. Schain (1954) claimed that brighter students did well in history whether or not they did homework, while average and poorer students did much better with homework.

RECENT STUDIES COMPARING
HOMEWORK AND NO TREATMENT

The Number of Studies, Samples, and Effect Sizes

Since 1962, 17 reports have detailed the results of studies comparing homework and no homework. One of these reports (Maertens, 1967) described a study that used a repeated measures design comparing two types of homework and no homework. No usable d-index could be retrieved from this study, so it will be dealt with separately. Another study (Nadis, 1965) did not contain enough information for the generation of an effect size. A third study (Koch, 1965) allowed the calculation of a d-index but only with additional variables partialed out of the error term. The latter two studies are included in the descriptive information given below, but not in the meta-analysis of unadjusted d-indexes. Summaries of 16 studies (excluding Maertens, 1967) can be found in Table 5.3.

The research reports contained a total of 22 independent samples. Because a single sample could have been used to test the effects of homework over multiple subjects and outcome measures (see Chapter 4), the actual number of d-indexes retrieved from the reports was 48.

The Type of Document

Six of the 22 samples were reported in journal articles, 12 in dissertations, and 4 in papers written for graduate-level classes.

The Geographic Location of Studies

All 16 studies were conducted in the United States. Three studies were conducted in California and Ohio, two in Michigan, and the rest in states represented only once.

The Sample Size

Fourteen of the samples were drawn from studies that were conducted in one school. Three samples were drawn from studies conducted in two schools, and four samples came from two studies that were conducted in eight schools. One report did not include information on the school sample size.

The average number of classrooms contributing to a sample was between 5 and 6, the median between 4 and 5. Nine of the samples were a part of a study including only 2 classrooms. One sample was drawn from 20 classrooms.

The average number of students in a sample was 107.7, with a range from 39 to 400. Eleven samples contained 60 or fewer students, and two samples contained more than 300 students.

The Research Design

Five methods for assigning students to treatment conditions were employed: random assignment of students (n = 5); computer assignment of students (n = 2); random assignment of classes (n = 3); nonequivalent control group with student matching (n = 4); and nonequivalent control group without student matching (n = 8).

Five of the samples came from studies that counterbalanced treatments, meaning that at different times the same students were in both the homework condition and the no-homework condition. These same five studies also took repeated measures of the treatments' effects.

The experimenter served as the teacher for 9 of the 22 samples.

The Nature of the Homework Treatment

The duration of the homework treatments ranged from 2 to 30 weeks, with an average length between 9 and 10 weeks. Five samples had homework treatments lasting 6 weeks, four had treatments lasting 10 weeks, and three did homework for 16 weeks before its effects were assessed.

Nine samples averaged three homework assignments per week. One

TABLE 5.3. Studies Included in the Homework Versus No-Homework Meta-
Analysis

Author (Year)	Type of Document	Location of Study (State)	Research Design	Counterbalancing/ Repeated Measures (used or not used)
Allison & Gray (1970)	Journal article	Calif.	Random assign. of students	Yes/yes
Ames (1983)	Paper	Ohio	Computer assign. of students	No/no
Doane (1972)	Diss.	N.Y.	NEC without matching	No/no
Foyle (1984)	Diss.	Kans.	Random assign. of classes	No/no
Grant (1971)	Diss.	Calif.	Random assign. of classes	No/no
Gray & Allison (1971)	Journal article	Calif.	Random assign. of students	Yes/yes
Hines (1982)	Paper	Ohio	Computer assign. of students	No/no
Hume-Cummings (1985)	Paper	Ohio	NEC with matching	Yes/yes
Koch (1965)	Journal article	Minn.	Random assign. of classes	No/no
Maertens & Johnston (1972)	Journal article	Ore.	Random assign. of students	No/no
Nadis (1965)	Diss.	Mich.	NEC with matching	Yes/yes
Parrish (1976)	Diss.	Tex.	NEC without matching	No/no
Rosenthal (1974)	Diss.	Mich.	NEC without matching	No/no
Singh (1969)	Diss.	Ariz.	NEC without matching	No/no
Whelan (1965)	Diss.	R.I.	NEC with matching	No/no
Ziebell (1968)	Paper	Wis.	NEC with matching	Yes/yes

sample did homework twice a week, three did homework four times a week, and four did homework every day. For five samples, the frequency of homework assignments was not reported.

The Outcome Measure

In the meta-analysis that follows, only achievement outcomes will be considered. Of the 48 effect sizes, 18 involved class tests or grades, and 30 involved standardized achievement tests.

Only three studies measured the effect of homework on attitudes.

TABLE 5.3. *Continued*

No. Schools/ Classes/ Students	Grade Level	Subject Matter	Treatment Duration (Weeks)	No. Assignments Per Week	Teacher as Experimeter	Outcome Measure
1/2/60	6	General math	4	3	No	Class test
1/2/54	7	Science	9	2	Yes	Class test
1/8/186	4	Computation	2	5	No	Class test
1/6/131	10	Social studies & history	6	5	Yes	Class test
8/17/386	5	Computation, concepts & problem-solving	10	3	No	Standard test
1/2/60	6	Computation	4	3	No	Class test
1/2/44	8	Social studies & history	10	NA	Yes	Class test
1/2/39	7	General math	12	NA	Yes	Class test
1/3/85	6	Concepts & problem-solving	10	5	No	Standard test
8/NA/387	4,5,6	Computation & concepts	6	4	Yes	Class test
1/2/80	9	Social studies & history	6	3	Yes	Class test
1/8/120	9	General math	2	3	No	Class test
1/2/175	6,8	Language & vocabulary	NA	NA	No	Class test
2/5/123	4,5,6	Computation, concepts, problem-solving, reading, language & vocabulary, spelling, science, social studies & history	16	3	No	Standard test
NA/20/400	6	Concepts, problem-solving, language & vocabulary	30	3	No	Standard test
1/4/40	10	Science	10	5	Yes	Class test

Note. NEC = nonequivalent control group; NA = not available.

These will be described separately. No other outcome variables were employed.

Subject Matter

Some 25 d-indexes related to achievement in mathematics. Of these, 3 involved general or unspecified math skills, 9 involved computation, 8 concerned concept learning, and 5 concerned problem-solving skills. Thirteen effect sizes related to reading and English. Ten related to science (n = 5) and social studies (n = 5).

The Average d-Index

The average magnitude of the 20 d-indexes calculated from independent samples was d = +.21. This means that the average student doing homework had a higher achievement score than 54.7% of students not doing homework. The 95% confidence interval revealed the lower estimate to be d = +.13 and the higher to be d = +.30. Thus, the probability is .95 that the true difference between the homework group and the no-homework group falls between these two values, and we can conclude that the difference is statistically significant (that is, not zero). Fourteen of the 20 d-indexes indicated a positive effect for homework. Figure 5.1 displays the distribution of the effect sizes.

As noted above, not included in the average d-index was a study by Maertens (1967) in which the effect of either teacher-prepared or experimenter-prepared math homework was compared to a no-homework condition using a repeated measures analysis of variance. In this study, none of

1.00 to .96	NN
.95 to .91	
.90 to .86	T
.85 to .81	
.80 to .76	
.75 to .71	
.70 to .69	
.65 to .61	
.60 to .56	T
.55 to .51	NTT
.50 to .46	
.45 to .41	
.40 to .36	NN
.35 to .31	N
.30 to .26	
.25 to .21	
.20 to .16	T
.15 to .11	
.10 to .06	NT
.05 to .01	N
.00 to −.04	
−.05 to −.09	NNT
−.10 to −.14	
−.15 to −.19	NT
−.20 to −.24	
−.25 to −.29	
−.30 to −.34	
−.35 to −.39	N

FIGURE 5.1.   Distribution of d-Indexes for Comparisons of Homework and No Homework. *Note.* The d-indexes are distinguished by whether the experimenter was also the teacher of the class: T = teacher; N = not teacher.

three math subskill tests produced significant results. However, because the results were based on F-tests with two degrees of freedom and because standard deviations were not given, it is impossible to tell if a simple contrast between homework and no homework would have revealed a significant result. In any case, five of the six comparisons favored the homework groups.

Also not included in the average d-index were two studies (Koch, 1965; Nadis, 1965) from which unadjusted d-indexes could not be computed. Both studies produced results indicating that homework led to higher achievement than no homework.

The homogeneity analysis indicated significantly more variability in the d-indexes than would have been expected due to sampling error alone, $\chi^2(19) = 57.41, p < .001$. Therefore, additional analyses were conducted to determine what might be causing this variability.

Moderators of the Effect Size

Twelve variables were examined to determine if they influenced the magnitude of the difference in achievement between homework and no-homework treatments. Ten of the potential moderators proved to be significantly related to the homework effect size. These are described in Table 5.4.

The size of homework's effect was related to the year in which the research report appeared, $\chi^2(1) = 8.00, p < .01$. Although studies conducted in the 1960s and 1970s revealed about equal average d-indexes— $d = +.16$ and $+.18$, respectively—the four samples collected in the 1980s revealed an average d-index nearly three times as large as the earlier estimates, $d = +.48$. The d-indexes did not differ depending on whether they were reported in journal articles or dissertations, $\chi^2(1) = 0.47$, ns (not significant).

Three of four factors related to the experimental procedures proved to be significant predictors of variance in effect sizes. First, no significant differences were found in the effect sizes generated by the five types of research designs, $\chi^2(4) = 8.58$, ns. The result was also not significant when a specific comparison was made between samples using random assignment (of students by the experimenter or computer, or of classrooms) and samples using nonequivalent control groups, $\chi^2(1) = 0.38$, ns.

Studies employing counterbalancing and repeated measures in their design revealed results that were significantly different from studies not employing these techniques, $\chi^2(1) = 4.68, p < .05$. Samples in which counterbalancing and repeated measures were used produced a negative d-index, $d = -.08$, indicating that students doing no homework outperformed students doing homework. Studies without these procedures produced effects favoring homework, $d = +.24$.

Whether or not the person conducting the study was the teacher of

TABLE 5.4. Effect Sizes for Comparisons of Homework Versus No Homework on Measures of Academic Achievement

		95% Confidence Interval		
	No. of Comparisons	Low Estimate	Mean	High Estimate
Overall ($\chi^2(19) = 57.41$, p < .001)	20	+.13	+.21	+.30
Year ($\chi^2(1) = 8.00$, p < .01)				
1960s	6	+.01	+.16	+.32
1970s	10	+.06	+.18	+.30
1980s	4	+.23	+.48	+.73
Counterbalancing and repeated measures ($\chi^2(1) = 4.68$, p < .05)				
Present	4	−.35	−.08	+.19
Absent	16	+.14	+.24	+.34
Experimenter ($\chi^2(1) = 9.52$, p < .01)				
Teacher	8	+.25	+.41	+.57
Not teacher	12	+.02	+.12	+.22
Duration of treatment ($\chi^2(1) = 3.89$, p < .05)				
<10 weeks	12	+.20	+.32	+.44
10 weeks or more	8	−.03	+.09	+.21
No. of Assignments ($\chi^2(1) = 15.43$, p < .001)				
1–3 per week	14	−.01	+.09	+.19
4 or 5 per week	6	+.30	+.44	+.58

Grade ($\chi^2(1) = 3.75$, p $< .06$)				
4–6	13	+.05	+.15	+.25
7–9	5	+.09	+.31	+.53
10–12	2	+.33	+.64	+.95
Subject matter ($\chi^2(2) = 19.13$, p $< .001$)				
Math	25	+.10	+.16	+.22
Reading and English	13	+.18	+.32	+.46
Science and social studies	10	+.38	+.56	+.74
Math areas ($\chi^2(3) = 6.79$, p $< .01$)				
Computation	9	+.12	+.24	+.36
Concepts	8	+.07	+.19	+.31
Problem-solving	5	−.12	+.02	+.16
General or unspecified	3	−.01	+.26	+.53
Outcome measure ($\chi^2(1) = 6.49$, p $< .02$)				
Class tests or grades	15	+.18	+.30	+.42
Standardized tests	5	−.07	+.07	+.21

the classes also influenced the research outcome, $\chi^2(1) = 9.52$, p < .01. The d-index was more than three times as large when experimenters were teachers, d = +.41, as when they were not, d = +.12.

Two aspects of the homework treatment were related to the outcomes of studies. Surprisingly, the effect of homework was negatively related to the duration of the homework treatment, $\chi^2(1) = 3.89$, p < .05, with longer treatments producing smaller effect sizes. Not surprisingly, however, homework produced larger positive effects if students did more assignments per week, $\chi^2(1) = 15.43$, p < .001.

The grade level of students had a nearly significant but certainly noteworthy effect on homework's effectiveness, $\chi^2(1) = 3.75$, p < .06. The d-index favoring homework was twice as large for junior high school students, d = +.31, as for elementary school students, d = +.15, and twice as large again for high school students, d = +.64.

Subject matter also influenced the outcome of comparisons, $\chi^2(2) = 19.13$, p < .001. Comparisons involving mathematics revealed the smallest d-indexes, d = +.16; those involving science and social studies revealed the largest d-indexes, d = +.56, while those involving reading and English fell in the middle, d = +.32. When comparisons involving the different subskills of mathematics were compared, a significant difference was also found, $\chi^2(3) = 6.79$, p < .01. It appears that the average effect of homework on problem-solving achievement was smaller, d = +.02, than on computation, d = +.24, or concepts, d = +.19.

Finally, how achievement was measured was significantly related to the outcome of homework versus no homework comparisons, $\chi^2(1) = 6.49$, p < .02. Homework had a larger effect when achievement was measured by class tests or grades, d = +.30, than by standardized tests, d = +.07.

Interrelations among the Moderator Variables

As noted in Chapter 4, before attempting to interpret the results regarding moderators of homework's effect it is important to examine the interrelation among the moderators themselves. Because different experiments often share the same procedures, it may not always be clear which procedure is responsible for a moderating influence, so chi-squares were calculated on the cross-tabulations of pairs of moderator variables. However, because expected frequencies in many cells were small, the chi-squares are only suggestive. For this reason, the results of the analyses will be described below in terms of the actual cell frequencies, not the precise chi-square values.

Whether or not the experimenter was the teacher of the classes proved to be a major source of confounding among the moderators. All four studies conducted in the 1980s were done with the experimenter as teacher, whereas in earlier years studies having teachers as experimenters were outnumbered three to one. Thus, it is not clear whether the effectiveness of homework has improved over the years or whether the possibility of biased treatment unrelated to homework has increased.

Experimenting teachers were also overrepresented in the earlier grades, with 11 such cases appearing in grades 4 through 6. These two influences, however, had opposite effects on the homework versus no homework comparison. Therefore, the revealed differences between grades and/or experimenting versus nonexperimenting teachers might have been larger had the confound not existed.

All eight samples with experimenting teachers used class tests or grades as outcome measures. Thus, the superior effect of homework on these measures may be due to teacher-experimenter biasing of treatments, or vice versa. Similarly, 11 nonexperimenting teachers gave only one to three assignments per week, confounding these two effects.

With regard to subject matter, experimenting teachers were underrepresented in both math and reading or English. Twenty math comparisons and 13 reading or English comparisons involved nonexperimenting teachers, but only 6 science and social studies comparisons (out of 10) were protected from this source of bias. Therefore, the subject matter difference may be due to factors unrelated to the homework manipulation.

Finally, the procedures of counterbalancing and repeated measures, which were themselves perfectly confounded, were also confounded with the type of outcome measure used and the math subskill. All samples using counterbalancing and repeated measures also used class tests or grades. No comparison involving problem-solving skills used counterbalancing and repeated measures. In both instances the potential effect of the confound would be to lessen the effect of each moderator.

Summary

Twenty independent comparisons revealed a d-index of +.21 favoring homework over no homework on measures of academic achievement. However, the effect was influenced by numerous third variables. Homework's effect was more positive in studies conducted in the 1980s than in earlier studies. It was smaller in studies using counterbalancing and repeated measures, and larger in studies where the experimenter was also the teacher of the involved classes. Homework treatments of shorter duration and those involving more numerous assignments per week were most effective. The effectiveness of homework improved as the grade level of students increased. Class tests and grades showed a greater difference between homework and no homework than standardized tests. Among the different subject matters, science and social studies revealed the largest homework effect, and math revealed the smallest. Math problem-solving revealed less of a homework effect than other math subskills. Finally, several confounds among the moderator variables, many of which involved the experimenting teacher, make the simple interpretation of these findings problematic.

HOMEWORK VERSUS NO-HOMEWORK STUDIES CONTAINING THIRD VARIABLES

Third variables can be entered into the analysis of homework's effect in two different ways. First, the variables can be used as covariates. One purpose of covariates is to control for potential differences between students in the homework and no-homework groups, as when nonequivalent groups are statistically equated for differences in ability. A second purpose of covariates is to reduce the size of the mean square error in order to increase the chance of finding statistical significance. Typically, when variables are used as covariates their interaction with the treatment of interest is not entered into the analysis.

Third variables can also be entered into analyses not only to examine their effect on the dependent measure but also to determine whether they interact with other variables in the model. In the present review, these analyses allow within-study determinations of whether the effect of homework varies for different types of students.

Eight of the studies included analyses of achievement scores that contained variables in addition to the homework versus no-homework effect. These analyses allow the examination of (a) the homework treatment with the influence of other variables removed from the standard deviation used in the d-index and (b) interactions between the homework treatment and other variables.

The Effect of Homework with Third Variables Controlled

The eight studies generated eight independent sample estimates of homework's effect with third variables controlled. Four samples controlled one extra variable (either as a covariate or potentially interacting effect), two employed two extra variables, and two samples included three or four extra variables.

The average weighted d-index from the studies was d = +.09. The eight effect sizes were found to be heterogeneous, $\chi^2(7) = 19.68$, p < .01. This is not surprising, considering that the d-index estimates controlled for different numbers and types of extra variables, in addition to other differences. In fact, the number of extra variables in the analysis was significantly related to the variance in effects, $\chi^2(1) = 13.14$, p < .001— studies that had more variables controlled also had less positive effects for homework.

Interactions between Homework and Other Variables

The gender of the student has been the most frequently examined moderator of homework's effects. Seven studies have included this variable in their analyses (Allison & Gray, 1970; Ames, 1983; Foyle, 1984; Grant, 1971; Gray and Allison, 1971; Hines, 1982; Whelan, 1965). Four of these studies formally tested the gender X homework treatment interaction, and all found the resulting F-value to be less than 1. (Since the value of an F-test is expected to be 1 when only chance is operating, we can assume these effects are trivial.) The other three studies examined the effect of homework separately for females and males; in no case was homework effective for one group but not the other. The effect of homework therefore appears to be independent of the gender of the student.

Four studies looked at whether the intelligence of the student influenced the homework treatment (Doane, 1972; Grant, 1971; Maertens, 1967; Whelan, 1965). Two of the studies formally tested the interaction on eight different measures. None of the tests proved significant, and only one had an F-value greater than 1. Doane (1972) did not test the interaction, but did report large differences in the effect of homework across four groups of students distinguished by I.Q. scores—the effect of homework grew more positive as the intelligence of the student increased. For the highest-ability group the d-index was +2.63, while for the lowest-ability group the d-index was −.35. Whelan (1965) also did not formally test the interaction, but found no consistent relationship between intelligence and the effects of homework across two math and three English subskill areas. There is at present no evidence that the effect of homework differs according to the intelligence of the student.

Finally, two personality variables have been examined as potential moderators of the homework effect. Allison and Gray (1970) examined both test and manifest anxiety and four interaction effects; all had F-values less than 1. Doane (1972) found a similar result for locus of control.

THE EFFECT OF HOMEWORK ON ATTITUDES

Three studies comparing homework and no-homework treatments included measures of the students' attitudes as outcomes.

Maertens (1967) created homework and no-homework conditions in third-grade arithmetic classes and measured the effect on six different attitude areas: the school, the teacher, homework itself, arithmetic, reading (a subject indirectly related to math homework), and spelling (a subject area unrelated to math). Attitudes toward each area were measured by 11 bipolar semantic differentials. Again, because Maertens conducted repeated measures analyses of variance with multiple degree of freedom F-tests and did not report standard deviations or simple comparisons, it is difficult to interpret his data unambiguously. However, five of the six attitude measures produced F-values (on two degrees of freedom) at or well below 1. The only test that approached significance involved the unrelated subject matter, spelling. The direction of the means indicated that students who did not do math homework had the least positive attitudes toward spelling.

A study by Maertens and Johnston (1972) also used bipolar semantic differentials to measure attitudes of fourth-, fifth-, and sixth-grade students doing and not doing math homework. Attitudes toward school, math, and homework revealed nonsignificant variation due to treatment condition and no consistent pattern in the direction of the underlying means.

Parrish (1976) measured ninth-graders' attitudes toward math after doing or not doing homework related to a unit on percentages. Attitudes were measured using the Aiken-Dreger Math Attitude Scale, which contains three independent attitude components. Analyses of all components revealed F-values close to or below 1. The direction of means on all three factors favored the no-homework group, with d = $-.20$ for enjoyment of mathematics, d = $-.14$ for apprehension about ability, and d = $-.09$ for security with mathematics.

SUMMARY

Studies comparing homework versus no homework prior to 1962 generally found homework had a positive effect on achievement in mathematics but no consistent effect in other subject areas. Since 1962, 20 independent comparisons revealed an average d-index of $+.21$ favoring homework with the 95% confidence interval ranging from $+.13$ to $+.30$. However, the positive effect was smaller in studies employing counterbalancing and repeated measures, and larger in more recent studies and studies where the experimenter was also the teacher.

The effect of homework was positively related to the grade level of the student—older students benefited most from doing homework. It was also most effective for shorter treatments and for treatments involving more assignments per week. Class tests and grades revealed a larger effect of homework than standardized tests did. Homework was more effective for science and social studies than for math, while the effect of homework did not vary for the different math subskills. Caution must be used in interpreting these findings because several of the moderator variables were confounded with one another.

The results were generally nonsignificant when studies examined the effect of third variables on the homework-achievement relation. Seven studies of gender and four studies of intelligence revealed no consistent pattern of results. Finally, the three studies looking at the influence of homework on attitudes suggested that homework has neither a positive effect nor a negative effect on how students feel about the school, teacher, or subject matter.

6

Homework Versus In-Class Supervised Study

The characteristic that distinguishes the studies to be reviewed in this chapter from those reviewed in Chapter 5 involves how the control group was treated. In the previous studies, no treatment was given to the control group. Control group students did not receive instruction meant to compensate for the fact that they did no homework. In the studies that follow, the control group was required to engage in some form of in-school supervised study not required of students who did homework. Thus, these studies compare the effects of two different treatments.

The definition of in-school supervised study varied from experiment to experiment. Essentially, three characteristics of the treatment are most germane. First, because homework requires that students spend additional time on academic material, some researchers have examined its effect compared to having students devote a similar amount of added time at school. This has been accomplished by lengthening the school day (e.g., Sutcliffe & Canham, 1937) or by shortening the time devoted to subjects or activities not covered in the homework assignments (e.g., Marshall, 1983).

Second, the type of supervision given students in the no-homework group has ranged from passive to active. Baxter (1973) had students complete math problems under the supervision of the teacher but without instructional assistance. Ten Brinke (1964) defined supervised study as students working on problems individually while the teacher moved around the room giving help. On the more active side, McGill (1948) had supervised study classes engage in activities that would be difficult to distinguish from additional class lessons.

Finally, supervised study can differ in how closely its content corresponds to that required of the students doing homework. In some studies the content was identical (e.g., students did the same math problems; Johnson, 1931; Marshall, 1983), while in other studies the material in the two treatments was related but not identical (e.g., teachers of classes in different conditions were allowed to develop homework assignments or to use the supervised study period however they saw fit; McGill, 1948).

EARLY STUDIES OF HOMEWORK
VERSUS SUPERVISED STUDY

These and other characteristics of six experiments involving in-school supervised study that were conducted prior to 1962 are summarized in Table 6.1. The first, by Hagan (1927), was described in a brief report containing little information about the nature of the supervised study treatment. However, because Hagan juxtaposed recitation (i.e., a "period for reports and discussions") with supervised study in his description of how time was allocated in classrooms, it might be assumed that supervised study meant silent, individual deskwork. Hagan reported the pretest to posttest gain scores of students in two pairs of sixth-grade classes and one pair of seventh-grade classes. Five subject areas were covered: fundamentals and problems in arithmetic, factual geography, problems in geography, and reading. The means of posttest scores were reported but not the standard deviations, and significance tests were not conducted. The direction of the gain scores favored the supervised study group in four of the five subject areas, the exception being arithmetic fundamentals.

Johnson (1931) compared homework and supervised study with sixth-grade history classes. Students were matched according to an intelligence test and scores on a history pretest. Supervised-study students not only completed assignments in class that homework students completed at home, but did so with the aid of the teacher and also received instruction in proper study habits. Johnson conducted the experiment over two history units and reversed the treatment groups for each unit. She also gave an immediate test of learning and a delayed test (four weeks after each unit), as well as a test of study skills.

No formal significance tests were carried out by Johnson, but raw data were included in the report, making the calculation of t-tests possible. These revealed no significant differences in achievement between the two treatments on either the first unit or the second for either the immediate or delayed tests (all t-test values were less than 1). The comparisons favored supervised study for the first unit ($d = +.38$ for immediate and $d = -.58$ for delayed) and homework for the second unit ($d = +.03$ for immediate and $d = +.29$ for delayed). Johnson argued that the training in study habits that the second unit homework group received when they were the supervised study group may explain why supervised study was not found superior

TABLE 6.1. Studies Comparing Homework to In-School Supervised Study Prior to 1962

Characteristics	Hagan	Johnson	Rosenstengel & Turner	Sutcliffe & Canham	Cooke & King	McGill
Year	1927	1931	1936	1937	1939	1948
Type of document	Book chapter	Master's thesis	Journal article	Book	Journal article	Dissertation
Location of study	Illinois	Illinois	Missouri	England	Tennessee	New York
Research design	NEC	NEC	NEC	NEC	NEC	NEC
Student equivalence procedure	None	Counterbalancing, matching	Matching	Counterbalancing, matching	Matching	Matching
Repeated measures	No	Yes	Yes	No	No	No
Grade level	6–7	6	6	11–15-yr.-olds	5–6	11–12
Subject matter	Math, geography, reading	History	Health	7 subjects	10 subjects	Economics, American history
No. schools/ classes/students	1/6/275	1/2/26	1/2/52	1/NA/50	1/6/156	1/16/370
Treatment duration	NA	4 weeks	2 units	1 year	1 year	14–20 weeks
Homework assignments per week	NA	5	NA	5	5	5
Added time for supervised study	None	None	15 min.	Yes	40 min.	NA
Type of supervision	NA	Active	NA	Passive	Active	Active
Similarity of assignments	Different	Same	Same	Same	Different	NA
Outcome measure	Standardized	Class tests	Class tests	Class tests	Standardized	Standardized

Note. NEC = nonequivalent control group; NA = not available.

during the second part of the study. It is equally plausible that matching failed to produce comparable groups.

Although they do not relate to the homework issue, Johnson did find significant differences on all four comparisons involving study habits, with the group that received training outperforming the control group on both the immediate and delayed tests for the first unit and on the immediate tests for the second unit. Of course, by the end of the second unit all students had received study habit training.

Rosenstengel and Turner (1936) conducted their experiment in two elementary school classes studying health. The supervised study class was given an additional 15 minutes of class time. Tests on two units were the measures of treatment outcome. These authors listed the raw scores of the 52 subjects in their experiment. On both tests the supervised study group outperformed the homework group. On the first test the d-index for the treatment comparison was $-.07$, and on the second test it was $-.97$.

Sutcliffe and Canham's (1937) research took place in a British secondary school for boys. The supervised study group stayed after school for an extra hour, while the homework group did about one-and-a-half hours of home study. Prior to the treatment, boys in the two groups were paired based on examinations constructed by their teachers. For statistical inference, the difference between the final marks of the pairs of students was analyzed in seven subjects. Four of the comparisons favored homework (history, geography, math, and French) and three favored supervised study (English, physics, and chemistry), though no comparison reached statistical significance. Only difference scores and their standard deviations were reported, so d-indexes for the unadjusted comparisons could not be computed.

Cooke and King (1939) divided fifth- and sixth-graders into two groups equated for mental age. Three classes then received regular homework assignments, and three received supervised study, but no additional instructional time. All students were given forms of the Unit Scales of Attainment Achievement Test as both pretest and posttest measures. Cooke and King analyzed their data by comparing the pretest and posttest measures of each class, not by comparing classes in the two treatment conditions with one another. They reported only the significance level of the pretest-posttest difference for 10 subjects. Using $p < .01$ as the criterion, 20 of the 30 comparisons for homework classes demonstrated significant gain in achievement, while 24 of 30 involving supervised study classes reached significance.

McGill (1984) matched high school students in 16 classes based on their scores on the Cooperative Test of Social Studies Ability. Half of the classes were studying economics, and half were studying American history. Half took part in the experiment in each of two terms. The outcome measures were posttest scores on the Cooperative Test and on one other standardized test specific to the subject matter. McGill examined matched students within subjects and terms separately, instead of including all students in a single overall analysis. Also, he reported the means of the outcome measures, the mean difference of paired students, and the standard deviation of the differences, but not the standard deviations of the raw scores. Thus, not enough data were reported to compute unadjusted d-indexes. Of the eight comparisons (two tests by two subject matters by two terms), five favored supervised study, including all four comparisons involving the Cooperative Test. However, the average value of the eight dependent t-tests was +.18, indicating that the mean effect size was likely near zero.

Inconsistent and incomplete data reporting make it impossible to generate comparable effect sizes and directly synthesize the early research using the supervised study control. However, the interpretation of the research as a whole seems clear. Few of the comparisons reached significance, and those that did could be explained as chance occurrences because of the large number of statistical tests that were conducted. Even when the simple direction of comparisons is examined, neither group appeared superior, though supervised-study students most often performed better. It seems safe to conclude, therefore, that experiments conducted before 1962 uncovered no meaningful difference between the two treatments.

RECENT RESEARCH COMPARING HOMEWORK AND SUPERVISED STUDY

Research conducted since 1962 yields only slightly different results. The eight studies conducted in the past 25 years are summarized in Table 6.2.

Ten Brinke's (1964) study of seventh-and eighth-grade math began with the random assignment of students to homework and supervised-study classrooms. Over the course of the treatments, students took tests on five units. Results were reported separately for the two grades and for the five units, as well as for the five tests aggregated into three skill areas—arithmetic facts, computation, and problem-solving. Not one of the 16 comparisons of treatments proved statistically significant. All three comparisons of skill areas for seventh-graders favored the homework students; for eighth-graders, two of the subskills (facts and computation) favored students receiving supervised study. Across all comparisons, the homework students outperformed the supervised-study students, with the magnitude of the effect being d = +.18.

In performing his analysis, Ten Brinke included a measure of the intelligence of the student that allowed tests of whether the effect of the treatments was moderated by the abilities of the students. On the six subskill comparisons, no interaction of treatment with student intelligence reached significance. The general direction of mean differences indicated that homework was more effective for brighter students and supervised study was

TABLE 6.2. Studies Comparing Homework to In-School Supervised Study After 1962

Characteristics	Ten Brinke	Hudson	Tupesis	Baxter	Marshall	Bird	Huddleson	Paulson
Year	1964	1965	1972	1973	1983	1983	1983	1983
Type of document	Diss.	Diss.	Diss.	Diss.	Diss.	Class paper	Class paper	Class paper
Location of study	Minn.	Ark.	Wis.	N.Y.	Calif.	Ohio	Ohio	Ohio
Research design	Random assignment	NEC	Random assignment by computer	Random assignment of classes	Random assignment of classes	NEC	NEC	NEC
Student equivalence procedure	None	Covariance	None	Counterbalancing	Covariance	None	None	None
Repeated measures	Yes	No	No	No	No	No	No	No
Grade level	7–8	7	10,11,12	6	5–6	High school	9	7
Subject matter	Math	Math	Math	Math	Math	French	English	Math
No. schools/classes/students	1/4/108	2/6/168	1/2/43	3/4/96	NA/21/499	1/2/44	1/2/58	1/2/57
Treatment duration	20 weeks	1 sem.	9 weeks	4 weeks	6 weeks	7 weeks	5 weeks	1 unit
Homework assignments per week	5	5	5	1	3	2–3	2	5
Added time for supervised study	No	No	No	No	Yes	No	No	No
Type of supervision	Active	Active	Active	Passive	Both	Active	Active	NA
Similarity of assignments	Same	Same	Same	Same	Same	Same	Different	Same
Experimenter as teacher	No	No	Yes	No	No	Yes	Yes	Yes
Achievement measure	Class tests	Standardized	Class tests, standardized	Class tests	Standardized	Class tests	Grades	Class tests

Note. NEC = nonequivalent control group; NA = not available.

more effective for slower students. Also, a secondary set of analyses was conducted in which test scores were analyzed using gender as a variable. For seventh-graders, all five comparisons involving girls favored homework, as did three of five comparisons for boys. For eighth-graders, all comparisons involving girls favored supervised study, while all comparisons for boys favored homework. However, none of the gender differences was significant (a total of 20 gender effects were tested), and because Ten Brinke analyzed the data separately for the two genders, no formal tests of the interaction were made.

Hudson (1965) instituted his treatments in six mathematics classes. The treatment involved supervised-study and homework students doing the same assignments, with the exception that homework students took home additional problems, averaging about 25% more work. Two subtests from the Iowa Test of Basic Skills, arithmetic concepts and problem-solving, served as dependent variables. Classrooms were paired according to pretest achievement levels. Means and standard deviations were reported separately for each pair of classes. The direction of effect of all six comparisons (three groups on two tests) favored the homework group, with an average effect size of $d = +.38$. However, because an overall standard deviation was not presented, this estimate controls for ability differences between the three groups of classes. To test for the significance of the treatment effect, Hudson performed six multiple regressions in which nine control variables were entered into the model before the homework versus supervised-study comparison. The control variables included gender, mental ability, socioeconomic status, attitude toward school, study skills, and pretest scores. Only one of the six analyses found a significant ($p < .05$) contribution to prediction by the treatments. The analyses did not test for interactions between the control variables and the treatment variable.

Hudson also examined the differences between the homework and supervised-study classes on attitudes toward school and study skills, as measured by the California Study Methods Survey. Across the three class pairings, students doing homework expressed higher morale and feelings of harmony with the school community, $d = +.10$, and showed more effective study skills, $d = +.43$, and more appropriate budgeting of study time, $d = +.20$.

Tupesis (1972) compared homework and supervised study in two high school geometry classes. Treatments were randomly assigned, and students were "computer assigned" to class. Pretest scores of students indicated no differences on several ability and achievement measures.

The homework treatment class spent 12 minutes of each class session correcting homework assignments, 15 minutes receiving new homework assignments, and 6 minutes reading. The supervised-study class spent 32 minutes in interactive problem-solving. The interactive problems were identical to the problems on the homework assignments. The remaining time in each class was spent on lecture, discussion, and oral exercises. The treatment lasted nine weeks.

Tupesis collected 10 different outcome measures, relating to achievements, attitude toward the subject matter, classroom interaction, and problem completion. A significant difference favoring homework was found on a standardized (textbook-supplied, norm-referenced) test, d = +.73. However, a nonsignificant difference favoring supervised study was found on a cumulative measure of class tests, d = -.17, and on a teacher-constructed test of retention given 10 days, d = -.49, after the material was covered. A retention test given nine weeks later significantly favored supervised study, d = -.76. The student means on the experimenter-constructed attitude test were exactly equal. Students doing problems at home completed significantly more of them, d = +.95. Finally, Tupesis found evidence that more indirect teaching occurred in the supervised study class than in the homework class. What is most striking about this study is the dramatic inconsistency in results for the standardized and teacher-constructed tests, with the former favoring homework and the latter favoring supervised study.

Baxter (1973) manipulated feedback about homework as well as homework and supervised-study treatments in sixth-grade classes. Students did comparable assignments at home or during class. They also received either feedback about the correctness of the solutions only or a description of the type of error that was made. The outcome variable was the number of correct solutions on the homework assignments. Data were analyzed separately for the first and second halves of the experiment, which lasted four weeks. Results for both analyses were nonsignificant (F < 1), with means for the first half favoring homework and means for the second half favoring supervised study, and the overall d-index equaling -.04. In addition, the interactions between the treatment, the feedback condition, and the week of the assignment were all nonsignificant.

Marshall (1983) randomly assigned classrooms to one of three treatment conditions. One treatment did homework in math computation while doing math word problems in class, a second group did word problems for homework and computation problems in class, and a third group did both types of problems in class. In the classwork-only treatment, word problems were treated as part of the normal class lesson, while computation assignments of about 20 minutes in duration were to be done in class but not during math lessons. From the description, it therefore appears that Marshall's experiment confounded the type ("activeness") of the supervision with the subject matter.

Marshall's intention in creating the two homework groups was to demonstrate that homework would be differentially effective, depending on the skill area involved. Drawing on social facilitation theory (Zajonc, 1965), Marshall reasoned that the learning of simple, rote tasks (e.g., math computations) would be improved by the presence of others, while more complex tasks (e.g., word problems) are best learned alone. Therefore, homework (which, Marshall showed through questionnaire responses, is normally done alone or with only one other person present) should be more effective than supervised study for word problems, and supervised study (done with classmates present) should be more effective for computation.

Marshall used three measures to assess computation and problem-solving achievement. Two measures contained standardized items taken from the State of California Inventory of Mathematical Achievement and the California Assessment Program. These were administered at the end of the treatment. A third measure contained items created by the experimenter to parallel items on the standardized tests. This measure was administered three weeks after the treatment ended. Data were analyzed separately for the fifth and sixth grades, using both the class and the student as the unit of analysis, and with and without covariates.

Across the two grades, comparisons of raw score measures indicated that, as predicted, the supervised study group had higher achievement on computation for five of six comparisons, with an average d-index of $-.19$ using students as the unit and $-.31$ using classrooms. The homework group did better on four of six problem-solving tests, but the average d-indexes were very small and favored homework only when the student was the unit of analysis ($d = +.03$, whereas $d = -.07$ when classrooms were used as the unit). Because the skill area comparisons were analyzed separately, there were no formal tests of the significance of the interaction. Also, the findings were more consistent with predictions for the delayed measure of achievement than for the measure taken immediately after the treatment, though again no interaction test was made.

Marshall also tested for the interaction of homework treatment and the student's mathematics aptitude, as measured by scores on the problem-solving section of the Iowa Test of Basic Skills. However, the actual aptitude-treatment interactions were never formally tested. Instead, the different magnitudes of regression slopes within conditions and grades were described and visually examined for crossovers. Based on these results, Marshall concluded that computation homework's effects were not influenced by the student's aptitude, but that problem-solving homework may be better for low-aptitude students while classwork may be better for high-aptitude students.

Finally, three studies of the difference between homework and supervised study (Bird, 1983; Huddleson, 1983; Paulson, 1983) were conducted as class projects at Wright State University in Ohio. All three studies involved two intact classrooms taught by the experimenter. Each class received one or the other treatment, with no other procedures used to produce equivalence between the students. In all three studies the material covered during supervised study and homework was identical. Teacher-constructed measures of achievement served as outcome variables. The subjects involved were French, English, and mathematics.

Bird (1983) found that French students received higher grades if they did homework (d = +.40). Huddleson (1983) found an effect favoring supervised study when grades in English were measured (d = −.06). Paulson (1983) found that class test scores favored homework both for a unit on percents (d = +.50) and for a unit on geometry (d = +.07).

SUMMARY (INCLUDING A META-ANALYSIS)

The eight recent investigations comparing homework and in-class supervised study contained 18 estimates of the treatment difference, drawn from 10 independent samples. These d-indexes were averaged and quantitatively analyzed to determine if seven different moderators explained variance in the effect sizes. Although the meta-analysis nicely summarizes the results of the eight studies, it should be viewed only as suggestive, considering the small number of studies and their qualitatively different methodologies. The results of the quantitative synthesis are summarized in Table 6.3.

The Average d-Index

Across the 10 independent samples, the average d-index for achievement measures was +.09, indicating that the average student doing homework had an achievement score about one-tenth of a standard deviation higher than the average student receiving in-class supervised study. In terms of distribution overlap, this means the average student in the homework condition outperformed about 53.6% of the supervised study students. The 95% confidence interval put the low estimate of homework's effect at d = −.05, thus favoring supervised study, and the high estimate at d = +.23. The 10 estimates of effect size were found to be homogeneous, $\chi^2(9) = 11.55$, ns.

Moderators of the Effect Size

The year in which a study was reported was not significantly related to the magnitude of its d-index, $\chi^2(1) = 3.37$, ns. However, the trend indicated that studies conducted prior to 1980 produced effect sizes larger than studies conducted in the 1980s. The d-indexes were +.31 and +.01, respectively.

Studies that employed some form of random assignment of students or classes to treatment groups produced a negative average estimate of homework's effect, while studies not using random assignment produced a positive one, $\chi^2(1) = 4.96$, p < .04. The average d-index for random assignment studies was −.04, while for studies not using random assignment it was +.28.

Whether or not the experimenter was also the teacher of the classes involved in the study was unrelated to the effect size estimate, $\chi^2(1) = 0.88$, ns.

TABLE 6.3. Effect Sizes for Comparisons of Homework Versus Supervised Study on Measures of Academic Achievement

		95% Confidence Interval		
	No. of Comparisons	Low Estimate	Mean	High Estimate
Overall ($\chi^2(9) = 11.55$, p < .3)	10	−.05	+.09	+.23
Year and duration of treatment ($\chi^2(1) = 3.37$, p < .08)				
Prior to 1980 (>10 weeks)	3	+.04	+.31	+.57
1980 or after (<10 weeks)	7	−.15	+.01	+.17
Random assignment ($\chi^2(1) = 4.96$, p < .04)				
No	4	+.06	+.28	+.50
Yes	6	−.21	−.04	+.13
Grade level ($\chi^2(1) = 5.89$, p < .02)				
5–6	3	−.27	−.08	+.11
7–9	5	+.03	+.24	+.45
10–12	2	−.10	+.33	+.76
Subject matter ($\chi^2(5) = 9.48$, p < .10)				
General math	4	−.12	+.14	+.40
Computation	4	−.38	−.17	+.04
Concepts	3	−.05	+.21	+.47
Problem-solving	5	+.00	+.18	+.35
English	1	−.57	−.06	+.45
French	1	−.20	+.40	+1.00

An initial analysis of grade level indicated no linear relation to homework's effect, $\chi^2(1) = 1.73$, ns. However, when grades were grouped according to elementary (grades 5 and 6), junior high (grades 7 through 9), and high school, a test for the linear relation proved significant, $\chi^2(1) = 5.89$, p < .02. Supervised study appeared to have a more positive effect than homework on the achievement of elementary students, d = $-.08$, whereas homework was more effective for junior high students, d = $+.24$, and for high school students, d = $+.33$.

The duration of the homework and supervised study treatments was perfectly confounded with the year in which a study was reported—all studies conducted before 1980 had treatment durations longer than 10 weeks, while studies conducted during the 1980s had treatments lasting less than 10 weeks. It is therefore impossible to determine whether the observed difference was due to a diminishing effectiveness of homework (or improved effectiveness of supervised study) over the years or to the longer treatments used in earlier studies.

The subject matter considered in a study had a nonsignificant but still noteworthy relation to the magnitude of the homework effect, $\chi^2(5) = 9.48$, p < .10. Furthermore, an analysis of only the math-related results indicated that these differences were significant, $\chi^2(3) = 8.13$, p < .05. Among the math subskills, supervised study was superior for computation, d = $-.17$, but homework was superior for concept learning, d = $+.21$, and problem-solving, d = $+.18$. In the only two comparisons not involving math, homework was superior to supervised study for French, d = $+.40$, but inferior for English, d = $-.06$.

There was no relation between the type of achievement outcome measure used in a study and the study's effect size, $\chi^2(1) = 0.10$, ns.

In addition to the confounding of the year in which a study was reported and the duration of the treatments, one other relation between moderators should be considered in interpreting these results. All the comparisons involving elementary school children were conducted in studies using random assignment. Therefore, it is not clear whether the lower d-index for random assignment studies was due to this factor or to the use of younger children, or alternatively, whether the negative effect for homework on younger children was due to the random assignment of these students to conditions.

Third Variable Interactions with the Treatment Effects

As noted in the descriptions of the individual studies, only one recent investigation examined whether the relative effect of homework versus in-class study was related to the gender of the student (Ten Brinke, 1964). This study found nonsignificant relations and no consistency in the direction of effect across mathematics subskills.

Two studies examined the moderating effect of the intelligence of the student. Marshall (1983) found homework better for low-ability students, and supervised study better for high-ability students on mathematics problem-solving, but the interaction was not directly tested. Ten Brinke (1964) found the opposite result across math subskill areas, but the interaction tests were nonsignificant. At present, then, there seems to be no evidence that the intelligence of the student affects the relative impact of homework and in-class supervised study.

Nonacademic Outcome Measures

Two recent investigations looked at student attitudes as a function of homework versus in-class supervised study. Hudson (1965) found that attitudes toward school were more favorable in the homework treatment group, while Tupesis (1972) found identical attitudes toward the subject matter expressed by both groups. Although the different results might be explainable by the various attitude referents, there are numerous other differences between the studies as well.

Finally, Hudson (1965) found better study mechanics and time-allocation among students doing homework than among students doing in-class study. This is the only instance of the use of study habits as an outcome variable in the literature.

7

Time Spent on
Homework Assignments

The research design used most often to assess the possible effects of home study is to correlate the amount of time students spend on homework with how well they are doing in school. In the past 25 years, more than half a million students have been asked to report the amount of homework they do, and this response has been related to some measure of academic achievement.

The problem is interpreting what the resulting correlation means. If time spent on homework and achievement prove to be positively related, does this mean that homework improves school performance, or does it mean that teachers assign more homework to better students? If the relation is negative, does homework have a detrimental effect on performance, or do brighter students simply finish assignments in less time? Both positive and negative correlations have been found in past research (though positive correlations dominate) and, not surprisingly, each interpretation has been invoked to make sense of the data.

As the above discussion implies, this literature confounds the variables of "amount of homework teachers assign" with "amount of time students spend on homework." There seems to be no study that attempted, either experimentally or statistically, to separate these variables. Thus, in the discussions that follow, the reader should remain alert to the possibility that when one of these variables is measured it may also be serving as a proxy for the other.

Discussion of the time on homework literature will be divided into five parts. First, three studies of historic interest conducted before 1962 will be briefly described. Second, the results of a quantitative synthesis of 17 more recent studies will be presented. All the studies (a) used the student as the unit of analysis and (b) calculated a zero-order (bivariate) correlation that estimated the simple relation between time on homework and student achievement or attitude. As part of this analysis, the effects of several moderators of the simple relation will be examined, including especially the subject matter, the type of outcome measure, and the grade level of the students. Third, a set of studies will be described that attempted to explain the time on homework and achievement relation by statistically controlling for third factors. Fourth, eight studies will be examined that reported mean achievement levels for each of several intervals of time spent on homework. These data allow an exploration of the hypothesis that the relation between time on homework and achievement might be curvilinear. Finally, two experiments in which time on homework was an independent variable will conclude the review.

EARLY STUDIES OF TIME ON HOMEWORK

In 1935, Cooke and Brown (1935) reported a study in which the number of minutes children spent "preparing each subject matter" at home was related to scores on the Stanford Achievement Test. Approximately 1,000 fifth- through eighth-graders from Birmingham, Alabama, supplied the data. Cooke and Brown claimed to have subjected their data to partial and multiple correlation and regression analyses, but they did not report any results. Instead, they simply said the results were of "no particular significance" and indicated that "it seems there is nothing to be gained, by way of achievement, in requiring elementary-school pupils to study at home" (p. 410).

In 1937 the Great Britain Board of Education issued a pamphlet entitled *Homework* (Great Britain, 1937). In the pamphlet several "experiments" in which there was a reduction in the amount of assigned homework were described. The experiences of 14 secondary schools were included, but although the effects of reductions in homework on school progress were measured in several instances, the actual data were not described. The report came to the general conclusion that "the total amount of time [on homework] demanded is excessive" (p. 66).

Finally, in 1951, Schunert (1951) compared the algebra and geometry achievement of students who reported doing less than 20 minutes and more than 40 minutes of homework a night. Students were randomly sampled, with stratification, from Minnesota's secondary schools. About 200 algebra students and 150 geometry students were given researcher-constructed achievement tests, and these were related to their teachers' reports of the length of homework assignments. Schunert's statistical analyses controlled for initial achievement differences, intelligence test scores, the size of the school, and the amount of college-level mathematics the teacher had taken. For both subject matters, the relation between achievement and time spent on homework was nonsignificant. In neither case did Schunert report the direction of the relation.

Thus, until 1962, there was little evidence in the research literature to support the notion that more time spent on homework was associated with higher achievement.

RECENT INVESTIGATIONS OF THE CORRELATES OF TIME ON HOMEWORK

In the past 25 years there has been a proliferation of data-collection efforts by school boards, state boards of education, and national assessments that attempt to identify the correlates of school achievement. Many of these surveys have included questions on the time students report spending on homework or on the amount of homework teachers report assigning. The results of the surveys have often contained correlation coefficients relating these variables to student achievement and/or attitudes. Other survey descriptions have provided enough information to allow calculation of an estimate of the simple linear relation between these two sets of variables.

The Number of Studies, Samples, and Correlations

Seventeen written reports describing 18 studies that included the correlations described above (not including multiple reports covering the same data) were located. The reports contained considerably more than 18 correlations, because data were often analyzed separately for different subsamples of students and for various grades, subjects, and outcome measures. For the present analysis, a total of 50 correlation coefficients were retained. Summaries of the 17 studies can be found in Table 7.1.

A single study could contribute more than one correlation to this analysis if separate correlations were presented for different grade levels. This convention does not greatly compromise the independence of the correlation estimates because they are based on different samples of students. It is more of a problem that some studies were allowed to contribute more than one correlation if they reported separate estimates for multiple levels of other variables that were of interest in the quantitative synthesis (see Chapter 4). For example, three classes of outcome measures (standardized tests, grades, and attitudes) were examined to see if they related differently to time on homework. Therefore, a study could contribute one correlation to each outcome class, even though the estimates were sometimes obtained from the same sample of students. In practice, the 50 correlations came from 27 separate samples, and no sample contributed more than five effect size estimates (which occurred in three cases). As a safeguard against non-independence, when each variable was tested for its effect on the correlation, the contribution from each sample was recalculated so that a sample

TABLE 7.1. Studies Included in the Time on Homework Meta-Analysis

Author (Year)	Type of Document	Geographic Area Covered	Sampling Design	No. of Students	Type of Respondents to Homework Questionnaire
Asp & Levine (1985)	Other	National	Random	2,300	Parents
Coulter (1980)	ERIC document	Multiple districts	Convenience	372	Students
Epstein (1983)	ERIC document	Multiple districts	Other	1,021	Parents
Fetler (1984)	Journal article	State	Random	10,603	Students
Fort Worth (1983)	School board report	Single district	Other	222	Students
Kohr (1979)	ERIC document	State	Random	9,805	Students
Nat'l Center for Education Statistics[a] (1972)	Report summary	National	Random	11,000	Students
Nat'l Center for Education Statistics[a] (1982)	Report summary	National	Random	15,000	Students
Natriello & McDill (1986)	Journal article	National	Random	12,146	Students
Raphael & Wahlstrom (1986)	State report	State	Total population	2,900	Students
Rhode Island (1978)	State report	State	NA	11,268	Students
Stennett & Racher (1985)	School board report	Single district	Total population	659	Teachers
Taylor (1971)	Diss.	Single district	Convenience	57	Students
Walberg, et al. (1982)	Journal article	National	Random	3,049	Students
Walberg, et al. (1986)	Journal article	National	Random	1,955	Students
Walberg & Shanahan (1983)	Journal article	National	Random	24,159	Students
Wolf (1979)	Book	National	Random	6,195	Students

[a] As reported in National Center for Educational Statistics (1985).

never contributed more correlations than the number of categories in the variable. For example, a sample could contribute only three correlations to the analysis examining outcome measures. If a sample had more than one correlation within an outcome category (e.g., two standardized measures in two subject areas), these were averaged before the analysis began.

The Geographic Location of Samples

At least a half-dozen nationwide surveys involving random samples of students have contained questions on time on homework. These include

TABLE 7.1. *Continued*

Measure of Homework	Outcome Measure	Grade Level	Subject Matter
Time spent	Standardized test	4	Other English
Time spent	Other	11	Science, math, other English, social studies
Amount assigned	Grades, other	3	Math, reading, multiple subjects
Time spent	Standardized test	6	Multiple subjects
Amount assigned	Standardized test	4,7,11	Multiple subjects
Time spent	Standardized test	5,8,11	Science, reading, other English, social studies, multiple subjects
Time spent	Standardized test	11	Multiple subjects
Time spent	Standardized test	11	Multiple subjects
Time spent	Grades	11	Other English
Amount assigned	Standardized test	8	Math
Time spent	Grades	4,6,8	Multiple subjects
Amount assigned	Standardized test	9	Math
Time spent	Other	10	Math
Time spent	Standardized test, interest	12	Science
Time spent	Standardized test, grades, attitudes, interest, other	12	Science, multiple subjects
Time spent	Standardized test	12	Math, reading, other English
Time spent	Standardized test	9,12	Science, reading, other English

Note. NA = not availabe; "Other English" = English skills other than reading.

several phases of the National Assessment of Educational Progress (e.g., ECS, 1977; Ward, Mead & Searls, 1983), the National Assessment in Science (e.g., Walberg, Fraser & Welch, 1986), High School and Beyond (both 1980 and 1982; e.g., Walberg & Shanahan, 1983), the International Evaluation of Achievement (e.g., Wolf, 1979), the Longitudinal Study of the High School Class of 1972 (e.g., NCES, 1985), and the National Survey of Children (e.g., Asp & Levine, 1985).

The nationwide surveys have been complemented by statewide surveys conducted in California, North Carolina, Pennsylvania, Rhode Island, and Washington and by numerous local school districts. In addition, research projects have sampled geographic areas ranging from nationwide (Natriello & McDill, 1986) to single districts (e.g., Taylor, 1971). Two studies were conducted in Canada (Raphael & Wahlstrom, 1986; Stennett & Rachar, 1985), and one was conducted in Australia (Coulter, 1980).

Of the 50 correlations, 18 came from studies on nationwide samples, 20 from statewide samples, 7 from samples including multiple school districts, and 5 from single school districts.

The Size of Samples

Few of the reports included information on the number of schools or classrooms that were sampled. The number of students sampled ranged from 57 to 24,159, with a median of 2,900 and a mean of 4,175. A total of 112,711 students were included in the 27 samples. In all estimates of average correlations the contribution of each sample was weighted by its size.

The Respondents and Measures of Time on Homework

Forty-one of the correlations were based on the responses of students to a question concerning how much time they spent on homework each night or each week. Four correlations dealt with student responses to a question about the amount of homework they were assigned. Three estimates of how much homework was assigned and one estimate of the time students spent on homework were provided by parents. One study asked teachers how much homework they had assigned.

The Measures of Academic Outcome

Thirty-three correlations employed standardized test scores as the measure of achievement, and another 7 correlations used class grades. For 10 correlations the outcome measure was the student's attitude toward school or the subject matter, expressed interest in the subject matter, or another measure of motivation to learn (e.g., hobbies, trips to museums).

The Subject Matter

The subject matter that each correlation related to was divided into six categories: multiple subjects (n = 14), science (n = 11), mathematics (n = 6), reading (n = 7), other English skills (n = 8), and social studies (n = 4).

The Average Correlation

The average correlation, weighted by sample size, across the 27 samples was r = +.186. The 95% confidence interval for this estimate ranged from r = +.180 to r = +.192. Twenty-two of the 27 correlations revealed a positive relation between time spent on homework and the outcome measure. Figure 7.1 displays the distribution of the 50 nonindependent correlations.

.39, .40	
.37, .38	S
.35, .36	
.33, .34	J
.31, .32	
.29, .30	J
.27, .28	SS
.25, .26	JJSSS
.23, .24	JSS
.21, .22	JJS
.19, .20	JSSSS
.17, .18	SS
.15, .16	SS
.13, .14	JSS
.11, .12	J
.09, .10	EJJJ
.07, .08	EEJ
.05, .06	EEEJS
.03, .04	
.01, .02	SS
.00	
−.01, −.02	E
−.03, −.04	
−.05, −.06	EE
−.07, −.08	J
−.09, −.10	
−.11, −.12	E
−.13, −.14	
−.15, −.16	J
−.17, −.18	J
−.19, −.20	

FIGURE 7.1. Distribution of Correlations between Time on Homework and Achievement-Related Outcomes. *Note.* Correlations are distinguished by grade level: E = grades 3–5; J = grades 6–9; S = grades 10–12.

The homogeneity analysis indicated that the correlation coefficients were significantly more variable than would be expected by sampling variation alone, $\chi^2(26) = 1683$, p < .0001.

Moderators of the Correlation

Six variables were tested to determine if they were associated with significant variation in correlations. All six variables proved significant. The average correlation and 95% confidence interval for five of these variables are presented in Table 7.2 (the sixth variable was continuous in nature). The variables concerning who responded to the homework question and how time on homework was measured were not analyzed because they lacked variation (i.e., the vast majority of cases involved students reporting the amount of time they spent on homework).

TABLE 7.2. Correlations between Time Spent on Homework by Students and Academic Outcomes

	No. of Comparisons	95% Confidence Interval		
		Low Estimate	Mean	High Estimate
Overall	27	+.180	+.186	+.192
Report outlet ($\chi^2(2) = 69.7$)				
Journal or book	7	+.17	+.18	+.19
ERIC document	8	+.10	+.12	+.14
State or local board report	8	+.10	+.12	+.14
Location ($\chi^2(2) = 841$)				
National	9	+.23	+.24	+.24
State	8	+.06	+.07	+.08
Local	10	-.02	+.02	+.06
Grade level ($\chi^2(2) = 1095$)				
3–5	5	+.01	+.02	+.04
6–9	8	+.06	+.07	+.09
10–12	14	+.24	+.25	+.26
Subject matter ($\chi^2(5) = 214$)				
Math	6	+.21	+.22	+.23
Reading	7	+.19	+.20	+.21
English	8	+.19	+.20	+.20
Multiple subjects	14	+.18	+.19	+.19
Science	7	+.12	+.13	+.14
Social studies	4	+.08	+.10	+.12
Outcome measure ($\chi^2(2) = 19.5$)				
Standard tests	17	+.18	+.18	+.19
Class grades	6	+.18	+.19	+.21
Attitudes and interests	8	+.11	+.14	+.16

The size of the correlation between time spent on homework and the outcomes was positively related to the year in which the correlation was reported, $\chi^2(1) = 9.80$, $p < .005$. Studies reported more recently contained more strongly positive estimates of the relation. This may be due to a changing relation over time or to recently improved measurement and research methods.

The size of correlations reported in three types of research outlets was compared. A significant chi-square, $\chi^2(2) = 69.7$, $p < .0001$, indicated that effect sizes reported in journals or book chapters, $r = +.18$, were larger than those reported in either ERIC documents, $r = +.12$, or in state or local school board reports, $r = +.12$. Although the difference is not dramatic, this result is consistent with the belief that published results constitute a sample biased toward larger effect sizes.

Analyses concerning the location of the sample indicated that studies conducted on national samples, $r = +.24$, produced the largest correlation coefficients, $\chi^2(1) = 841$, $p < .0001$. A possible explanation for this finding might be that studies done at the state or local level had their correlations restricted because they did not contain the range of homework or achievement behaviors sampled at the national level. This may be a partial explanation, but it cannot suffice alone because of the diverse nature of the populations of some states and districts reporting data. Another possibility is that the national studies used measures of time spent on homework and achievement that were more valid. Of course, it must also be kept in mind, for this finding as well as the other, that the relation between sampling breadth and the time on homework correlation may be spurious, or caused by other variables confounded with the geography of the student sample.

The subject matter under consideration also was associated with significant variation in the correlations, $\chi^2(5) = 214$, $p < .0001$. Mathematics produced the strongest correlation, $r = +.22$. Reading, $r = +.20$, English, $r = +.20$, and correlations based on multiple subjects, $r = +.19$, produced slightly smaller estimates that all fell with the 95% confidence range of one another. Science, $r = +.13$, and social studies, $r = +.10$, produced the smallest correlations. Examining the order of effects leads to an interesting observation: the correlations get larger as the homework assignments are more likely to involve rote learning, practice, or rehearsal. Put differently, subjects such as science and social studies, which often involve longer-term projects, integration of multiple skills, and/or creative use of nonschool resources, show the smallest correlations, though in absolute magnitude the differences are not great.

A significant relation was also revealed when the type of outcome measure was related to the time-on-homework correlation, $\chi^2(2) = 19.5$, $p < .0001$. Although standardized tests, $r = +.18$, and grades, $r = +.19$, produced nearly identical correlations, the estimate associated with attitudes and interests was somewhat smaller, $r = +.14$. This again may be due to less valid means for testing attitudes and interests. Alternatively, affective and motivational responses to academic work may be less responsive to homework variations, or teachers may not take a positive attitude into account as much as strong achievement when they decide how much homework to assign. Again, however, while the difference in correlations is significant, the magnitude of difference is not great.

Finally, the most dramatic influence on the magnitude of the time-on-homework relation to outcomes was grade level, $\chi^2(2) = 1,095$, p < .0001. For high school students, grades 10 through 12, a moderate correlation was found, r = +.25. For students in grades 6 through 9 the correlation was small, r = +.07, and for elementary school students, grades 3 through 5, it was nearly nonexistent, r = +.02. A discussion of this finding will be postponed until the analyses of a possible curvilinear relation between time on homework and achievement are presented, because those findings bear on the interpretation.

Because significant effects were found for both grade level and subject matter, the possible interaction between these two moderators of the homework effect was examined. To do so, average correlations were calculated for high school (grades 10 through 12) and pre-high school students in the following subject classifications: mathematics, English-related (reading and English), and a combination of science and social studies. Some categories were collapsed to increase the number of correlations and stabilize the average estimates. As might be expected, the effect of subject matter was due entirely to variation among high school students. For pre-high-school students, correlations were r = +.06 for math, r = +.11 for English-related, and r = +.09 for science and social studies. For high school students, the correlations were r = +.25 for math, r = +.23 for reading, and r = +.16 for science and social studies.

Finally, it is important to determine whether the different moderators of the homework effect are intercorrelated with one another. Because the expected cell frequencies were quite low when the moderators were cross-tabulated, chi-square statistics should be viewed as suggestive only. Publication outlet and location were confounded, with a disproportionate number of national surveys appearing in journals (n = 7) and local surveys appearing in reports (n = 6). Also, many of the surveys using local samples were conducted with high school students as respondents (n = 5). These two variables, however, had opposite effects on the magnitude of the homework correlation.

In sum, analyses of 50 correlations based on more than 112,000 students revealed a positive relation between the time spent on homework a student reported and several academic outcomes. The correlation, averaging about r = +.19 across the estimates, cannot be interpreted as demonstrating a causal effect of homework on academic achievement or attitudes. It is equally plausible, based on these data alone, that teachers assign more homework to students who are achieving better or who have better attitudes, or that better students simply spend more time on home study. In addition, the magnitude of the relation appears to be modified by several variables. These include the type of outcome measure (with achievement showing larger relations than attitudes), the subject matter (with math showing the largest correlation and science and social studies the smallest), and grade level (with high school students showing the only substantial estimated correlation).

Two studies not included in the quantitative synthesis deserve separate mention. These studies, by Rutter et al. (1979) and by Bailey (1981), also examined the simple linear relation between time on homework and academic outcomes, but they employed the classroom or the school as the unit when the strength of the relation was estimated. Rutter et al. conducted their study in 12 secondary schools in London, England. Fourteen-year-old students and their teachers were the participants. Using the school as the unit of analysis, they reported relatively strong positive correlations between teachers's reports of how many minutes of homework had been assigned and student achievement in multiple subjects, $r + = .46$, attitudes toward school, $r = +.49$, absence of behavior problems, $r = +.41$, and attendance, $r = +.42$.

Bailey's (1981) study was conducted in 70 classrooms of fifth-, eighth-, and eleventh-graders in school districts in western Connecticut. For English and math classes separately, two measures of time spent on homework were correlated with student scores on the Otis-Lennon I.Q. test and achievement tests. When time spent on homework was measured by the number of assignments teachers gave, the correlations ranged from $r = +.37$ to $r = +.52$. When the measure was the number of minutes students reported spending on homework, the estimates ranged from $r = +.10$ to $r = +.38$. Therefore, results of studies of high school students that use the classroom or school as the unit of analysis are quite similar to studies that employ students as the unit.

TIME-ON-HOMEWORK STUDIES STATISTICALLY CONTROLLING THIRD VARIABLES

Table 7.3 presents nine studies that reported analyses of the time-on-homework relation to academic outcomes that statistically controlled for other variables. The techniques employed in the analyses included multiple regression, with both standardized and unstandardized regression coefficients reported, variance partitioning, path analysis, and analysis of covariance. The control variables ranged from pretest scores, to ability measures, to gender, race, and economic background, to classroom and home conditions. The number of additional variables included in the analyses ranged from 1 to 16. Because of the incompatibility of the studies' designs and analyses, no attempt was made to generate an overall estimate of the adjusted relation between time-on-homework and academic out-

TABLE 7.3. Correlational Studies of Time on Homework in which Third Variables Were Statistically Controlled

Author (Year)	Location	Sample Size	Grade Level	Third Variables[a]	Direction	Significant
Walberg et al. (1986)	National (NAS 1981–82 data)	1,955	12	Ten variables, including previous grades, voluntary participation in activities, attitude, gender, race.	+	Yes, achievement Yes, attitude
Keith et al. (1986)[a]	National (HSB, 1980)	28,051	12	Varying third variables. All included ability, race, family background.	+	Yes
Keith (1982)[a]	National (HSB, 1980)	20,364	12		+	Yes
Tarbuck (1984)[a]	National (HSB, 1980)	42,724	12		+	Yes
Natriello & McDill (1986), (data collected 1964–65)	National	12,146	10–12	Sixteen variables, including ability, gender, parent education, no. of siblings, parent and student expectations.	+	Yes
Fetler (1984)	California	10,603	6	TV viewing, parent occupation reading for pleasure, ease of schoolwork.	−	Yes
Walberg et al. (1982)	National (NAEP, 1976)	3,049	12	Parent education, motivation, quality of instruction, class morale, home characteristics, gender, race.	+	Yes, in 6 of 8 analyses

Study	Location	Sample	Grade	Controls	Effect	Additional
Wolf (1979)	National (IEA)	2,665–5,550 (varies by grade)	5,9,12	Entered in blocks: background, type of school or program, instructional procedures, teacher and student characteristics.	+	Assessed as part of block
Raphael & Wahlstrom (1986)	Ontario	113 classrooms	8	Pretest, SES, teacher experience, opportunities to learn.	+ in 6 of 8 outcome measures.	Yes, in 1 of 5 achievement Yes, in 1 of 3 attitude
Harding (1979)	Pennsylvania	299	4	I.Q.	– for 6 of 8 teacher preferences for types of homework	All ns
Singh (1969)	Arizona	127	4–6	Pretest, I.Q., grade level.	+ for 9 subjects	Yes, in 7 of 9 analyses

Note. Unless otherwise noted, the measure of time on homework was student report and the outcome measure was either achievement test scores or grades. NAS = National Assessment in Science; HSB = High School and Beyond; NAEP = National Assessment of Educational Progress; IEA = International Evaluation of Achievement.
[a] Keith et al. (1986), Keith (1982), and Tarbuck (1984) all used the same database.

come measures. Instead, Tables 7.3 presents only the direction of the adjusted relation and whether the estimate was significantly different from zero. Seven of the studies (excluding Harding, 1979, and Singh, 1969) were also included in the synthesis of simple correlations described above.

The results of the nine studies indicated overwhelmingly that the relation between time-on-homework and academic-related outcomes remains positive and significant even when a host of potential third variables are statistically controlled. However, similar to the results concerning the simple relationship, two of the three studies conducted on students in primary school grades reported predominantly negative results (Fetler, 1984; Harding, 1979). Only one study (Singh, 1969) showed a positive relation using elementary school students.

One purpose of including additional variables in such an analysis is to attempt statistically to rule out plausible rival explanations for the relation under study. By doing so, the case is strengthened for the "independent" variable of interest (time on homework) being a cause of the "dependent" variable (academic-related outcome). For instance, in the present example most of the studies include some measure of the students' ability or past achievement as a control variable. This is a principal third variable because the argument can be made that past achievement or ability causes both present achievement *and* time spent on homework. Therefore, researchers hope that the relation between time spent on homework and present achievement will remain positive and significant even after ability or past achievement has been controlled. If this is so, the claim can be made that ability or past achievement cannot fully explain the "effect" of homework on present achievement and therefore the case that time on homework is a causal agent of achievement is strengthened.

Although it is extremely appealing, reasoning in this manner is not as straightforward as it seems. Without becoming too technical, Cook and Campbell (1979) note that the adjustment does not work as hoped except under rare circumstances. They point out that the statistical approach fails unless the controlled variables "model the selection process whereby different kinds of persons came to be in different groups, or provide an acceptable causal model of the dependent variable" (p.298). In the present example, this requirement means that, for the estimate of the homework effect to be taken as causal, the list of controlled variables must fully and exactly include all the differences between students who achieve differently. Otherwise, the estimate of homework's effect may overestimate or underestimate its true effect and may even possess the wrong directional sign, depending on what variables have been omitted. A complete understanding of the determinants of achievement still eludes us. As Cook and Campbell say of the more general case, "The only way such covariates can provide an adequate adjustment is for one or more of them to be a perfectly reliable and valid measure of the latent common factor. Such covariates simply do not exist" (p. 300).

In sum, these studies indicate that the relation between time on homework and academic outcomes for high school students remains positive and significant even after a host of rival explanations has been statistically controlled. However, the statistical adjustment for the other determinants of academic outcomes is probably inadequate, so this result cannot of itself be taken as evidence that increases in time on homework cause higher achievement or better attitudes. It can only be stated cautiously that the evidence is consistent with such an interpretation. Furthermore, no such claim can be made for students in elementary school grades, since these results produced both positive and negative relations.

EVIDENCE FOR A CURVILINEAR RELATIONSHIP

In addition to the 17 studies that contained data estimating the simple correlation, and the 9 studies controlling for third variables, a different set of 9 studies was found that reported mean levels of achievement for different amounts of time spent on homework. For instance, the state of North Carolina issued two reports (North Carolina, 1983, 1985) in which the mean scores of sixth-graders and ninth-graders on the California Achievement Test were presented for students reporting six different amounts of time on homework—no homework, less than 1 hour a week, 1 to 3 hours, 3 to 5 hours, 5 to 10 hours, and more than 10 hours. The nine studies included a total of 13 independent samples. The studies are described in Table 7.4.

Because none of these reports included standard deviations, their results could not be used to generate a reliable estimate of the simple linear relationship. However, by making some considered assumptions, they could be used to assess the possibility that the relation between time on homework and achievement was curvilinear, or negatively accelerating. Such a hypothesis would be consistent with results in related areas. For instance, Fredrick and Walberg (1980) noted that the relationship between time-on-task and achievement seemed to reach a plateau at which increases in time had a marginal effect on learning. This could also be the case with time spent on homework, and the present set of studies might shed first light on the idea.

In order to carry out the analysis, three steps were taken to get the 12 sample results into comparable form. First, the mean achievement scores for each amount of time on homework were standardized for each sample separately. This was done so that the grand mean for the sample was zero and the standard deviation of the means was 1. The standardization involved calculating the unweighted grand mean and standard deviation of the means, subtracting each mean from the grand mean and dividing by the standard deviation.

Second, the time-on-homework intervals were examined to determine which were used most frequently, and samples that did not use these intervals were converted to the closest corresponding interval. For instance,

TABLE 7.4. Studies of Time on Homework Used in the Analysis for Curvilinearity

Author	(Year)	Location[a]	Sample Size	Grade Level	Measure of Achievement
Education Commission of the States	(1977)	National (NAEP, 1976)	10,014	12	Standard math tests developed for project
Ward et al.	(1980)	National (NAEP, 1979)	a. 30,488	8	Standard reading tests developed for project
			b. 25,551	12	Standard reading tests developed for project
Young & Kehoe	(1982)	Rochester, N.Y.	1,102	7–12	Type of courses taken (i.e., honors, regents, nonregents)
Brouillet et al.	(1982)	Wash.	1,800	12	Class grades
North Carolina DPI	(1983)	N.C.	a. 87,000	6	California Achievement Test
			b. 83,700	9	California Achievement Test
Nat'l Center for Education Statistics	(1984)	National (HSB, 1980)	12,664	10	% of "A" grades
North Carolina DPI	(1985)	N.C.	a. 79,666	6	California Achievement Test
			b. 84,814	9	California Achievement Test
James	(1986)	Seattle, Wash.	a. 905	9	Grade point average
			b. 764	9	Standardized reading test
Hinckley et al.	(1979)	National (SES)	7,000	1–6	Comprehensive Test of Basic Skills

Note. For all studies, time spent on homework was measured by student self-report. NAEP = [a]National Assessment of Educational Progress; HSB = High School and Beyond; SES = Sustaining Effects Study.

two of the frequently used intervals were "between 5 and 10 hours of homework per week" and "more than 10 hours." However, James (1986) did not use these intervals but reported an interval of "more than 4 hours per week." For purposes of this analysis, it was assumed that most of the students falling into James' interval would have fallen into the 5-to-10-hour interval.

Third, the standardized achievement scores, both weighted and unweighted by sample size, were averaged across samples for each time-on-homework interval. Because of the earlier reported findings concerning grade level, this was done separately for high school (grades 10 through 12) and junior high school (grades 6 through 9) samples.

Only one study was available for grades 1 through 6. This study involved a nationally representative sample of children that was part of the Sustaining Effects Study evaluation of compensatory education (Hinckley et al., 1979). Like the other results, however, students of all abilities and economic levels were included in the sample.

The single study examining time spent on homework and achievement for elementary school children revealed a strong and negative accelerating relation. Although students who reported doing no homework had standardized achievement scores approximately equal to the scores of students reporting less than one hour a night (+1.00 versus +.87, respectively), the relative achievement of students reporting one to one-and-a-half hours a night dropped markedly (−.44) and continued to drop for students reporting more than one and a half hours a night (−1.42). This result contradicts that obtained from the larger database described above, which showed a relation close to zero for elementary students. The finding is also qualified because students performing better in school spent more time in recreational reading. It is therefore unwise to draw any conclusions about possible curvilinear relations for elementary school students based on this single study.

Figure 7.2 presents the results of the analysis for junior high and high school students weighted by sample size. The curves produced by the unweighted analysis were nearly identical to the curves in this figure. It is important to note that the axis for the variable of hours spent on homework contains nonequal intervals. In determining the spacing for intervals, (a) a convenient distance was chosen to represent the difference between no homework and less than 1 hour of homework a week; (b) 1 to 5 hours was placed at twice this distance, assuming that students choosing this interval averaged about 3 hours; (c) 5 to 10 hours was placed at four times this distance (about 7 hours); and (d) more than 10 hours was placed about four times this distance yet again (about 11 hours). These estimates were based on the common-sense belief that as the intervals represented more time, more precise measures would have placed student responses closer to the lower end of the range.

Figure 7.2 clearly reveals the general linear relation between time on

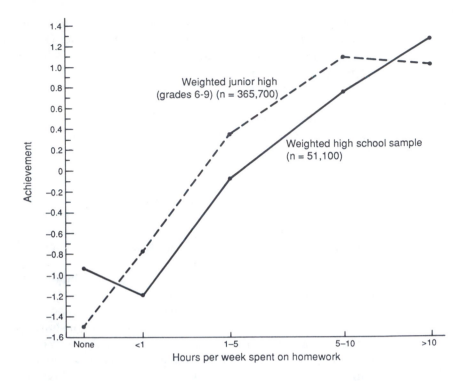

FIGURE 7.2. The Relation between Achievement and Time Spent on Homework. *Note.* The achievement scale is based on standardized, within-study mean achievement for each level of homework.

homework and achievement. It also reveals interactions between the two variables and grade level at both ends of the time-on-homework dimension. Specifically, for high school students the positive relation between the variables does not appear until at least one hour of homework per week is reported. Then it continues to climb unabated to the highest interval. On the other hand, for junior high students the positive relation appears for even the most minimal level of time spent on homework, but it disappears entirely at the highest interval.

Again because the results are correlational, a causal interpretation of these data can be framed in at least three ways. First, it is possible that the results are spurious, or caused by some third, unmeasured variable. Second, it is possible that achievement has an effect on time spent on homework. If this is the case, then teachers of junior high students might use achievement as a guide for how much homework to assign until students are among the brightest in the class. Then distinctions in amount of homework are no longer made among the brightest students, at least not based on achievement differences. For high school students, achievement is not used for assigning homework at the lower levels, but it becomes a causal factor as performance improves. A similar set of arguments could be fashioned by hypothesizing that students at different achievement levels choose to spend more or less time on homework.

The third way to construe these data is to view homework as the cause of achievement. When this approach is taken, an interpretation of the data that could have significant implications for homework policies emerges. If homework is viewed as causal, the figure indicates that small amounts of homework for high school students are of little utility. However, once a critical amount is reached, perhaps about 1 hour a week, increases in time spent on homework, up to more than 10 hours a week, cause improvement in achievement. No data are available beyond this point. For junior high students, even less than 1 hour of homework a week might improve achievement, until between 5 and 10 hours a week are assigned. At this point, there is no advantage to increases in time spent on homework.

These data should be viewed as only suggestive. There can be no reliable formal test of the difference between the high school and junior high school curves, so the interpretation rests on a visual inspection of the data. Also, the data on time spent on homework are based on self-reports of students. However, a pattern across three sets of data has emerged. When the simple linear relation between academic outcomes and time spent on homework was estimated, a strong positive relation was found for high school students, but not for earlier grades. When third variables were controlled, the positive relation remained significant for older students, but again was not evident before high school. Finally, an examination for curvilinearity suggested that the relation reached an asymptote for junior high school students but not for high school students, at least within the time ranges measured. If homework is taken as the causal agent in the relation, then together the results suggest that increases in time spent on home study have more of a positive effect on the achievement of students at higher grades. Increasing the amount of homework for middle-grade students may be efficacious up to a certain point, but after that point more time spent on assignments is of no value. There is no evidence that any amount of homework improves the academic performance of elementary students.

EXPERIMENTAL STUDIES OF
TIME SPENT ON HOMEWORK

Two studies experimentally varied the amount of homework students were assigned. In neither study were students randomly assigned to treatments, although other experimental controls were employed.

Koch (1965) varied the amount of homework assigned to three sixth-grade arithmetic classes in Minnesota, with between 26 and 30 students in each class. Homework treatments were assigned to classes on a random basis. One class received about 20 to 30 minutes of homework a night, a second class received half this amount, and a third class received no homework at all. Students in the "half-homework" condition did the same problems as those contained in the first half of the "full-homework" assignments. All three classes used the same textbook, and teachers agreed to cover the same material. An analysis showed that the three classes did not differ significantly in I.Q. before the experiment began.

The effect of amount of homework was measured by examining pretest to posttest differences in student scores on the arithmetic concepts and problem-solving sections of the Iowa Test of Basic Skills. Using the student as the unit of analysis, a significant difference between the three groups was found for concepts, $p < .001$, but not for problem-solving. For concepts, students receiving the longer homework assignments outperformed those receiving the shorter assignments ($d = +.63$ for gain scores). However, students given shorter assignments outperformed the longer-assignment students on problem-solving ($d = -.41$). (Results for comparisons involving the no-homework conditon were included in the homework versus no homework analysis described earlier.)

Anthony (1977) performed his study in 18 sections of ninth-, tenth-, and eleventh-grade algebra at a high school in Piscataway, New Jersey. Each section contained about 20 students. Eight teachers participated, and each had one experimental class and one control class—except for one teacher, who had two experimental and control classes. Although it was never explicitly stated, it appeared that, for each teacher, which section would receive the experimental or control treatment was randomly determined.

In the short homework assignment condition, students were required to do no more than five homework problems, while in the long assignment condition three times as many problems were assigned. How homework was assigned and treated in class was held as constant as possible between the two conditions. Achievement was measured by using tests prepared by the textbook companies.

Anthony performed an analysis of covariance on pretest to posttest difference scores, using I.Q. and math grades from the previous year as covariates and entering the level of the algebra course and the teacher as additional factors. The student was the unit of analysis, and no advantage was taken of the fact that treatments were nested within teachers. Anthony found a singificant effect ($p < .05$) favoring the short homework assignment condition. If all sources of variance were returned to error and the student was used as the unit, the d-index equaled $-.18$. If sources of variance associated with teachers only were used as the estimate of error, the d-index was $-.31$. Anthony also reported that the difference between the treatments became smaller as the level of the algebra course got higher.

Taken together, the two experimental studies lend no support to the notion that longer homework assignments lead to higher achievement, at least in mathematics. This result is especially interesting because math generated the largest estimate of relation among the correlational studies described above. It lends some support to the notion that the results of correlational studies are due to (a) the existence of a third variable affecting both time spent on homework and achievement or (b) higher achievement causing more time spent on homework, but there are no experimental tests of either of these hypotheses. In addition, the two experimental studies contained serious methodological flaws.

Part IV

Variations in the Homework Process

8

Variations in Homework Assignment Content

The research reviewed in the previous three chapters looked at the general effectiveness of homework. In the last chapter a variation in homework assignments was examined, but this variation—the time spent on homework—was free of content considerations. In fact, with the exception of subject matter, all the potential moderators of homework's effects examined so far have been external to the homework assignment itself (e.g., grade level, outcome measures, characteristics of the research).

In this chapter, four aspects of homework that concern variations in the content of homework assignments are considered. Thus, the underlying question now changes from "Is homework effective?" to "Are some kinds of homework assignments more effective than others?" The variations examined are (a) the instructional purpose, (b) the skill area, (c) individualization, and (d) the degree of student choice.

INSTRUCTIONAL PURPOSE

Preparation and Practice

Eight dissertations have examined whether the amount of dispersion of content across homework assignments influences homework's effectiveness. The dispersion strategies have been given different labels in the literature, sometimes being referred to as massed versus distributed homework, or standard versus spiral exploratory homework, and sometimes referred to as vertical versus oblique or semi-oblique homework. It is conceptually clearest to think of these dispersion strategies as ways of implementing the instructional purposes of preparation and/or practice of material presented in class. For instance, the massed or vertical strategy uses assignments requiring students to do homework problems that pertain only to the material presented in class on the day the problems are assigned. On the other hand, distributed homework involves assignments that may include the introduction of material that has not yet been covered in class (also called semi-oblique) and/or that was covered in lessons prior to the current day (also called oblique). In terms of instructional purposes, distributed strategies that include material not yet covered in class are meant to prepare students for upcoming topics, while coverage of previous material is meant as practice or review. Thus, it is possible to describe the eight studies of dispersion strategies as comparing same-day or current-content homework with homework that involves preparation for future lessons, and/or practice or review of past lessons.

Table 8.1 presents a brief description of each study. Seven of the eight studies used as a control group students who received homework that pertained only to the content of the current day's lesson. The exception was Peterson's (1969) study, which employed two control groups, one with an unspecified treatment in which teachers assigned homework "in the same manner" as before the experiment began (p. 47), and one in which students were assigned "placebo" homework that involved using mathematical principles different from those being taught in class. For purposes of this review, the "same as before" group was considered most likely to be receiving homework on current class content.

In two studies, students in the treatment classes received preparation and practice homework in addition to current-content homework. In four studies, current-content homework was supplemented with practice homework only, and in two studies it was supplemented with preparation homework only. These variations allowed for tests of (a) whether preparation or practice homework is more efficacious than current-content homework and (b) whether the joint effect of both is greater than either alone. It is also possible to compare the relative effect of the preparation versus practice strategies.

In addition, five of the studies included achievement outcome measures given some time after the conclusion of the treatment, as well as tests given immediately after the completion of a topic or chapter. This allows for a test of whether the different instructional purposes of homework have differential effects on the longer-term retention of material.

The eight studies also contained some commonalities. All the studies were performed in classes at the junior or senior high school level (grades 7 through 11), and seven of the studies were conducted in mathematics classes (e.g., algebra or basic math), the exception being one study of history classes (Foyle, 1984). All the studies randomly assigned treatments at the classroom level, with several authors pointing out that assignment of students to classes was performed by computer, on a presumably random basis. All but one study (Urwiller, 1971) reported results using the stu-

TABLE 8.1. Studies Comparing Preparation and/or Practice Homework with Current-Content Homework

Author (Year)	Location	Sample Size (Schools/Classes/Students)	Grade	Unit of Analysis		Treatment Duration	Treatments		Delayed Measurement
				Class	Student		Preparation	Practice	
Peterson (1969)	Ohio	3/12/260	8	Yes	Yes	18 days	Yes	No	Yes
Laing (1970)	Ohio	5/20/456	8	No	Yes	2–4 weeks	No	Yes	Yes
Urwiller (1971)	Midwest	20/40/732	10–11	Yes	No	1 year	No	Yes	Yes
Camp (1973)	N.J.	6/22/529	9	Yes	Yes	1 month	No	Yes	Yes
Butcher (1975)	N.J.	8/26/587	9	Yes	Yes	Varied	No	Yes	Yes
Friesen (1975)	Nebr.	3/6/143	7	Yes	Yes	6 weeks	Yes	Yes	Yes
Dadas (1976)	N.Y.	3/6/112	9	No	Yes	½ year	Yes	Yes	No
Foyle (1984)	Kans.	1/6/93	10	No	Yes	6 weeks	Yes	No	No

Note. In all cases the control treatment involved students doing homework on the content of the same day's lesson. All studies randomly assigned classes to treatments.

dent as the unit of analysis. Six of the studies (excluding Urwiller, 1971, and Dadas, 1976) used tests constructed by the researcher as measures of achievement, although most of these studies employed some procedure to ensure the validity of these measures (e.g., reliability estimates, review by panels of experts). Finally, all but one study (Peterson, 1969) had treatment and control groups perform assignments of equal length, and across the entire duration of the study both groups received identical sets of problems. However, the studies did differ in the procedure used to disperse content throughout the homework assignments (e.g., the number of problems done relating to a particular topic on a given night).

A Meta-analysis of Preparation and Practice Research. The results of the eight studies were quantitatively combined. To accomplish this, up to three d-indexes were generated for each study: one for the comparison of instructional purposes involving tests of achievement administered immediately after the treatment, one for the delayed effect of treatment on achievement, and one for the effect of the treatment on students' attitudes. In some cases, studies contained multiple analyses within each of these categories of effect. For instance, Camp (1973) reported separate analyses of immediate achievement effects for three student ability levels and two textbook chapters. These six effect sizes were averaged to obtain a single immediate achievement effect size. Thus, the effect size for Camp's study controls for differences in student ability. In a similar manner, five of the studies reported the results of analyses of covariance, controlling for I.Q., standardized achievement test scores obtained before the experiment began, and/or pretest differences. However, in four of these instances (Friesen, 1975, being the exception), the complete Analysis of Covariance (ANCOVA) tables were presented, so d-indexes could be computed as though no other effects were removed from the error term or measure of dispersion about the treatment means. In these cases, d-indexes were computed from the unadjusted sums of squares or from unadjusted means and standard deviations. Finally, Peterson's (1969) three-level treatment comparing preparation homework, "same as before" homework, and placebo homework could not be reduced to single degree of freedom comparisons. In this case, because the placebo group's scores always fell between the preparation and "same as before" scores they were assumed to have contributed nothing to the sums of squares.

The two studies that included a measure of student attitudes produced negligible effects. Dadas (1976) reported a d-index of +.02 favoring the group that received preparation and practice homework in addition to current-content homework. Friesen (1975) reported an identical d-index favoring the current-content-only group. It appears that the instructional purpose of homework assignments has little effect on students' attitudes toward the covered material.

An initial analysis of the immediate and delayed achievement measures together revealed an average d-index of +.14 favoring homework that included preparation, practice, or both types of instructional materials, compared with homework on current content only. All eight studies produced positive treatment effects. The effects were homogeneous, $\chi^2(11) = 12.70$, ns, and the immediate versus delayed measurement variable was a nonsignificant predictor of variance in d-indexes, $\chi^2(1) = 0.94$, ns. However, for conceptual clarity all subsequent analyses were separately conducted on the immediate and delayed achievement measures.

The seven studies that used the student as the unit of analysis and an immediate measure of achievement revealed an average d-index of +.11 favoring homework that included preparation or practice. The average student who did preparation, practice, or both types of homework in addition to current-content homework outperformed 54% of students who did current-content homework only on tests of achievement given immediately after the topic lessons were completed. The 95% confidence interval ranged from +.03 to +.20. The chi-square measure of homogeneity for the seven effects (df = 6) was 4.49, which does not approach significance. It can therefore be assumed that random sampling error is the cause for the variation in effect sizes.

The average d-index in the two studies of immediate effects containing both preparation homework and practice homework did not differ from the effect in studies containing either preparation or practice, $\chi^2(1) = 0.01$, ns. However, the two studies comparing preparation homework with current-content homework revealed an average d-index of +.30, while the three studies comparing practice and current-content homework revealed a d-index of +.07. This difference approached significance, $\chi^2 = 3.66$, $p < .07$, giving some indication that preparation homework may be more effective than practice homework in increasing students' scores on immediate measures of achievement. Neither the year the report appeared nor the duration of the study was related to the magnitude of the study's effect.

The five measures of achievement that were taken some time after a topic was completed revealed an average d-index of +.18. Thus, the average student in the experimental classrooms scored higher on the delayed measures of achievement than 57% of students in the control classrooms. This effect was significant at $p < .0005$, two-tailed, with a 95% confidence interval ranging from +.08 to +.27. The d-indexes associated with delayed measures of achievement were homogeneous, $\chi^2(4) = 7.26$, $p < .20$.

The one delayed-measurement study that examined a treatment including both preparation and practice homework revealed a larger d-index, $d = +.52$, than the four studies that examined one or the other instructional purpose, which had an average d-index of +.15, $\chi^2(1) = 4.41$, $p < .05$. The two studies that included preparation homework only did not differ in effect from three studies that included practice homework only, though a trend indicated that preparation homework, d = +.30, may be more effective than practice homework, d = +.07.

The above analyses employed the student as the unit in the calculation of effect sizes. However, five of the dissertations reported the classroom means for treatment and control groups and for immediate and delayed measurements, so it was possible to use these means as raw data in a repeated measures analysis of variance. This analysis would test for the significance of treatment differences and time-of-measurement differences, as well as generate an effect size that used the classroom as the unit of analysis.

The analysis included 53 teachers as a between-units factor, with treatment versus control classroom and immediate versus delayed measurement as within-units factors. Three of the studies from which classroom means were drawn used practice homework as the treatment, one used preparation, and one employed both instructional purposes. All five studies utilized both immediate and delayed measures of achievement, although in one instance the length of these tests had to be equated.

The analysis revealed a significant time-of-measurement effect, indicating that students scored higher on tests given immediately after a topic was covered, $F(1,52) = 18.16$, $p < .0001$, d = 1.18. The effect for treatment was nonsignificant, $F(1,52) = 1.04$, $p < .31$, but the d-index of +.28 indicated that the average class receiving either preparation homework, practice homework, or both outscored 61% of the classes receiving current-content homework only when variation due to teacher differences was statistically controlled. The interaction of treatment with time of measurement was also nonsignificant, $F(1,52) = 1.54$, $p < .22$.

Influence of Student Characteristics on the Effect of Preparation or Practice Homework. Four of the dissertations examined whether the effect of preparation and/or practice homework on achievement was moderated by the intelligence of students.

Laing (1970) stratified the five schools that took part in his study according to their average student's score on the California Test of Mental Maturity—Short Form and on the three subsections of the California Test of Basic Skills that relate to mathematical abilities. The interaction of average school test score with the instructional purpose of homework was nonsignificant for both immediate and delayed tests, with F-test values near 1. Laing did not report the means underlying these interactions.

Camp (1973) reported separate analyses for the effect of instructional purpose on students categorized as scoring relatively high, middle, or low on the Henmon-Nelson Test of Mental Ability. Because the data were analyzed separately for the three groups of students, no test of the interaction of student intelligence with the instructional purpose of homework was presented. However, the underlying means indicated that the positive effect of practice homework as compared with current-content homework was greatest for students in the middle-ability group for both immediate and delayed measurements.

Butcher (1975) also used the Henmon-Nelson Test of Mental Ability to categorize students. He reported no significant interaction of intelligence and instructional purpose on either immediate or delayed measures of achievement, though for one of four immediate measures the interaction approached significance ($p < .07$). The means and separate analyses for three levels of intelligence showed no consistent pattern of results.

Dadas (1976) grouped students according to scores on the Otis-Lennon Test of Mental Ability. In this study the relevant two-way interaction again produced an F-test value of less than 1. Contrary to the Butcher (1975) study, however, the middle-ability group did not have the largest effect; it had only a small effect favoring current-content homework.

In sum, there appears to be no indication that the effect of preparation homework and practice homework on achievement is moderated by student intelligence.

Foyle (1984) included the gender or the student in his analysis of the effect of instructional purpose. The F-test value for the relevant interaction was near zero.

Peterson (1969) had teachers rate students on their "dependence-proness" and included this variable in several analyses. The effectiveness of preparation homework did not differ for independent and dependent students ($F < 1$). The interaction was not tested for control group students.

Extension Homework

Two studies have examined whether homework meant to extend material learned in class is more effective or less effective than homework with other instructional purposes. However, the two studies did not replicate the same comparison.

Baughman and Pruitt (1963) compared assignments meant to reinforce text materials, or what was early termed "practice homework," with assignments meant to encourage students "to explore in depth and breadth an area of study" (p. 155), a combination of what was earlier called "extension and integrative homework." No further description of the treatments was given in the experimental report.

The study was conducted in seventh-grade and eighth-grade social studies classes at four Illinois junior high schools. A total of 397 students participated in the study. The number of participating teachers or classes was not reported. The treatment lasted eight weeks.

Teachers were given identical instructions, and each teacher taught both a reinforcement class and an enrichment class or classes. Classes in different treatments were roughly equivalent, but no mention was made concerning whether classes were randomly assigned to the two experimental conditions. The Stanford Social Studies Test was used as the measure of achievement.

The data were analyzed with the student as the unit of analysis, even though the treatment was at the classroom level. On the other hand, the researchers employed a chi-square test of the difference in percentages of students in each condition who showed either gain or no gain from pretesting to posttesting. Thus, the analysis was probably less sensitive to changes in achievement than a dependent sample t-test, which could have legitimately been used with these data.

The chi-square test proved nonsignificant, with the percentage of improving students equaling 61% for enrichment homework and 69% for reinforcement homework. The mean pretest and posttest scores for each treatment group were not reported, but the range of raw change in test scores was nearly identical for the two groups. It appears safe to conclude, therefore, that had a more appropriate analysis been conducted the conclusion would still have been that the two types of homework did not differ in effectiveness.

The Peterson (1969) study described above and in Table 8.1 included a placebo condition in which students were assigned "mathematical puzzles" that did not involve the same mathematical principles being taught in class and were the topic of assignments in the other homework conditions. The puzzles had been constructed by the experimenter or were adapted from puzzle books or math texts. It is therefore reasonable to contend that students in this condition received a form of homework meant to extend or enrich the curriculum.

On both immediate and delayed tests of achievement, students receiving preparation homework scored highest, students receiving homework according to the undefined pattern used by teachers before the experiment scored lowest, and students receiving math puzzles scored between the two extremes. Both achievement tests also produced significant, multi-degree-of-freedom F-test values in analyses of covariance. However, a range test, applied to the underlying means, indicated that only the preparation and "same as before" homework strategies were significantly different from one another, and this effect appeared only on the delayed tests of achievement. Because Peterson did not report standard deviations, the precise magnitude of the differences between the math puzzles and other homework groups could not be calculated.

Summary

The eight studies examining practice and preparation homework provide a convincingly consistent pattern of results. With regard to achievement, all eight studies found that homework involving preparation for new material or practice of old material led to higher scores on tests than homework that dealt solely with the content of the present day's lesson. This finding held true for tests given immediately after the conclusion of a topic (d = +.10) or with some delay (d = +.20). Although the effect was larger for delayed measurements, the difference was not so large as to be statistically reliable. What is certain, however, is that the greater relative effectiveness of preparation and/or practice homework appears not to diminish over time.

When the data underlying these findings were converted to the classroom unit of analysis, the superiority of preparation or practice homework became nonsignificant (p < .14). However, the magnitude of effect, with variance due to teacher differences statistically controlled, nearly doubled (d = +.28), indicating that the lack of significance could be easily attributed to the relatively low power of the analysis.

Comparisons of preparation homework with practice homework revealed some trends, but these were statistically nonsignificant and based on a small number of studies. Therefore, it seems most appropriate at present to view these differences as requiring further study before they are accepted.

Two studies that examined differences in students' attitudes toward the subject matter as a function of preparation or practice versus current-content homework revealed no differences. Similarly, two studies comparing assignments meant to extend the content covered in class with "same as before" or practice homework showed no differences.

As a whole, the studies were well-controlled for threats to internal validity (i.e., treatments were randomly assigned to classes, and students were apparently assigned to classes without bias), and the achievement measures appeared to be carefully constructed. In addition, the findings seem to be robust across different levels of student intelligence. However, certain precautions need to be taken in the generalization of these findings. The studies were conducted on a relatively narrow population of students and subjects. Specifically, no study has examined the effect of the instructional purpose of homework on students in elementary school. Also, mathematics was the predominant subject of instruction.

SKILL AREA UTILIZED

Two studies have examined whether the skill area that students are asked to utilize in carrying out an assignment influences the effect of homework.

Nadis (1965) conducted a study in which assignments requiring reading only were compared with assignments requiring reading plus the answering of related questions or reading plus outlining of the material read. Two classes in ninth-grade world history taught by the experimenter at a Detroit junior high school served as the experimental setting. Each class, consisting of over 40 students, was divided into two "equivalent" groups based on reading and I.Q. scores, not on random assignment. In one class, one group was assigned only reading homework, while the other group did the same reading but also answered questions provided by the teacher. In the other class, one group did reading only, while the other group read the same material and prepared outlines of it. After six weeks the two groups within each class reversed treatments. The measure of the homework strategies' effect was student scores on three teacher-developed tests given at two-week intervals and a fourth review test.

Nadis reported that t-tests of the differences between groups were nonsignificant. This was true for both classes during both the initial and reversed-treatment phases of the study. The actual t-test values, degrees of freedom, and standard deviations were not reported, but Nadis did describe the direction of group differences and provided an unstandardized measure of effect. The effect size was expressed as the difference in average percentage of correct answers calculated over all four tests for each comparison group during each phase of the study. For the class in which reading-only was compared with reading-plus-questions, Nadis found that the reading-only group got 3.9% more questions correct than the reading-plus-questions group during the initial phase. The reading-plus-questions group score was 5.7% higher during the reversed-treatment phase. Because this result indicated that the same group of students performed best during both phases of the study, Nadis speculated that the two groups might not have been initially equivalent. He also interpreted the fact that the size of the difference was greater when the superior group did reading-plus-questions as an indication that this treatment may have been more effective.

The comparison between reading and reading-plus-outlining favored the latter group during both phases. During the first period, the difference was 3.7% more correct, and during the second period the difference was 3%. Nadis also reported that most students believed that written homework assignments of either type were more effective because (a) without it students might not bother to read the material and (b) it helped them remember the material.

It is difficult to interpret Nadis' results because the design and analysis strategy did not allow a strong test of his hypotheses. Specifically, had random assignment been used to place students in groups, reading and I.Q. scores could have been used as covariates. In addition, the four tests could have been analyzed as repeated measures, allowing an assessment of the changing effect of the treatment over time. These strategies would have resulted in a much more sensitive test of the hypotheses.

Perry (1974) examined the effect of three homework procedures on the achievement of second-semester high school students in shorthand classes. The three procedures involved (a) traditional homework involving both the reading and copying of shorthand letters, (b) homework assignments that established reading goals but did not require writing of connected matter, and (c) homework requiring reading goals and the writing of outlines of material students felt was especially difficult under the pressure of dictation. Thus, the object was to discover whether homework writing assignments in conjunction with reading assignments enhanced shorthand speed and learning of shorthand theory over reading assignments only. In addition, Perry examined whether the student pretest level of shorthand competence moderated the effectiveness of the three procedures.

Perry contacted shorthand teachers throughout the country, and 33 agreed to cooperate, giving this study exceptional population validity. However, Perry did not describe the procedure by which teachers were assigned to the three conditions, so it is not clear whether random assignment was used. Also, even though conditions were assigned at the teacher level, students (totaling 252 in the traditional homework condition, and 105 in the other two conditions) were used for establishing degrees of freedom in the data analysis.

Perry concluded that (a) reading-only homework can serve as a legitimate substitute for reading-and-writing homework when the goal is accurate, high-speed reading of shorthand, (b) homework involving reading plus outlining of difficult material led to significantly higher dictation speeds than reading-only homework or reading-and-writing homework for the top two-thirds of the students in pretest dictation speed, while for the bottom third homework procedure made no difference, and (c) reading-only homework led to more theoretically correct outlining of material for students in the top third (according to pretest theory mastery), while homework procedure did not affect the outlining ability of other students.

The unique subject area and the analytic flaws in Perry's research make strong inferences from his study problematic. However, the results of the Nadis (1965) and Perry (1974) studies taken together suggest that the effectiveness of homework requiring different skills may depend on the nature of the material under study. Accordingly, the influence of the skills utilized on the effectiveness of homework may best be understood by examining research on more general study techniques.

DEGREE OF INDIVIDUALIZATION

Whether individualizing homework for students at different performance levels improves achievement has been the topic of four previous studies.

Schunert (1951) included a question on his survey of Minnesota high school teachers asking whether the homework they assigned was identical for all students or differentiated for various students (see Chapter 7 for the details of this study). Schunert found 25 classes in which homework was regularly differentiated, and 45 in which identical homework for all students was the norm, although only 32 classes were used in these analyses. Achievement differences in algebra and geometry were measured on tests constructed by the experimenter and administered to students at the beginning and end of the school year. Before examining for the effects of individualization, Schunert adjusted year-end achievement scores for initial achievement and I.Q. differences among students and for the size of the school and the amount of college mathematics the teacher had. Schunert reported that algebra classes where homework was differentiated outperformed undifferentiated classes (d = +.78), but no significant difference was found for geometry classes (it is regrettable that Schunert reported the size of the associated F-test but not the direction of effect).

Bradley (1967) compared group homework assignments in arithmetic with assignments designed to meet the needs of individual pupils. In the individualized condition, (a) students played a role in determining what the assignments would be, (b) assignments were sometimes remedial and sometimes for enrichment, and (c) assignments varied in length. In the group condition, homework came primarily from the textbook and was identical for all students.

Participants were 202 fifth-graders drawn from eight classrooms, two each from four schools in Lancaster County, Pennsylvania. The four schools were chosen to represent different communities and income levels. Students were matched before the experiment according to gender and scores on the Metropolitan Achievement Test (MAT). One classroom in each school was assigned to each condition based on a coin flip. The treatment lasted eight weeks.

Bradley employed three indices of the treatment effect: (a) achievement change, measured by posttest minus pretest gains on mastery tests accompanying the textbook; (b) interest levels, measured by the frequency with which students chose math-related materials from an "interest table" set up in each classroom for use when students were not otherwise occupied; and (c) time spent on homework, both for students to complete assignments and for teachers to create and correct them.

The analysis of achievement-gain scores, using the student as the unit of analysis even though the treatment was administered to classrooms, revealed a significant treatment effect favoring the individualized homework group, d = +.32, U3 = 66.7%. However, this main effect was accompanied by a significant interaction involving the school—relatively large gains for the individualized homework were found in two schools, and relatively small gains for group homework were found in two schools. Furthermore, separate analyses for subgroups revealed that individualized homework was significantly more effective than group homework for girls and for students scoring in the top third on the MAT. The two types of homework did not differ for boys or for students scoring in the bottom two-thirds on the MAT.

Chi-square analyses of the interest data revealed no difference between the treatments with regard to how many times math-related activities were chosen. Separate analyses by gender showed that boys receiving individualized homework chose math activities more often than boys receiving group homework, while the opposite was true for girls. Achievement did not relate to activity choices. It must be kept in mind that the chi-square analysis treated each choice at the interest table as independent, even though the same student may have made numerous choices over the course of the experiment.

Data concerning the number of minutes students spent on homework were analyzed by examining how many students reported spending between 25 and 35 minutes on each assignment. This amount of time was considered to be the desirable time allotment. No overall difference was found between the homework treatments, but boys more frequently spent time above the desired range when given group homework than when given individualized homework. Most important, almost half the bottom-third achievers spent more than the desired time on group homework, compared with only one in six when it was individualized.

The number of minutes of out-of-school time that teachers spent preparing and correcting homework was 47 minutes per assignment in the individualized condition and 29 minutes in the group homework condition. However, as the experiment progressed the difference between treatments diminished.

A third study (Singh, 1970), purporting to test the effects of individualized enrichment homework, defined individualization similarly to Bradley's treatment. However, Singh did not describe how the students in the control condition were treated, how assignment to treatments was accomplished, or how treatment differences were statistically analyzed.

Finally, a study by Grant (1971) defined individualized homework in a somewhat different fashion. In this study, students in the individualized homework condition were allowed to choose between two types of assignments that varied in level of difficulty but were similar in format and covered the same material. These assignments were prepared by the experimenter, not by the classroom teachers. The experiment also contained (a) a condition in which all students did the same homework taken from the text and (b) a no-homework condition.

Seventeen fifth-grade classrooms drawn from three school districts were included in the study. Classrooms were randomly assigned to homework conditions, except in one district where assignment occurred at the school level (in order to avoid parental complaints about differing treatment of students). In all, 386 students participated. Students were stratified according to intelligence using the Lorge-Thorndike Intelligence Test. Gender was also examined as an interacting variable. The experiment lasted 10 weeks.

The measure of achievement in Grant's study was scores on the Comprehensive Test of Basic Skills subtests for arithmetic computation, concepts, and applications. Parallel forms were used to pretest and posttest students. Pretest scores were used as a covariate. Intelligence level, gender, and homework treatment were independent variables. Students were used as the unit of analysis.

Grant reported no significant differences between treatments as a main effect or in interaction with gender and intelligence. However, these conclusions were based on the outcomes of tests involving two degrees of freedom (individualized versus group versus no homework). Single degree of freedom comparisons were not computed. Inspection of the 12 sets of means for the two types of homework broken down for the three subtests by the two genders and intelligence levels (high versus low) revealed six comparisons favoring individualized homework and six favoring group homework. Also, contrary to Bradley's (1967) finding, four of the six comparisons involving girls favored the group homework.

Summary

The Bradley (1967) and Grant (1971) studies are among the best-designed examinations of variations in homework, although their data analyses leave something to be desired. Bearing in mind that the studies used quite different treatments, together they indicate few benefits of individualizing homework. The Bradley study deserves special commendation for having assessed the treatments' effects on multiple outcomes. The interest measure revealed no treatment effect, but choices at an interest table probably constituted a strong test of the effect, given the short length of treatment and the number of other factors that might influence such behavior. The measures of student and teacher time raise some interesting ancillary issues in that they indicated that slower students may require considerable time to complete group homework, while individualized homework may burden the teacher.

DEGREE OF STUDENT CHOICE

Three studies have examined the relative effectiveness of compulsory homework and voluntary homework, but the studies varied dramatically in scope and one study was conducted more than 30 years after the others.

Abramowitz (1937) conducted a study in three Spanish classes that he taught. In one class, written grammatical exercises were given as optional homework, while in the other two classes the exercises had to be handed in. No attempt was made to match or equate the classes. The optional homework class demonstrated the smallest gain in test scores when mid-term tests were compared with average test grades from the prior term. However, Abramowitz presented no standard deviations or inference test results and he labeled the difference as negligible.

DiNapoli (1937) performed one of the largest, best-controlled quasi-experimental studies of homework. Beginning in 1905 the New York City school system required primary-grade students to perform homework that would count toward the students' standing in class. Employing six schools chosen to represent three different levels of economic background, DiNapoli tested the notion that students' achievement and interest in academic subjects would not be affected if compulsory homework was replaced by homework that was not scored and did not contribute to grades.

Three schools were chosen to institute a voluntary homework program. The choice of voluntary-homework schools was made not through random assignment but through "conference with the principals" (p. 19). A total of 1,200 students in grades 5 and 7 constituted the initial sample. Students in voluntary-homework schools were matched with students in compulsory-homework schools based on (a) chronological age, (b) scores on the Otis Test of Mental Ability, and (c) average scores across nine subtests of the Metropolitan Achievement Test. The matching procedure resulted in 398 matched pairs of students. The number of teachers or classrooms involved in the study was not reported.

The study lasted from February to June 1935. Teachers in the voluntary condition were instructed not to assign any homework, to praise voluntary homework if it was praiseworthy, and to assign any studying they felt was necessary during school hours. Teachers in the compulsory condition were given recommendations concerning appropriate homework strategies. The curriculums in all six schools were the same.

The outcome measure was a posttreatment administration of the Metropolitan Achievement Test and a specially prepared inventory designed to measure childrens' interest in the course of study used in New York City schools.

DiNapoli considered the student as the unit of analysis and reported results separately for boys and girls at the two grade levels. He found that compulsory homework led to greater achievement in fifth grade, where compulsory homework students gained an average 1.3 months more in achievement than voluntary homework students, though the difference only approached significance. When subject matter was taken into account, eight of nine subtests favored compulsory homework, with arithmetic fundamentals being the only subject to favor the voluntary group. In seventh grade, the voluntary-homework students outperformed the compulsory-homework students (by .43 months gained on average), but the difference was nonsignificant. The effect of degree of choice in homework was approximately equal for boys and girls.

DiNapoli also compared the achievement gained by students in the experiment with the gain expected by the norms of the test. He found that all students surpassed the normative gain, except for fifth-graders in the voluntary-homework condition. These students achieved only 86% of the normative gain.

With regard to interest in academic subjects, DiNapoli reported a complex set of findings involving gender, grade, and the subject matter covered. At the most general level, the data seemed to indicate that compulsory homework tended to accentuate (a) a general loss of interest in arithmetic over the course of the study and (b) a general gain of interest in history.

The DiNapoli study is frequently cited as an early example of empirical research on homework. It is also cited for the divergence between the researcher's findings and recommendations. Based on the evidence cited above, DiNapoli recommended "the abolition of compulsory homework in favor of voluntary homework" (p. 43). Goldstein (1960) commented that this final recommendation was "entirely unwarranted" (p. 215) and "bears so little relationship to these findings as to make one wonder how the same author could have written both" (p. 214). Goldstein also pointed out that the students in the voluntary-homework condition had experienced several years of compulsory homework before it was discontinued. He wondered what the effect of voluntary versus compulsory homework might be if students were exposed to one strategy or the other for their entire school. career.

Taylor (1971) conducted a study of compulsory versus voluntary homework in two introductory algebra classes and two introductory geometry classes at a California high shool. The compulsory-homework class in each subject area was required to hand in assignments that were spot-checked and constituted 20% of the students' grades. The voluntary-homework class received the same assignments on the same day, but these were not collected or graded.

Students were not assigned to classes at random, but the researcher randomly determined which class within each subject area would receive which treatment. Also, a pretest revealed no significant differences between classes with regard to prior knowledge of the subject areas, but the pretest was not used as a covariate in the posttreatment analyses. The texts used were identical within each subject area. The study lasted one semester, or about 4.5 months. The experimenter was the teacher of all four classes. A total of 113 students took part in the study.

Achievement was measured using tests constructed by the authors of the textbooks used in the classes. Students were used as the unit of analysis, and algebra and geometry classes were analyzed separately. Taylor reported no difference between the achievement scores of compulsory-homework classes and those of voluntary-homework classes. However, both comparisons favored the compulsory-homework group, and the effect for algebra was quite large ($d = +2.15$ for algebra and $d = +.11$ for geometry). Attitudes were assessed using the Ellington Attitude Inventory, a measure of high school students' opinions about mathematics. This measure also revealed no significant differences between compulsory-homework groups and voluntary-homework groups, but again the mean direction favored the compulsory group, and for algebra the effect was greater than for geometry ($d = +.44$ and $d = +.09$, respectively).

Summary

The Abramowitz (1937) study, which favored compulsory homework, should probably be discounted because of its age, small number of classrooms, and lack of experimental control. The DiNapoli (1937) study also generally favored compulsory homework for its effect on achievement, but it too must be interpreted with caution because of its age. Furthermore, because the voluntary-homework treatment is not described clearly, we cannot tell whether this group was exposed to a different level of choice or to a no-homework condition.

The nonsignificant effects on achievement found in the Taylor study favoring compulsory homework are easily attributable to chance or to imprecise matching. It is curious that these directional effects appeared for mathematics instruction, the one subject for which DiNapoli found effects favoring voluntary homework.

Neither the DiNapoli study nor the Taylor study produced evidence that compulsory homework leads to poorer attitudes toward the covered subject matter. Such an outcome might have been predicted based on the hypothesis that obvious external causes for pursuing a task (i.e., required home study) diminish intrinsic interest in the task (cf. Deci & Ryan, 1985). Although the DiNapoli study did find that compulsory homework led both to a greater loss of interest and to poorer achievement in arithmetic, the broader pattern of results indicated that for other subjects compulsory homework enhanced both achievement and interest.

In sum, in the past 40 years only one study has compared the effects of compulsory homework versus voluntary homework, and that small investigation reported nonsignificant differences. However, it would be imprudent to conclude that the two practices had equal effect until larger and more varied studies are conducted.

9

Home and Community Factors and Classroom Follow-up

In this chapter the final two stages in the homework process will be examined. These stages involve the influence of home and community factors and the follow-up procedures employed by the teacher after the homework assignment is completed.

In Table 1.3 three home-community factors were identified: leisure activities that compete for students' time; conditions in the home environment that either facilitate or inhibit students' opportunities to study (e.g., adequate space and light, a quiet atmosphere, the availability of necessary materials); and the involvement of others. Of these three classes of variables, only one question relating to home factors has been the focus of research—Does the involvement of parents in the homework process affect the achievement or attitudes of students? The relation of competing leisure-time activities, home environment, and the involvement of people other than parents to the effects of homework has yet to be examined. However, there is a large and growing nonexperimental literature that relates to issues of parents and other family members as educators, to family literacy in general, and to the family as a source of informal education. Although these issues are considerably broader than our subject of homework, a short description of some related research will be given. Also, several communities have instituted programs that provide after-school telephone assistance to students with homework problems. These have never been formally evaluated for their influence on achievement, but a description of some of the programs is in order.

With regard to classroom follow-up of homework assignments, several studies have examined the effects of instructional feedback, grading, and incentives on subsequent performance. These studies are reviewed in the final section of this chapter.

PARENT INVOLVEMENT

Eight studies have examined whether parent involvement in homework relates to achievement. Six of these studies were correlational in design, and two involved experimental manipulations.

Correlational Studies

The value of having parents participate in homework was the focus of one of the earliest empirical investigations in this area. In 1916, Brooks reported a study that examined whether parental supervision of homework related to the class standing of the student. The study was conducted in the Durham, North Carolina, school district and involved 268 fourth-, fifth-, and sixth-graders.

Each home was visited, and the visitor recorded whether the parents provided assistance with homework. Unfortunately, Brooks did not state (a) an operational definition for "parental assistance," (b) how long the home visit lasted, (c) what rationale was given for the visit, (d) who or how reliable the observers were, or much other procedural information that might help assess the validity of the parental supervision data. Also, supervision was treated as a categorical (present/absent) rather than continuous variable in the analyses. Principals provided the students' class standing, also dichotomized for the analyses, after the homes were visited.

Brooks presented his results separately for each grade and for two classes within each grade. No statistical tests were performed, but the entries in his 2×2 contingency tables permit easy calculation of chi-square statistics. These revealed a highly significant overall effect indicating that students in homes where parental supervision was present had higher class standing than their counterparts whose homework went unsupervised (χ^2 (1) = 42.35, p < .0001, r = +.40). The effect was consistent across grades.

Another difficulty in interpreting Brooks' results, aside from the lack of detail about the meaning and measurement of "parental supervision," stems from the correlational nature of the data. The data cannot reveal whether parental supervision of homework caused higher class standing, whether high class standing encouraged parental supervision, or whether both variables were caused by a third, more diffuse home environment effect. It should also be kept in mind that Brooks' study is more than 70 years old. The societal and familial variables surrounding homework have undoubtedly changed over the years, as has perhaps the meaning of homework itself.

Rankin (1967) presented the results of a study examining the difference between the behavior of parents of underachievers and parents of overachievers. Thirty-two children of each type were identified by comparing the aptitude and achievement scores of 241 third-graders and fourth-graders from Detroit inner-city schools. Aptitude and achievement were measured across multiple subjects using standardized tests (e.g., the California Achievement Test and the Iowa Test of Basic Skills for achievement). Parents were asked 123 questions, 38 of which related to their interest in school activities. The interview was administered by the experimenter, leaving open some possibility of experimenter bias. However, parent responses were validated by comparing them with student responses to similar questions, and although parents tended to report more involvement than their children, the difference appeared to be unrelated to the achievement status of the child.

Rankin used chi-square statistics to anlayze data measured at the interval level. Neither the means and standard deviations of responses nor the precise inference test values were presented. Of the 123 items, only the 17 that reached statistical significance were described. Among the 5 items related to school activities that proved significant, one measured parents' attempts "to find the reason for poor work and helping the child correct it when he did a poor job on a school assignment" (p. 4). Assuming that no other question measured homework involvement in a more precise manner (a liberal assumption), and assuming a chi-square value equal to 3.84 (exactly $p < .05$; a conservative assumption), the correlation between parental involvement and overachievement versus underachievement would be $r = +.24$.

Wolf (1979) reported data from the United States students participating in the International Achievement Project (IAP). The study involved a national random sample of more than 11,000 10- and 14-year-olds and twelfth-graders. Standardized tests developed specifically for this project were related to four sets of variables: student background, type of community, learning conditions, and kindreds. One of the kindred variables in some of the analyses involved parent help with homework, though Wolf did not report whether this variable was measured continuously or as simple presence versus absence. He also did not state whether the parent-involvement measure was omitted from some of the analyses because the question was not asked or because of nonsignificance in data analyses. (The IAP study also included a variable concerning the amount of homework done by students. These findings were included in the earlier analysis.)

The analyses were carried out separately for each subject and each age or grade level. For 10-year-olds, parent help with homework revealed a negative relation to achievement scores in science ($r = -.06$) and in reading comprehension ($r = -.07$). For 14-year-olds, parent involvement was negatively associated with reading comprehension ($r = -.20$) but positively associated with French reading ($r = +.06$) and French listening ($r = +.03$). Similar positive relations were found for high school seniors for French reading ($r = +.11$) and French listening ($r = +.29$).

A study by Harding (1979) also revealed different outcomes, depending on the subject matter involved. He performed an interesting analysis on a cross-sectional data set. The analysis was meant to determine if several years of parental participation in homework had a cumulative effect on achievement. He identified 299 fourth-grade students who had been in the same Souderton, Pennsylvania, school district for first, second, and third grades. He asked all teachers who had taught these grades during the appropriate years questions about their attitude toward parent involvement and about the frequency with which they assigned homework that called on parents to take part. Students were then matched with their teachers for the past three grades. A cumulative score expressing each student's teacher's favorableness toward parental involvement was generated. The rating was based on a combination of both the attitude measure and the frequency measure, but it can be assumed these were highly correlated. For entry into analyses of covariance, students were divided into three groups, depending on whether their teachers had been strong, moderate, or weak advocates of parent involvement. Teachers were labeled strong or weak advocates if their scores were one standard deviation above or below the mean of the distribution.

The outcome measure was the students' scores on the Stanford Achievement Test. The analyses of covariance, employing I.Q. as the controlled variable, produced nonsignificant effects for parent involvement for both reading ($F < 1.00$) and math ($F = 1.40$). Examination of the means for reading indicated that students whose teachers weakly and moderately favored parent involvement had similar test scores, while students whose teachers strongly favored involvement scored lowest. Comparing the strongly favored with the weakly favored groups revealed a correlation equal to $r = -.50$. For math, students whose teachers strongly and weakly favored parent involvement had similar test scores ($r = +.06$, favoring involvement), while students of teachers who moderately favored involvement scored highest.

Beyond the confounding of attitude and frequency in the measure of parent involvement, Harding's study had two other weaknesses. First, the teacher's reports concerning parent involvement measured their attitudes and practices at the present time, not when they in fact were the teachers of the students in the study. Second, the procedure of defining strong and weak advocacy of parent involvement as being one standard deviation above or below the distribution mean created highly discrepant cell sizes. Thus, only 20 students were categorized as having teachers who were strongly favorable, and 12 were categorized as weakly favorable, while 267 students fell in the moderate group. Had the favorability-toward-parent-involvement variable been left in its continuous form, a much more trustworthy conclusion could have been drawn.

A study of the sustaining effects of compensatory education included an examination of student home environments (Hinckley et al., 1979). In this phase of a much larger study, visits were made to the homes of more than 15,000 students selected through a careful sampling of all elementary schools in the United States. During the visits, parents took part in face-to-face interviews that included many measures of home environment.

One of the measures derived from the interviews was called "homework activity." Parents were asked five questions about their child's reading and math homework routine. These included whether or not the child (a) brought homework home frequently, (b) very frequently got help with homework, (c) spent more time than the average student doing homework, and (d) did *not* get assistance from his or her mother and/or father. The problem in interpreting the parent involvement issue is that the five responses were summed, so that receiving help from parents was considered an indication of *low* homework activity, while a parent's report of more frequent help in general (question *b*) was taken as an indication of high homework activity. Beyond this confusion, there is also the problem that the homework-activity index confounds the amount of homework done with the involvement of others. (Results concerning a measure of time spent on homework, also collected in this study, were described in Chapter 7).

The homework activity index was correlated with students' scores on the Comprehensive Test of Basic Skills. Over all students, homework activity related negatively to both reading achievement ($r = -.10$) and math achievement ($r = -.16$). The effect was negative at all grade levels, but slightly more so in first and second grades than in the fifth and sixth grades. The effects were also slightly more negative for white students than for members of ethnic minorities.

If the homework acitivity index total score had correlated positively with its parent involvement component, this would have indicated that students receiving more help from parents had higher achievement scores. Although this is a legitimate assumption, it should also be kept in mind that this study found a strong negative relation between achievement and time spent on homework (see Chapter 7). Therefore, the frequency and amount-of-time components of the homework activity measure may best explain the negative relation.

A study by Epstein (1983) involved questionnaire responses provided by 82 teachers and 1,021 parents in 16 Maryland school districts during 1980 and 1981. Teachers were chosen to represent different levels of experience and various types of school communities. (Epstein also reported negative relations between total minutes spent on homework and achievement. These data were included in the analysis reported above.)

The questions asked about homework included (a) how many minutes parents spent helping their children with homework and (b) how frequently the teacher requested such parent involvement. These were related to teacher-provided measures of achievement in reading and mathematics and to classroom discipline problems.

Epstein found that the number of minutes parents spent assisting with homework was negatively associated with the child's reading achievement ($r = -.18$; a correlation of $\pm.08$ was significant at the $p < .01$ level) and math achievement (r = −.19), and positively associated with discipline problems (r = +.13). Similarly, children of parents who received more frequent requests for involvement had lower reading (r = −.14) and math (r = −.12) achievement.

A difficulty in interpreting correlational results, beyond spuriousness and directionality, is highlighted by the Epstein study. Although Epstein found results that, at face value, might be interpreted as arguing against parent involvement in homework, she chose to cast her findings in a different light. She suggested that "these negative relationships indicate teachers are reaching out to parents to obtain extra help for children who need additional time, or that parents are recognizing students' weaknesses and helping on their own" (p. 14). She held out the hope that future longitudinal analyses would tell whether the extra assistance paid off. Thus, although Epstein found correlations whose directions were opposite to those obtained by Brooks (1916) and Rankin (1967), all three researchers interpreted their results as supporting parent involvement in homework.

One way to reconcile the correlational literature would be to suggest that parent involvement has different effects for various subjects. However, with regard to math learning, the Harding (1979) and Epstein (1983) studies differed in the direction of their results. Reading skills are more consistently related to parent involvement, with three of the correlational studies reporting negative correlations. However, it is not possible to test fully the notion of subject matter dependence with the present body of studies because of the small number of studies, confounded variations in definitions of parent involvement and achievement, and markedly different sample sizes and methodologies.

It is important to note a strong temporal trend in the data. As time has passed, studies have moved from reporting positive relations to reporting negative relations. The average correlations between parent involvement and subject matter achievement in five studies (excluding Hinckley et al., 1979), presented in temporal order, are +.40, +.24, +.02, −.22, and −.16. Again, the body of evidence is not large enough or homogeneous enough to invest great meaning in this finding, and an explanation of why the relation of parent involvement to achievement might have changed over time is not readily apparent.

Experimental Studies

A study by Maertens and Johnston (1972) is often cited as bearing on the issue of parent involvement in homework, but this study did not contain a pure test of involvement versus no involvement. Instead, three treatments were compared for their effect on achievement in and attitudes toward fourth-, fifth-, and sixth-grade arithmetic: (a) no homework, (b) homework involving feedback on the correctness of arithmetic story problems and computations administered by parents immediately following completion of the problem, and (c) delayed feedback of a similar nature delivered by parents after all homework problems are completed. Therefore, this study contained no direct comparison of homework with and without parent involvement, but instead compared two strategies for parents' delivery of similar feedback. Also, parents were explicitly instructed to inform their children only of the correctness of their responses and not to give assistance or praise and criticism.

Maertens and Johnston measured the effects of their treatments using (a) an achievement test, (b) the cumulative score on experimenter-prepared weekly tests, and (c) semantic differentials measuring attitude toward arithmetic, school, and homework (e.g., good or bad, hard or easy). About 400 students from a rural Oregon community, randomly assigned to conditions, took part in the six-week treatment.

The immediate and end-of-assignment feedback treatments did not differ significantly in their effectiveness, whether the effect was measured by achievement or by attitudes. Examination of the underlying means also revealed no trend. (The researchers did find that homework combined with either type of parent feedback had a significant positive effect on computational and problem-solving performance. The homework manipulation had no significant effect on attitudes toward the subject matter. These results were included in the homework versus no homework analysis described above.)

Paulukaitis and Kirkpatrick (1986) also manipulated parents' involvement in homework. One group of children was required only to read assigned stories to their parents. Another group of children first reviewed words with their parents, then the children read them stories, and finally parents and children discussed interactive questions provided by the experimenters.

The study was conducted over two school years in a rural Louisiana community. Students, 38 first-graders in all, were exposed to both treatments. The teacher was also one of the researchers. During the first year of the study, students received the reading-only treatment in the fall and the more interactive treatment in the spring. Treatment order was reversed during the second year. Homework was assigned two or three times a week. Some poorly performing students were excluded from the study for fear that the procedures might frustrate them and their parents.

Several measures of reading achievement, varying in degree of standardization, were used to assess the treatment effects. In the primary analysis, nonsignificantly different and nearly identical mean achievement scores were found on tests constructed by the textbook company and given on a periodic basis when units of the reading text were completed. However, the authors report that vocabulary and comprehension subtests favored the more interactive parental assistance strategy, although no data to substantiate these claims were presented. Also, when a prereading skills inventory was used as a covariate to control for initial differences between the first-year and second-year groups, highly significant treatment effects were found on the number of reading units completed: students whose parents took a more active role in homework completed more units than students who simply read to their parents. Finally, three other tests of achievement (one standardized) revealed no effect for type of parent involvement. However, the group of students who received more interactive homework in the fall outperformed students receiving this treatment in the spring.

The authors interpret their results as supportive of greater parent involvement in homework. Considering (a) the failure of the treatment to produce differences in the primary variable of interest, (b) use of the student as unit of analysis when the treatment was administered at the group level, and (c) preexisting differences between the first- and second-year groups, this assessment seems risky.

Summary

It appears that there is as yet no reliable evidence on whether parent involvement in homework affects student achievement. No study directly manipulating the presence versus absence of such involvement has been conducted. Six correlational studies, causally ambiguous by nature, have produced conflicting results, with the authors of the most divergent findings each claiming that their results support parent involvement. One well-controlled experimental study manipulated such a small component of parent involvement (whether or not feedback on correctness was immediate or delayed, with no parental instructions or affect allowed) that it is irrelevant to the larger question. Finally, the one experiment that did manipulate the level of parent involvement in a meaningful fashion is fraught with interpretation difficulties.

HOMEWORK HOTLINES

One type of community-based effort related to homework involves the establishment of homework "hotlines." These are telephone services in which teachers are available to answer questions related to homework problems.

Probably the first such effort was the Dial-a-Teacher program instituted by the School District of Philadelphia (Blackwell, 1979). In this program, eight teachers with different areas of expertise answered telephones. The idea behind the service was to help callers who did not have available at home the resources necessary to solve problems encountered in doing homework, or students who might have forgotten the procedure to be employed to complete an assignment. Teachers did not complete the homework assignment. Instead, they (a) helped callers understand the concepts or process they were working with, (b) helped callers find sources of information or supplemental materials, and/or (c) led callers to alternate solutions.

It is difficult to assess the effectiveness of such programs using the outcome variables that appear in other types of homework research. However, the Philadelphia program did monitor the type and number of calls. The service was used by students of all ages, from kindergarten through high school, as well as by parents assisting their children with homework. The subject area receiving the most calls was mathematics. During the first semester of operation (beginning January 1979), the number of calls per week reached a peak about a month after the program began, following considerable publicity in the local media. A precipitous decline occurred after the first spring recess. The decline was attributed to (a) varying school vacation dates, (b) decreased media attention, and (c) the onset of warm weather and longer daylight hours. However, when the program was reinstituted during the next semester (September 1979), the number of calls quickly exceeded the first semester, increasing by nearly 60%.

The school district of Norfolk, Virginia, operated a homework hotline from mid-April to early June 1985 (Gay, 1985). This service included two teachers receiving calls and was restricted to elementary school grades. In order to assess the effects of the program, questionnaires were administered to 865 students, parents, teachers, and administrators. All parties involved found the hotline useful.

Perhaps most instructive about the Norfolk evaluation were the recommendations concerning how the hotline could be made more effective. These included (a) increased teachers and telephone lines to make access easier, (b) longer hours of operation so that students doing homework later could use the service (especially in the warmer months), and (c) increased public awareness of the hotline's existence. It seems that these would be key elements to the effectiveness of any homework hotline service.

It should be noted that New York City ran several programs for low-achieving students that were called Homework Helper or High School Homework programs (Heintz, 1975; Joiner, 1970; U.S. Department of Health, Education & Welfare, 1969). However, these programs contained tutorial components that were probably more central to their goals than help with homework. Evaluations of their effects on measures of achievement, involving both matched control groups and regression discontinuity analyses, produced positive results.

FAMILIES AS EDUCATORS

Just as homework hotlines blur the distinction between families and schools by bringing the teacher into the home, there is a corresponding line of inquiry examining how families act as educators (Leichter, 1974). Much of the associated research involves observation of children in the home, often when they are doing homework. For instance, McDermott, Goldman, and Varenne (1984) observed two families from the same neighborhood with similar economic and religious backgrounds. They found differences between the two families in the physical arrangement, temporal pattern, and attention paid to procedural matters in doing homework. In particular, they found that one family had a difficult time integrating homework into the flow of family events, while the other family easily shifted between homework and other social forms. They conclude that teachers "without knowing it, of course, have a rather different fabric into which they would like to weave their design" (pp. 405–406).

Other studies have employed larger samples and more controlled observation. For instance, Chandler et al. (1983) observed the interactions of 32 low-income parent-child dyads. Observations were done in the home, but involved a standard homework-like lesson. Chandler et al. wanted to test the "discontinuity hypothesis," which claims that low-income families and schools emphasize different functions of literacy and language and different teaching and learning experiences. They found the interactions in general to be positive, cooperative, and productive. Chandler et al. concluded that there was no evidence of home-school discontinuity, but instead labeled the interactions "strikingly similar to what [students] experience in school" (p. 21). Epstein (1986) has broadened the concept of continuity or discontinuity between families and schools by introducing the notions of school-like families and family-like schools.

The families-as-educators line of inquiry is not bound by issues related to homework. In fact, homework is but a small area of concern. Researchers and educators interested in the home as a site for learning go well beyond examining the work students bring with them from school. In this vein, Leichter (1985) noted that an ethnographic study meant to examine the "literacy resources" within the home found that "even those families that relied to a large extent on conversation for communication, rather than reading or writing, were inundated by print both in the home and in the community outside the home" (p. 89).

Finally, there is a large and growing literature relating to how parents can become involved in school issues beyond simply assisting with homework (see Epstein, 1987a, 1987b) and how parents can be trained to be better transmitters of knowledge (see, e.g., Levenstein, 1983). However, these efforts go well beyond the study of homework and deserve fuller attention than can be given here. For the present purpose, these lines of inquiry point out the importance of viewing homework as only one avenue of cooperation between school and home, viewing the school as only one of many sites for learning, and viewing the teacher as only one conveyor of knowledge.

TEACHER FEEDBACK AND INCENTIVES

The response of teachers when homework assignments are collected can vary in four different ways. First, teachers can provide students with instruction on ways the assignment could have been more accurately completed. This can be done by reviewing all or a portion of the assigned work with the class as a whole or by providing individual students with comments describing their errors. Second, teachers can provide letter or numerical grades, which can then be used as part of the student's overall performance evaluation. Third, teachers can provide praise or criticism, either verbal or written, meant to reward correct responses and/or punish incorrect ones. Both grades and reinforcement can be based simply on whether the homework was completed or on the accuracy of the responses. Finally, teachers can provide nonverbal incentives, such as candy or early dismissal, dependent on the completeness or accuracy of the homework. The four strategies can be applied in combination and with varying frequencies, ranging from continuous to intermittent use of any given strategy.

Nine studies have examined the effects of teacher-provided homework feedback on subsequent student performance. Considering the number of possible combinations of feedback strategies, it is not surprising that no two studies replicated a conceptually identical comparison. Tables 9.1 and 9.2 summarize the methodological characteristics of the studies and the nature of the strategies they examined. Eight of the studies used a design in which (a) multiple classrooms or students were assigned to different feedback conditions, (b) conditions were run simultaneously, and (c) inferential statistics were used to compare the feedback conditions. A study by Harris (1972) employed several replicates of a single-case, time series design and relied on visual inspection of graphed data to draw inferences.

A study by Lash (1971) is often listed among feedback studies, although its inclusion as such is debatable. Lash prepared three booklets for students to take home with them that contained either hints about how to solve geometry homework problems, answers to the problems, or full problem solutions. The effects the three booklets had on test scores were compared with each other as well as to a no-booklet control. Results from unit progress tests did not consistently favor any treatment. A test of change scores on a standardized test revealed that students given booklets including full solutions showed the least improvement in performance, while the other three treatments—hints, answers, and no booklet—did not differ.

Lash's study is probably best construed as an examination of study aids, but it is mentioned here because the answers and full-solutions booklets could be considered forms of teacher feedback, if students referred to them only after having worked the problems. However, the findings suggest that this was not the case—students with full solutions may have copied these without working the problems on their own.

The first notable aspect of the feedback research is that all studies dealt with mathematics. One study (Stewart & White, 1976) looked at both math and spelling but did not distinguish between the two in the analyses, and another (Harris, 1972) looked at math and social studies. There is therefore little evidence concerning the effects of homework feedback on performance in subject areas other than math. Second, although only four of

TABLE 9.1. Studies Comparing the Effects of Types of Instructional Feedback or Grading of Homework Assignments

Characteristics	Baxter (1973)	Austin (1976)	Dick (1980)	Austin & Austin (1974)	Small et al. (1967)	O'Connor (1985)
Document type	Diss.	Journal	Diss.	Journal	Journal	Thesis
Location	N.Y.	Ga.	Ky.	Ind.	Fla.	Tex.
Research design	NEC	RA	NEC	RA	NEC	NEC
Student equivalence procedure	Counter-balancing	Blocking	Covariates, counter-balancing	Blocking	Matching	Matching
Grade level	6	4,9,10	9	7,8	10	10,11,12
Subject matter	Math	Math	Algebra	Math	Geometry	Algebra
No. schools/classes/students	3/4/96	NA/9/222	1/2/38	1/2/51	1/2/36	1/2/50
Treatment duration	8 weeks	6 weeks	1 year	7 weeks	1 year	5 weeks
Homework assignments per week	1	3–4	5	3–4	5	5
Treatment 1	Description of error	Correctness indication	Solve and explain all problems	Every problem graded	Spot graded for completeness	Irregular grade for accuracy
Treatment 2	Correctness indication	Correctness and encouragement and how to get right	Solve and explain student requests	Random half graded	All graded for accuracy	Grade every day for completeness
Homework performance measure	Accuracy	None	None	None	None	None
Unit performance measure	None	Teacher constructed	Teacher constructed	Teacher constructed	Teacher's manual	Teacher constructed
Comprehensive exam measure	None	None	None	None	Standardized	Teacher constructed

Note. NEC = nonequivalent control group design; RA = random assignment; NA = not available.

144

the studies used random assignment to place students in feedback groups, all used some technique to enhance the equivalence of students in the different feedback conditions. Also, as with other areas of homework research, most of the studies administered the feedback treatment at the classroom level but used the student as the unit of analysis.

Another notable aspect of the feedback research is that only two studies, by Fink and Nalven (1972) and Harris (1972), contained a comparison in which no feedback was compared with a feedback strategy, and both these studies dealt with the provision of incentives. Thus, no study has examined how instructional feedback, grading, or verbal or written praise and criticism compare with no feedback at all. Instead, studies examining these strategies compare variations in how the particular type of feedback is used.

Instructional Feedback

Three studies have examined the effect of instructional homework feedback on subsequent performance (see Table 9.1). Baxter (1973) compared a strategy in which students were simply given an indication of whether a math problem was right or wrong with one in which errors were classified into five types (i.e., error of fact, renaming, algorithm, omission, or blunder). Baxter found that students receiving only feedback on correctness solved more problems correctly, but the difference between treatments was minuscule—that is, the F-test value was less than 1 in both of two phases of the experiment.

Austin (1976) had one group of students receive feedback only on whether a problem solution was right or wrong, while another group received three types of feedback—correctness feedback, indications of how to get wrong answers right, and written encouragement. In five of nine classes the multiple feedback strategy proved more efficacious, with two classroom comparisons reaching significance, using a nonparametric analysis strategy.

Dick (1980) looked at whether in-class solving and explaining of all homework problems the day after an assignment was completed produced more learning than solving and explaining only those problems requested by students. Results gauged by performance on unit tests favored reviewing all problems, but again the associated F-test barely reached the chance value of 1.

Grading

Three studies compared different strategies for grading homework (see Table 9.1). Austin and Austin (1974) examined whether grading every homework problem differed from grading only a randomly selected half of problems. For seventh-graders, a nonsignificant ($p < .12$) effect on unit tests was found favoring the grading of all problems ($d = +.78$), while for eighth-graders a difference between strategies was undetectable ($p < .50$, $d = 0$).

Studies by Small et al. (1967) and O'Connor (1985) confounded grading strategy with whether homework was graded for completeness or for accuracy. Specifically, Small compared irregular grading for completeness with grading all problems for accuracy, while O'Connor compared irregular grading for accuracy with everyday grading for completeness. Both researchers examined the strategies' effects on unit tests and comprehensive exams. Both reported no differences between the strategies, again with inference test values hovering around $t = 1$.

Evaluative Comments

Two studies have examined the effect of verbal or written evaluative homework comments (see Table 9.2). One was the 1976 study by Austin described above, in which instructional feedback and encouragement were varied together. The other, conducted by Stewart and White (1976), involved use of evaluative comments not only on homework but on classwork as well. These authors reported no difference on both unit and comprehensive test performance for students receiving grades, grades and evaluative comments, evaluative comments only, or positive evaluative comments only. This conclusion was based on an overall comparison between the four strategies ($df = 3$), revealing F-test values of 1.19 and 0.37 for unit and comprehensive tests, respectively.

It is also interesting to note that Stewart and White performed a meta-analysis of 13 other studies of the effect of evaluative comments on performance, including research not involving homework and studies of college students. The test they used employed the hypothesis that students who received no comments would perform more poorly than (a) students receiving comments specified by the researcher to reflect varying performance (for example, "excellent" when a student received a grade of A, "you must do better next time" for a grade of D) or (b) students receiving comments generated by the teacher, called the "free comments" condition. A summation of the rank order of these three conditions across the 13 studies revealed nonsignificant overall discrimination, though the researcher-specified evaluative feedback condition did rank highest.

Incentives

Finally, two studies have examined whether nonverbal incentives for homework completion affect subsequent performance (see Table 9.2). Fink and Nalven (1972) claimed that, for the economically disadvantaged children who were the participants in the study, verbal praise and candy produced more homework completion than either no feedback or verbal praise alone. This study suffered from the fact that a baseline period in which all students received no feedback indicated that the four groups of students used in the

TABLE 9.2. Studies Comparing the Effects of Evaluative Comments and Incentives on Homework Assignments

Characteristics	Austin (1976)	Stewart & White (1976)	Fink & Nalvin (1972)	Harris (1972)
Document type	Journal	Journal	Journal	Diss.
Location	Ga.	N.J.	N.Y. City	Kans.
Research design	RA	RA	NEC	TS
Student equivalence procedure	Blocking	Blocking	Matching	Counterbalancing
Grade level	4,9,10	5,7	3	6
Subject matter	Math	Spelling, math	Math	Social studies, math
No. schools/classes/students	NA/9/222	NA/17/415	1/5/137	1/3/77
Treatment duration	6 weeks	6 weeks	4 weeks	10–12 weeks
Homework assignments per week	3–4	varied	5	5
Treatment 1	Correctness indication	Letter grades	No feedback	No homework
Treatment 2	Correctness and encouragement and how to get right	Grades and evaluative comments	Verbal praise	Early recess or candy
Treatment 3	No third treatment	Evaluative comments	Verbal praise and candy	Late recess
Treatment 4	No fourth treatment	Positive comments only	No fourth treatment	No fourth treatment
Homework performance measure	None	None	Completion	Completion, accuracy
Unit performance measure	Teacher constructed	Teacher constructed	None	None
Comprehensive exam measure	None	Teacher constructed	None	None

Note. NEC = nonequivalent control group design; RA = random assignment; TS = time series; NA = not available.

study may have been initially nonequivalent, though they did not test for equivalence and did not report how students were assigned to conditions. They also combined two conditions, one in which two weeks of verbal praise were followed by two weeks of praise plus candy, and one in which two weeks of praise plus candy were followed by two weeks of praise alone, to form an overall praise-plus-candy condition. This creates problems in interpreting the results.

The direction of effect indicated that homework completion rates dropped when feedback began, regardless of the feedback strategy. Yet when treatments administered simultaneously were compared, Fink and Nalven found that students receiving verbal praise did not differ from students receiving no feedback, but that students receiving verbal praise and candy completed their homework more often than either the praise-only or no-feedback group.

Harris' (1972) single-case, time series studies also employed disadvantaged children as participants. Three types of incentives—early recess or candy for successful assignments, and delayed recess for unsuccessful ones—were compared with no-incentive baseline conditions.

Harris administered multiple combinations of treatments to each of three classes over the course of a semester. The classroom was used as the unit of analysis, and visual inspection of changes in problem completion and accuracy served as the basis for inferences. Completion and accuracy of homework assignments, and accuracy of in-class problems, were the dependent variables.

At the broadest level, Harris' results revealed that (a) consequences for completing homework increased assignment completion but did not affect in-class performance and (b) consequences for accuracy of homework assignments enhanced accuracy of in-class performance.

Summary

The research on variations in feedback strategies reveals little reason to choose one strategy over another. Whether or how much instructional feedback is given, whether all or only some problems are graded, and whether the teacher provides evaluative comments appear to have little relation to homework's effectiveness for improving performance. In fact, though common sense dictates that some monitoring of homework assignments is important, there is as yet no credible empirical test of this assumption.

Finally, taken together, the Fink and Nalven (1972) and Harris (1972) studies indicate that the use of incentives to increase the completion or accuracy of homework by disadvantaged children may enhance school performance. It should be kept in mind, however, that in both studies the measures of effectiveness were either (a) responses on the homework assignments themselves or (b) in-class assignments that were similar or identical to those given as homework. Although both authors assert that demonstrating improvement on such measures by poor-performing students is a step in the right direction, the effectiveness of the procedures on more distal and global measures of achievement (i.e., unit, comprehensive, or standardized tests) remains to be demonstrated. Also, because of methodological problems with both studies, the results should be viewed as only suggestive.

Part V

Implications for Practice and Research

10

A Summary of Conclusions

Summarization occurs at several points in the research process, and each time it occurs information is lost. A primary researcher calculates the mean score of students receiving and not receiving a treatment and often ignores the variation around those means. The means are then statistically compared, and if a significant difference is found a conclusion is drawn that the treatment is effective. The fact that a large segment of students in the group with the lower mean may actually have performed better than many students in the higher-mean group is given little attention. A reviewer then takes a set of studies and averages their results. Some differences between studies are ignored; others are tested, found to be statistically nonsignificant, and brushed aside.

The slighting of variation in the summarization of research is mirrored in the way educational policies—indeed, all social policies—are typically implemented. The response of every student to an instructional innovation is unique, yet educators cannot tailor pedagogical practices to each student. Instead, teaching strategies are applied to groups of students in full knowledge that the practice will be more successful with some than with others. Educators hope that *in general* the *net effect* of the strategy will be beneficial. Likewise, researchers hope that their results will prove more often than not to be transferable to other settings.

The more complex the phenomenon under study, the more tenuous generalization becomes. With complicated issues, researchers and research synthesizers are more likely to miss important distinctions among persons and places that determine whether a generalization is accurate. Homework is an extremely complex teaching strategy. Yet homework researchers and research reviewers offer general conclusions. Decisions about whether and/or how to assign homework continue in the schools. These policies need to be informed by the best data available—however crude, and even misleading in some circumstances, they may be.

This chapter contains yet another level of summarization of homework research. The process of selective integration and ignoring that began in the preceding chapters is taken one step further. More damage is done to the unique responses of individual students, so that some general conclusions can be drawn that are serviceable at the national, state, district, school, and classroom levels. Even at these levels, the conclusions will fail a distressing number of times.

PARTS OF THE HOMEWORK
PROCESS YET TO BE RESEARCHED

In Table 1.3 a temporal model of the factors influencing the homework process was presented. Eighteen classes of influence were identified, based on theoretical approaches to homework and past reviews of the homework research. In addition, four classes of outcome measures were introduced. Table 1.3 is reproduced here as Table 10.1.

An examination of the homework research indicates that many components of the homework process have never been the focus of scientific study. Among factors exogenous to the process, student ability, grade level, and the subject matter of homework assignments have frequently been examined as potential moderators of homework's effects. However, differences among students with regard to motivation and study habits have never been tested to determine whether they play a role in the home study process. At present we have no data on whether students with greater motivation or better study skills benefit more from doing homework.

Of the seven characteristics that define homework assignments, two have gone unresearched. The roles of (a) completion deadlines and (b) the social context of doing individual or group projects have never been systematically scrutinized. In addition, although the instructional purposes of homework have been researched numerous times, no study has examined whether noninstructional purposes (e.g., creating parent awareness, punishment) have their intended effects.

Neither set of initial classroom factors that might influence homework's effects—the provision of materials and facilitators—has received research attention. It has been suggested that these variables are of special importance if homework is to have the desired effects on students from poor families and students who are slow learners.

The home-community factors of competitors for student time and home environment have been similarly ignored. Although numerous studies have looked at the relationship between the time children spend watching television and achievement (Williams et al., 1982), no study has examined how

TABLE 10.1. A Process Model of Factors Influencing the Effectiveness of Homework

Exogenous Factors	Assignment Characteristics	Initial Classroom Factors	Home-Community Factors	Classroom Follow-Up	Outcomes or Effects
Student characteristics	Amount	Provision of materials	Competitors for student time	Feedback	Assignment completion
Ability	Purpose	Facilitators	Home environment	Written comments	Assignment performance
Motivation	Skill area utilized	Suggested approaches	Space	Grading	Positive effects
Study habits	Degree of individualization	Links to curriculum	Light	Incentives	Immediate academic
Subject matter	Degree of student choice	Other rationales	Quiet	Testing of related content	Long-term academic
Grade level	Completion deadlines		Materials	Use in class discussion	Nonacademic
	Social context		Others involvement		Parental
			Parents		Negative effects
			Siblings		Satiation
			Other students		Denial of leisure time
					Parental interference
					Cheating
					Increased student differences

television-watching affects the relation between homework and achievement. Other competitors for student time, such as clubs and sports teams, have never been related to the home study process. Likewise, we have only informal knowledge of whether the physical surrounding in which homework is carried out (space, lighting, noise level) affects the value of homework. Finally, research into the influence of assistance from others has never extended beyond the involvement of parents to include siblings and peers.

One of three classroom follow-up factors—teacher feedback—has been the focus of past research. The effects of using homework content in subsequent class discussion and of testing related material have gone largely unstudied. These factors share the underlying rationale of ensuring that homework is appropriately integrated into classroom instruction and that students perceive it as such. To date there are few data concerning whether such efforts at integration influence the value of homework.

The most distressing omissions from past research relate to the outcome measures that have been used to gauge homework's effects. Table 1.2 listed 21 potential positive and negative effects of homework, yet only 4 have appeared with any regularity in the literature. Three of these involve immediate academic outcomes (i.e., better retention of factual knowledge, increased understanding, and better critical thinking, concept formation, and information processing), and one involves a long-term academic outcome (improved attitude toward school). A few studies of time spent on homework have related this variable to inquisitiveness and independent problem-solving, and one investigation comparing homework with in-class supervised study looked at study habits and time organization. In both instances the database is too small to warrant any assertion about homework's effect. All the nonacademic effects, including the effect of homework on parents, the satiation-related measures, the denial of access to other activities, the heightened pressures associated with parental interference, and cheating, remain unmeasured.

Finally, it is plausible to speculate that many of the factors thought to influence the homework process will have interactive effects. They may be effective in some circumstance or in tandem with one another. For instance, it could be that the effectiveness of individual versus group contexts for homework assignments depends on the subject matter. Such interactive effects have rarely been studied, except for the combining of exogenous factors (e.g., student ability, grade level, subject matter) with other factors in the process.

Summary

Table 10.2 summarizes the parts of the homework process that have yet to be researched. The list suggests that most of the conceptual thinking surrounding the homework process has not been translated into systematic, empirical research. This is especially true if the numerous potential interactions among the factors are considered. Most problematic is the number of homework outcomes that remain unresearched, even in simple homework versus no homework comparisons. Although much of the debate surrounding homework focuses on long-term and nonacademic implications, research can only speak about its effects on short-term academic and attitude measures.

THE VALIDITY OF HOMEWORK RESEARCH

Before summarizing the results of research on homework, it is important to evaluate the quality of the studies making up this body of evidence. To do so, I use the four types of validity defined by Cook and Campbell (1979) to assess the trustworthiness of research results.

The four types of validity include internal, external, measurement, and statistical validity. Briefly, internal validity refers to the assurance with which a conclusion about causal relations can be drawn from the studies. Studies using random assignment of students to experimenter-controlled homework treatments are more internally valid than correlational or quasi-experimental studies. Random assignment studies establish the temporal precedence of homework and rule out many rival explanations for findings. External validity refers to the generalizability of results across people,

TABLE 10.2. Parts of the Homework Process Yet to Be Researched

Distinctions in homework assignments
    Noninstructional purposes
    Completion deadlines
    Sibling assistance and group projects

Factors influencing the effectiveness of homework
    Student motivation and study habits
    Initial classroom factors
    Competitors for student time
    Home environment
    Use and testing of homework content

Positive and negative effects of homework
    Positive effects
        Curriculum enhancement
        Learning during leisure time
        Better study habits and skills
        Greater self-direction, self-discipline, time organization
        More inquisitiveness, independent problem-solving
    Negative effects
        Physical and emotional fatigue
        Denial of access to leisure-time activities
        Parental pressure and instructional confusion
        Cheating

TABLE 10.3. Summaries of the Validities of Research on Different Homework Topics

Topic	Internal Validity	External Validity	Measurement Validity	Statistical Validity
Homework versus no homework	Fair	Outcomes: poor Subject matter: good Grade level: poor Student differences: good	Good	Poor
Homework versus supervised study	Poor	Outcomes: poor Subject matter: poor Grade level: fair Student differences: poor	Good	Poor
Time spent on homework	Poor	Outcomes: good Subject matter: excellent Grade level: excellent Student differences: poor	Achievement: excellent Attitudes: poor	Excellent
Instructional purpose (preparation and/or practice homework versus current-content homework)	Very good	Outcomes: poor Subject matter: poor Grade level: poor Student differences: poor	Very good	Fair

settings, and times. External validity is better established if an effect of homework has been tested and is shown to hold for different types of students in different schools at varying times. Measurement validity refers to the correspondence between the variables that are measured and the variables about which inferences will be drawn. The outcomes of homework studies will be more trustworthy if the measures of achievement and attitude have been shown to relate to the constructs they are meant to measure. Statistical validity refers to the appropriateness of the statistical procedures employed to analyze data. Appropriateness involves such issues as whether assumptions are met, whether tests have acceptable statistical power, whether correct units of analysis are employed, and whether probability levels are protected across all tests in a study.

Table 10.3 summarizes my assessments of the validities of research associated with the four homework topics that have received the most attention. For each topic the research is evaluated on a scale ranging from poor to excellent.

Taken as a whole, the studies comparing homework with a no-treatment control can best be described as having fair internal validity. This judgment is based on the fact that (a) about half these studies did not employ random assignment of students to treatment conditions; (b) about half were conducted by experimenters who were also the teachers of the classes in the study; (c) few studies included counterbalancing or repeated measures; and (d) the homework treatment was generally short in duration, with more than half the treatments lasting less than 10 weeks.

Homework versus no-treatment comparisons fared poorly with regard to their potential for generalizing results across outcomes and grade levels. Only three tests of attitudes were conducted; the remaining tests all involved immediate measures of achievement. Nearly two-thirds of all tests occurred at the elementary school level (but none earlier than fourth grade), while only two tests were conducted on high school students. Coverage across subjects was good, and the student differences of intelligence and gender were often used to test for interaction effects.

The measurement validity of homework versus no-treatment studies was generally good, with most studies employing standardized and teacher-developed tests of achievement. However, statistical validity was poor because most studies were conducted on small samples and used the student as the unit of analysis even though the treatment was administered at the classroom level.

Studies comparing homework to supervised study suffered from the same internal validity problems as studies using no-treatment controls, but for the former group the problems were even more severe. The design of supervised study research, primarily involving quasi-experiments with no counterbalancing, did an even poorer job of ruling out rival explanations for outcomes. The potential for these studies to be generalized across outcome types, subjects, and student differences was also poor. Only three tests of outcomes other than achievement were made, only two tests dealt with non-mathematics-related subject matter, and individual differences between students rarely appeared in analyses (twice for intelligence and once for gender). Measures were again good, and statistical procedures were poor, for the same reasons mentioned above.

Studies of time spent on homework had the poorest rating for internal validity. Nearly all these studies were correlational, although some performed analyses meant to eliminate rival explanations statistically. Because they are correlational, these studies cannot even establish the temporal precedence of homework; it is plausible that in these studies achievement caused time spent on homework. External validity is another matter. Grade levels and subjects were well represented in time-on-homework studies. Types of outcomes included ample achievement and attitude indices, but as with other topics, only these. However, tests of interactions between student differences and time spent on homework were nonexistent. The statistical validity of these studies was excellent. Large samples of students were used, and time spent on homework was both measured and tested at the student level of analysis.

Studies comparing preparation and/or practice homework with current-content homework were the only ones that fared well in internal validity. These studies all randomly assigned treatments to classrooms, accounting for teachers. In many studies the number of classrooms was generally large and students were assigned to classes by computer. Steps were taken to ensure that assignments given to the two conditions were of equal length and even that assignment problems were identical, with only their distribution across days being manipulated. However, the generalizability of these studies was poor. Although both immediate and delayed measures of achievement were tested, few other types of outcomes were assessed. All studies but one were conducted in math classes, and all classes were seventh through eleventh grade. Tests for interactions with student individual differences were rare, with the exception of student intelligence.

For the remaining six topic areas, few studies relate to each question, making superfluous any detailed assessment of the individual topic areas. The two areas with the largest body of evidence varied in internal validity. Studies of parent involvement had generally poor internal validity. These studies were either correlational or poorly controlled quasi-experiments. About half the research on teacher feedback employed well-controlled designs involving random assignment. The other half employed more suspect designs.

It also can be said that research on the six topics shares poor external validity. This is because studies are sparse—that is, a broad representation of people and places is missing. Measurement validity is good across the areas, based on the routine use of standardized and teacher-developed tests. Statistical validity is generally poor because of small sample sizes and incorrect use of the student as the unit of analysis.

Summary

As Table 10.3 reveals, it is impossible to characterize the quality of homework research with a single descriptor other than to say that the situation is far from ideal. The validity of outcomes varies for different topics and different criteria. Statistical validity is hampered by small sample sizes. This means that the tests of homework's effect should lack statistical power. However, because students are so frequently used as the unit of analysis, even though treatments are administered to classes, statistical power is probably greater in these studies than it ought to be. Measurement validity is good, reflecting the fine array of standardized and teacher-developed tests available to assess achievement. Generalizability across outcome types is poor because the vast majority of all measures relate to immediate achievement. Other types of external validity vary across topic areas. This is also true concerning internal validity.

Considering the variation in quality of research across topics and types of validity, it is best not to attempt to characterize the field as a whole. Instead, the integrated conclusions concerning each topic area should be judged relative to the quality of the specific research on which they are based.

EVIDENCE ON THE EFFECTIVENESS OF HOMEWORK

Three types of homework research can be used to help draw conclusions about the overall effectiveness of the practice. The three topics are the comparisons of homework and no treatment, homework and in-class supervised study, and the relation between time spent on homework and academic-related outcomes.

Table 10.4 summarizes the effect sizes in each area of research. In the original presentation of this material, the results associated with no-treatment and in-class supervised study control groups were expressed using the d-index. This metric, which describes the effect in terms of the number of standard deviation units that separate the group means (see Chapter 4), is retained in Table 10.4. Results concerning time spent on homework were originally presented using correlation coefficients. These results have been transformed in Table 10.4 to d-indexes to make them comparable to the other two types of research.

Examining the overall results, all three types of research reveal positive effects of homework. The largest effect belongs to research on time spent on homework. The average student doing relatively more homework scores about .39 standard deviations higher on academic-related outcomes than the average student doing less homework. Put differently, the average student doing more homework outperforms about 65% of students doing less homework. Of course, as noted in the earlier discussion of research validity, the time-on-homework studies suffer from an inability to establish

TABLE 10.4. Effect Sizes for Research Bearing on Homework's Effectiveness

Moderators	Homework vs. No Homework	Homework vs. Supervised Study	Time Spent on Homework
Overall	+.21	+.09	+.39
Grade level			
Elementary	+.15	−.08	+.04
Junior high	+.31	+.24	+.14
Senior high	+.64	+.33	+.53
Subject matter			
Math	+.16	+.10	+.46
Reading and English	+.32	−.06	+.42
Science and social studies	+.56	—[b]	+.24
Math areas			
Computation	+.24	−.17	—[b]
Concepts	+.19	+.21	—[b]
Problem-solving	+.02	+.18	—[b]
Outcome measure			
Standard tests	+.07	—[c]	+.37
Class tests or grades	+.30	—[c]	+.39
Attitudes	—[b]	—[b]	+.29

[a] Effect sizes for time spent on homework are d-indexes calculated from the r-indexes presented in Table 7.2.
[b] Effect sizes for these subgroups of moderators were unavailable.
[c] The outcome measure moderator for supervised study comparisons was nonsignificant.

causal direction. In the simplest terms, this means that if homework does improve performance, *and* if students who perform better tend to do more homework, then both these causal mechanisms are reflected in the time-on-homework effect size.

The smallest effect belongs to comparisons of homework and in-class supervised study. About one-tenth standard deviation separates these two groups, meaning that the average student doing homework outperforms about 54% of students doing supervised study. It should not be surprising to find that supervised study comparisons reveal the smallest effects. They are really comparisons of two alternate treatments. Recall that the definition of supervised study was not consistent across investigations. For instance, in some investigations homework and in-class assignments were related, and in other research they were not. Some researchers added instructional time for supervised study, while other researchers did not. It is therefore easy to imagine ways to manipulate homework assignments and/or the definition of supervised study to produce results favoring one treatment or the other. Perhaps the best way to interpret these comparisons, then, is to search for studies that find no difference and ask "How much and what type of homework is equivalent in effect to how much and what type of in-class study?" In this framework, the effect size reveals that homework had a more positive, but small, effect on academic-related measures than did the form of supervised study offered by researchers as its approximate equivalent.

The comparison of homework and no-treatment controls, the most easily interpretable type of research, revealed a d-index of +.21. The average student doing homework outperformed about 60% of students not doing homework. This effect size falls neatly between the high and low estimates, as the analysis presented above suggested it should. However, when the homework versus no-homework effect size is examined in light of some research validity considerations, several concerns are raised. First, only about half these comparisons employed random assignment, although type of assignment procedure was unrelated to the size of an experimental effect. Second, few studies employed counterbalancing and repeated measures, and those that did actually revealed a negative effect for homework ($d = -.08$). Finally, studies in which experimenters did not serve as teachers revealed a smaller than average effect size ($d = +.12$).

Taken as a whole, it appears that homework has a positive effect on academic-related outcomes. Bearing in mind the qualification that the relevant research is of generally poor internal validity, the magnitude of the effect is best estimated at .2 standard deviations. This estimate is based not only on the outcome of homework versus no homework comparisons but also on the lower estimate provided by research using supervised study controls and the higher estimate from studies of time spent on homework. The estimate is also bound by the duration of the homework treatment. *Thus, a teacher might expect that the average student assigned homework* relevant to a class unit lasting about 10 weeks will perform better on a related outcome measure than approximately 60% of students not doing homework. This being said, the accuracy of estimating the effect of homework can be improved by taking into account some contextual factors.

EVIDENCE ON MODERATORS OF HOMEWORK'S EFFECT

There is one moderator of homework's effect that reveals a remarkably consistent influence across the three types of research summarized in Table 10.4—the grade level of the student. Upper-level elementary school students, encompassing fourth grade through sixth grade, show the smallest effect of homework, while high school students show the largest effect.

In attempting to estimate the different magnitudes of effect, an appropriate algorithm is not as clear as with the overall effect estimated above—the estimate from studies involving no-homework control groups does not fall between the other two. One reason for this may be a procedural confound. In homework versus no-homework studies, a disproportionate number of comparisons in which experimenters served as teachers were conducted in elementary school classrooms. This means that the elementary school effect size could be an overestimate relative to the junior and senior high school effects. In general, it may be best to offer only rough estimates of effect size that are somewhat lower than those revealed in the homework versus no-treatment studies. I will place these estimates at about one-twentieth standard deviation for elementary school students, one-quarter standard deviation for junior high students, and one-half standard deviation for high school students. *Therefore, a teacher might expect the average student doing homework over a 10-week unit to outscore about 52% of no-homework students if the class is in the upper elementary grades, about 60% in junior high grades, and about 69% in high school grades.*

How the achievement outcome is defined may also influence the effect of homework. Homework versus no-homework studies showed a clearly stronger effect of homework on class tests and grades than on standardized achievement tests. This seems logical, considering that material on homework assignments should correspond more closely to material that was taught in class and that appeared on tests than to content covered on achievement tests. Yet the lack of difference between standardized and teacher-developed measures in time-on-homework studies reminds us that the two indices can differ in measurement validity. Standardized measures may be generally more trustworthy than teacher-constructed ones. *Thus, a teacher might expect the effect of homework to be relatively equal on self-developed and standardized measures of achievement, though the mechanisms producing these empirical results might be quite different.*

With regard to attitudes, the only area of research on homework's effectiveness that has included such measures involves time spent on homework.

A somewhat smaller effect of homework on attitudes than on achievement was found, though again it is not clear if this is due to a less direct causal mechanism or to a lesser trustworthiness in how attitudes are measured. What is certain is that this body of evidence cannot rule out the (likely) possibility that students with better attitudes do more homework. *Therefore, a teacher should expect the estimates of homework's effect to pertain primarily to outcomes related to achievement, since their relevance to student attitudes is not yet clear.*

There is also evidence that subject matter influences homework's effectiveness. Again, however, the interpretation is not straightforward. Investigations comparing homework to no homework and to in-class study produced nearly opposite orderings of effect sizes for different subjects and mathematics subareas. The reason for this may again lie in the nature of control groups. Studies employing no-homework controls may reveal a "pure" estimate of homework's relative effect across subjects, but research using supervised-study controls produces an effect influenced by both the relative effect of homework and the relative effect of supervised study. Therefore, it would take, at a minimum, a set of investigations comparing supervised study to no treatment to begin untangling these effects.

The confounding of treatments cannot explain the reversal of orderings for no-homework and time-on-homework studies. In studies using no-homework controls, the effect sizes for science and social studies were twice as large as effects for reading and English, which were twice again as large as math effects. For time-on-homework studies, math, reading, and English effects were twice the size of social studies and science effects.

There are three reasons for placing more faith in the time-on-homework estimates. First, the no-homework estimates in math, reading, and English may be relatively small, compared with their social studies and science counterparts, because they were less often confounded with teachers who also serve as experimenters. Second, the methods used in no-homework studies generally were heterogeneous, whereas methods were quite similar across time-on-homework studies. This does not imply that time-on-homework studies are more valid. It simply means that subject matter is less likely to be confounded with other design characteristics that may influence the relative order of subject matter effects. Finally, no-homework effect sizes were based on considerably smaller samples of students, making them less reliable.

Turning to the math subareas, the relation of effect sizes when homework and supervised study were compared was exactly as Marshall (1983) predicted. Recall that she suggested, based on social facilitation theory, that homework would be more effective for math concepts and problem-solving and that supervised study would be more effective for computation. This would occur because the presence of others is hypothesized to interfere with the learning of complex material. However, the results of no-homework comparisons contradicted the social-facilitation hypothesis.

These studies indicate that simple concepts are learned best at home. This finding is congruent with the notion that homework is a good vehicle for teaching simple skills and concepts that depend heavily on practice. The findings of the time-on-homework studies concerning more general subject matter differences are also compatible with this principle, if one assumes that math homework most often includes learning simple skills.

In sum, then, interpreting the pattern of results related to subject matter is fraught with difficulty. Sense cannot be made of the findings without highlighting the strengths of some data sets while downplaying their weaknesses, and doing the opposite with other data sets. Obviously, these decisions could vary from interpreter to interpreter. Therefore, if the decision rules outlined above are valid, the research indicates that *a teacher might expect larger positive effects of homework on the learning of simple skills that require practice and rehearsal than on complex tasks that require higher-order integration of knowledge and skills.* It should be kept in mind, however, that this effect may again be a measurement artifact, since simple skills can generally be measured with less error than complex ones. It also does not rule out the use of homework that requires the integration of skills (e.g., research reports) or imagination (e.g., creative writing). The finding does suggest that such assignments build skills that are already well-learned.

Finally, three individual differences among students—gender, intelligence, and personality—have been examined as moderators of homework's effect. Tests of gender differences have been uniformly nonsignificant. Formal tests of interaction with intelligence also have been nonsignificant. The means underlying intelligence comparisons revealed inconsistency in direction of effect—some comparisons showed homework to be more beneficial for high-ability students, and others showed more benefit for low-ability students. The two personality differences examined—anxiety level and locus of control—also proved unrelated to the effect of homework. *Therefore, a teacher might expect the effects of homework to be similar for different types of students.* Although it is reasonable to expect some differences in student responses, they may not be large enough within a given class to be of great significance.

Interpreting the Magnitude of Homework's Effect

In the previous discussion the relative magnitude of d-indexes was used to compare homework's effect across different grade levels, outcomes, and subjects. Effect size estimates can also be used to gauge the consequences of homework compared with other instructional techniques (see Cooper, 1984). This allows the placing of homework into a broader educational context, thus permitting a more informed judgment of its value.

In the third edition of the *Handbook of Research on Teaching*, Walberg (1986) presents the results of selected quantitative research reviews.

TABLE 10.5. Selected Effect Sizes from Meta-Analysis Examining Influences on Achievement[a]

Author (Year)	Independent Variable	Effect Size[b]
Bangert et al. (1981)	Individualized vs. conventional teaching	+.10
Carlberg & Kavale (1980)	Special- vs. regular-class placement	−.12
Johnson et al. (1981)	Cooperative vs. competitive learning	+.78
Kulik & Kulik (1981)	Ability grouping	+.10
Kulik et al. (1982)	Programmed instruction	+.08
Luiten et al. (1980)	Advance organizers	+.23
Pflaum et al. (1980)	Direct instruction	+.60
Redfield and Rousseau (1981)	Higher cognitive questions	+.73
Wilkinson (1980)	Praise	+.08
Williams et al. (1982)	Amount of television watching	+.10
Willson & Putnam (1982)	Pretests	+.17

[a] Topics are those listed by Walberg (1986) as involving achievement as the dependent variable.
[b] Effect sizes are expressed in d-indexes.

Included are several meta-analyses that examine the effect of instructional strategies and teaching skills on measures of student achievement. These are listed in Table 10.5. I have used Walberg's list instead of generating one specifically to evaluate homework because Walberg (a) exployed systematic retrieval procedures and (b) attempted to demonstrate the viability of quantitative synthesis as a research tool rather than evaluate the value of any particular instructional technique. Thus, it cannot be claimed that contrasting instructional techniques were chosen purposely to make homework look good or bad.

Based on a comparison with the entries in Table 10.5, the effect of homework on achievement can best be described as *above average*. The median effect size in the table is d = ±.10, whereas homework's effect is +.20. If grade level is taken into account, homework's effect on achievement of elementary school students could be described as *small*, but on high school students its effect would be *large* relative to the effect of other instructional techniques.

Methodology should also be taken into account when making judgments across research domains. It is likely that the quality of the measures of achievement was relatively equal across the studies underlying the entries in Table 10.5. However, other aspects relating to the integrity of research designs undoubtedly vary considerably from area to area. It is not clear whether biases in the homework literature would make homework's effect smaller or larger than those listed—that is, in relation to biases present in other literatures. Finally, recall that a conservative assumption was imposed on the estimate of homework effect sizes—all effects were calculated so as to gauge homework's influence against an error term unreduced by the removal of other sources of variance. In addition, the average effect size estimates were reduced somewhat to reflect internal validity problems associated with the research designs employed. Therefore, the synthesizing methods used to derive the homework effect size are probably among the most conservative approaches represented in Table 10.5.

A final aid in interpreting the magnitude of an effect is to compare it with the cost of implementing the treatment. Here, most of the entries in Table 10.5 fare well. The cost of instituting these treatments is small, with the possible exceptions of special-class placement and individualized and programmed instruction. Homework certainly can be regarded as a low-cost treatment. The major costs involved in giving homework assignments would be (a) a small loss in instructional class time because time must be allocated to homework management and (b) additional outside-class preparation and management time for teachers.

In sum, it appears that the effect of homework on the achievement of high school students is impressive. Relative to (a) other instructional techniques, (b) the associated research and synthesis methods, and (c) the costs involved in its implementation, homework can produce a substantial positive effect on adolescents' performance in school. For young children the effect may be small, even bordering on trivial.

EVIDENCE ON VARIATIONS IN HOMEWORK ASSIGNMENTS

Seven of the 10 areas of homework research relate not to the general effectiveness of homework but to the relative effect of different strategies for constructing and evaluating assignments. One topic area—time spent on homework—bridges both questions.

Time on Homework

In Chapter 7, studies correlating the amount of time a student spends on homework with achievement were used to help determine whether the idea of assigning homework was a good one. To do this, it was assumed that if homework was beneficial then students doing more of it would reap more benefit. In the context of assignment variations, the question becomes, "Is there an optimal amount of time for students to spend on homework?" If an optimum exists, teachers could use it to help determine how much homework to assign.

Studies of time on homework that gauged the linear relation with achievement uncovered a strong positive relation for high school students $(d = +.53)$, an average relation for junior high students $(d = +.14)$, and a weak relation for upper-level elementary school students $(d = +.04)$. Studies that attempted to rule out rival explanations for the relation in high school demonstrated that it held up even after statistically controlling third variables.

However, the conclusion that for older students more homework is better is not totally accurate. A set of nine studies permitted the plotting of achievement scores for students spending different amounts of time on homework. This permitted an analysis meant to discover whether a curvilinear relation existed. The curves were displayed in Figure 7.2. They demonstrated that junior high school students (sixth through ninth grade) reporting more than 10 hours a week spent on homework had achievement scores slightly lower than those reporting 5 to 10 hours. Thus, it appears that for junior high school students homework may reach its optimum effect when one to two hours of homework is reported each night.

No such asymptote appeared for high school students. Instead, there was evidence that tenth-, eleventh-,and twelfth-graders need to do a minimum amount of homework before it begins to have a beneficial effect. Students reporting doing less than one hour of homework a week had lower achievement scores than students reporting none at all. However, once the beneficial effect took hold, at one to five hours a week, it appeared to increase unabated through the highest interval on the scale. Of course, logic dictates that the relationship should become curvilinear at some point, even if we do not yet know where the asymptote will be.

As yet another reminder, interpretation of the time-on-homework literature is clouded by the poor internal validity of the common research design. The possibilities that higher achievement causes students to do more homework or that both achievement and homework are caused by third factors—for instance, the ability level of the student and/or the home environment—cannot be ruled out. However, most of the time studies have excellent external, measurement, and statistical validity and are consistent with related data sets. In addition, accepting their findings would lead to a more cautious interpretation of homework's benefits.

In light of the evidence, then, it seems reasonable to suggest that *time on homework and achievement are curvilinearly related and that the curve is different at different grade levels. An elementary school teacher might expect little relation to exist. For teachers of junior high school students, a linear relation might be expected to peak at 5 to 10 hours of homework a week, after which more homework would have no benefit. For teachers of high school students, homework may not have a positive effect until somewhere between 1 and 5 hours a week are done. However, once the critical amount is reached, additional homework appears to have accumulating positive effects on achievement, at least through 10 hours a week.*

Instructional Purpose

The least ambiguous conclusion to be drawn from homework studies comes from studies of whether it is better to have assignments reflect only the current day's lesson or to distribute content to include preparation and practice of future and past lessons. In general, the average student doing preparation and/or practice homework scores about .14 standard deviations higher on tests of achievement than the average student doing current-content homework. The effect appears to hold whether achievement is measured immediately after a topic is completed or after some delay. There is some evidence that preparation homework is more effective than practice homework, but the body of evidence is small and the difference is statistically unreliable.

The studies leading to these conclusions were well-designed and consistent in their results. Their sample sizes were generally small, but a re-analysis of data indicated that the effect probably held at the classroom unit of analysis (d = +.28) as well as the student unit of analysis. Their major deficiency involves external validity—all but one study concerned math, and all studies were conducted in junior and senior high schools.

In sum, *a teacher of mathematics in junior or senior high school could expect a student doing preparation and/or practice homework to outperform about 55% of students doing homework based only on the current day's lesson. This effect would not disappear on delayed measures of achievement.* Nothing can be said on the distribution of content in subjects other than mathematics.

Two studies comparing extension or enrichment homework with preparation and practice homework revealed differences favoring the latter types, but the differences were not significant. Only one of these studies included a current-content homework condition, and it found a nonsignificant effect favoring enrichment homework. However, the database seems too small for any firm conclusion to be drawn. Likewise, the only two studies to examine the effects of homework's instructional purpose on students' attitudes found no significant effects.

Skill Area Utilized

Only two studies have looked at whether having students do reading or reading-plus-outlining homework assignments had a more positive effect. Both studies had design flaws, and only two subjects were represented—history and shorthand. Therefore, it seems advisable to eschew drawing any conclusions on this topic. Instead, examinations of the effectiveness of general studying techniques probably provide the best guidance for teachers.

Degree of Individualization

Four studies with diverse methodologies have examined whether tailoring homework assignments to the needs of individual students is more effective than homework geared to the class as a whole. One correlational study found a positive effect for individualization in algebra but not in geometry. Another study gave no information on critical aspects of its methodology.

Two well-conducted studies found different results, including numerous conflicting interactions. Thus, *teachers might expect no consistent positive effect associated with individualization of homework assignments*. Past research hints at individualization being effective in some subjects and with certain subgroups of students, and logic demands that individualization would be appropriate in some circumstances, but replication of these findings is needed before conclusions can be drawn. In addition, individualization may significantly increase the cost of homework in terms of the time teachers spend preparing and correcting assignments.

Degree of Student Choice

Only one study in the past 40 years has examined the effect of compulsory versus voluntary homework assignments. This small study, involving 113 students, found no differences between the two approaches. Drawing conclusions about student choice, then, would certainly be premature.

Parent Involvement

Five correlational studies relating the level of parent involvement in homework to students' achievement have produced three positive and two negative r-indexes, with the negative relations appearing in more recent studies. Interpretation of these findings is complicated by the possibility that achievement is the cause and parent involvement the effect—parents of students who are doing poorly in school may be asked more often, or may volunteer, to get more involved in homework.

The only study that attempted to manipulate parent involvement found no effects on the primary achievement measures employed, but that study had several design flaws and only a small sample of students and classrooms.

Thus, although parent involvement in homework has received more attention than several other topics, the generally poor internal validity of the studies again makes it unwise to draw any conclusions about the strategy's effectiveness.

Teacher Feedback and Incentives

No study has examined whether instructional feedback, evaluative comments, or grading has a positive impact on the effectiveness of homework when compared with the absence of these strategies. Studies comparing different types of instructional feedback, grading procedures, and evaluative comments, although scarce, generally have sound methodologies. This is because the different feedback strategies have been experimentally manipulated within the same classroom, with students randomly assigned to conditions. Taken as a whole, the seven feedback studies indicate that *a teacher might expect no differential effects on achievement related to the kind of instructional or evaluative comments provided, or whether grading of homework assignments is frequent versus infrequent or based on completeness versus accuracy.* It should be kept in mind, however, that in these studies instructional and evaluative comments were written on homework sheets. These studies do not relate to the effect of using homework to guide more interactive instruction with individual students.

Finally, the two studies conducted to examine the effect of incentives suggest that provision of rewards for handing in homework can increase completion rates among disadvantaged students. The methods of these studies were poor, however, and the dependent variable—rate of homework completion—is only indirectly related to the measures of achievement used in other homework studies.

SUMMARY

The temporal model of the homework process presented in Chapter 1 includes 18 classes of influence. An examination of the related research revealed that many of these have gone unstudied. Especially troubling was the lack of breadth in dependent measures of homework's effect. Of 21 potential positive and negative effects of homework found in the literature, only 4 have been the object of repeated study.

Three areas of research were found to bear on the question of whether homework is a generally effective instructional strategy—investigations comparing homework to no homework and to in-class supervised study, and investigations relating time spent on homework to academic-related outcomes. The results of this research indicated that homework does have positive effects on achievement. However, the effect was moderated by several interacting characteristics of students and settings. First, compared with the effect of other teaching and instructional techniques, homework's effect on the achievement of high school students was appreciable, about average for junior high students, and negligible for upper-level elementary school students. Studies of homework effects in the earliest grades of school are nearly nonexistent. Second, there was some evidence that the effect of homework varies depending on the subject matter. It appears that homework's effects might be more positive on the learning of simple tasks than complex ones. Finally, homework's effects appeared similar, regardless of whether achievement was measured by standardized or teacher-developed tests, and regardless of the gender or intelligence of the student.

Eight variations in homework assignments were the topic of past research. The conclusions concerning these are summarized in Table 10.6. Evidence suggested that the generally trivial relations between homework and achievement for elementary school students was not modified by the time spent on assignments. For junior high students, the positive effect of homework appeared to peak at between 5 and 10 hours a week, with assign-

TABLE 10.6. Summary of Findings Concerning Variations in Homework Assignments

Topic	Conclusion
Time on homework	a. For elementary school, no effect. b. For junior high school, positive effect up to 5–10 hours a week. c. For high school, no effect until 1–5 hours, then positive effect.
Instructional purpose	a. Preparation and/or practice more effective than current-content only. b. Few data on other purposes.
Skill area utilized	Not enough data to draw conclusions.
Degree of individualization	a. No difference between individual versus group assignments. b. More data needed on possible interactions.
Degree of student choice	Not enough data to draw conclusions.
Parent involvement	Poor methodology prevents conclusions.
Teacher instructional and evaluative comments, grade	a. No data on effectiveness per se. b. No difference in effect of different strategies.
Incentives	Poor methodology prevents conclusions.

ments lasting beyond this amount having no added benefit. For high school students, a minimal amount of homework, less than 1 hour a week, had no positive effect, but once time spent surpassed 1 hour, its beneficial effect continued unabated through the measurement scale, with an as yet undetermined asymptote.

Preparation homework and practice homework proved more effective than homework restricted to current-day lesson content, though studies were conducted almost exclusively in junior and senior high math classes. This effect held for both immediate and delayed measures of achievement, but not for attitudes. Little research has examined other instructional and noninstructional purposes of homework.

Most of the other topics of homework research are plagued by small samples of studies and/or poor methodology, making any assertions about their cumulative findings unwise. It can be tentatively concluded that individualizing homework assignments had little positive effect on achievement. The same is true for variation in teacher feedback, whether in the form of instructional and evaluative comments or in the form of grades, although the presence versus absence of feedback per se has yet to be tested.

11

Homework Policy
Recommendations

The previous chapter contains an apologia concerning the pitfalls associated with the summarization and integration of research. I pointed out that at each level of synthesis (a) damage is done to the unique responses of individuals and (b) the potential exists that conclusions are overdrawn. The rationale for making any general assertions about homework was that the practice continues and homework policies should be informed by the best evidence research has to offer, even if this contribution is slight.

In this chapter, the final inferential leap is taken. I will attempt to answer the question "What guidelines ought to be contained in a homework policy?" The suggested guidelines would be quite short if they were based only on conclusions that can be drawn firmly from past research. Furthermore, such a strategy would deny me the opportunity to utilize the "tacit knowledge" that I acquired through reading more than 200 empirical research reports, nonempirical journal articles, books, and policy statements and through discussing homework issues with friends and colleagues. Therefore, my recommendations are grounded in research in that none of them contradicts the conclusions of my review. However, I will not hesitate to suggest policies that relate to aspects of homework neglected by past research if my reading of the literature so warrants.

The best place to start when developing a set of homework guidelines is to look at the recommendations others have made. In the next section, I describe a sample of homework policy recommendations offered by national organizations. These statements are examined for their correspondence with research results and to identify aspects of the homework process that those before me have suggested are in need of policy guidance. A second section briefly describes some sources of help in developing policies that are available to the interested reader. The chapter concludes with a summary of my recommendations.

POLICY GUIDES FROM NATIONAL ORGANIZATIONS

"What Works"

The most popular publication ever printed by the United States government is a booklet entitled *What Works* (U.S. Department of Education, 1986). *What Works* was intended to be a distillation of research on teaching and learning. In compiling the topics for the booklet, the Department of Education included "only those findings about which research evidence and expert opinion were consistent, persuasive, and fairly stable over time" (p. 1). However, the booklet also contains the caution that some research findings may "seem to be oversimplifications of complex phenomena or premature resolutions of hotly contested disputes" (p. 1).

What Works contains sections that relate to both the quantity and the quality of homework assignments. Figure 11.1 reproduces the section on homework quantity. Based on my findings, there is a major qualifier to the booklet's assertion that amount of homework and achievement are positively related—it applies only to high school students. The graph in Figure 11.1 portrays a linear relation between amount of homework per week and test scores. My review showed that junior high school students doing 5 to 10 hours of homework a week performed no better on achievement tests than students doing 1 to 5 hours a week. In the upper-level elementary school grades there was no relation between time on homework and achievement, and only a trivial effect on achievement when homework and no homework were compared in experiments or quasi-experiments. No data exist for lower-level elementary school grades.

The comments on homework quantity in *What Works* seem justified. The first paragraph contains an easily understood description of homework's effect size (based on a single study's results). The second paragraph presents a reasonable theoretical rationale for the homework-achievement link. The third paragraph points out that teachers report assigning more homework than students report doing. In the context of high-school-level education, the booklet's comments are sound, but if applied to other grades they may be misleading.

Figure 11.2 contains the section in *What Works* on the quality of homework. The paragraph on the research findings suffers from a vagueness in the description of homework's effect. No outcome measure is mentioned for gauging the influence of well-designed—that is, carefully prepared, thoroughly explained, and promptly commented on or criticized—homework. The booklet's comment is more specific. However, only one outcome measure of well-designed homework appears to have withstood

Research Finding: Student achievement rises significantly when teachers regularly assign homework and students consciously do it.

Comment: Extra studying helps children at all levels of ability. One research study reveals that when low-ability students do just 1 to 3 hours of homework a week, their grades are usually as high as those of average-ability students who do not do homework. Similarly, when average-ability students do 3 to 5 hours of homework a week, their grades usually equal those of high-ability students who do no homework.

Homework boosts achievement because the total time spent studying influences how much is learned. Low-achieving high school students study less than high achievers and do less homework. Time is not the only ingredient of learning, but without it little can be achieved.

Teachers, parents, and students determine how much, how useful, and how good the homework is. On average, American teachers say they assign about 10 hours of homework each week–about 2 hours per school day. But high school seniors report they spend only 4 to 5 hours a week doing homework, and 10 percent say they do none at all or have none assigned. In contrast, students in Japan spend about twice as much time studying outside school as American students.

References: Coleman, J.S., Hoffer, T., and Kilgore, S. (1982) *High School Achievement: Public, Catholic and Private Schools Compared.* New York: Basic Books.

Keith, T.Z. (April 1982). "Time Spent on Homework and High School Grades: A Large-Sample Path Analysis." *Journal of Educational Psychology,* Vol 74, No. 2, pp.248-253.

National Center for Education Statistics. (April 1983). *School District Survey of Academic Requirements and Achievement.* Washington, D.C.: U.S. Department of Education, Fast Response Survey Systems. ERIC Document No. ED 238097.

Rohlen, T.P. (1983). *Japan's High Schools.* Berkley, CA: University of California Press.

Walberg, H.J. (1984) "Improving the Productivity of America's Schools." *Educational Leadership,* Vol. 41, No. 8, pp. 19-36.

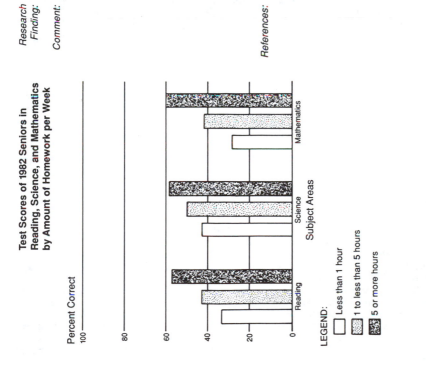

Test Scores of 1982 Seniors in Reading, Science, and Mathematics by Amount of Homework per Week

FIGURE 11.1. "What Works" on Homework Quantity. *Source:* U.S. Department of Education, National Center for Education Statistics. (1986). *Condition of Education, 1985.*

empirical testing—well-designed homework is more likely to be completed by students than homework that is not well designed (Coulter, 1980). The nonacademic effects cited in the second and third paragraphs of Figure 11.2 under "comment" have never been the focus of homework research.

The booklet carefully avoids making assertions about the effect of well-designed homework on achievement. Of the several components of well-designed homework, only comments and criticisms have been tested for their influence on test scores. However, these studies have examined different feedback strategies rather than the presence versus absence of feedback per se. Both the Austin (1976) and Dick (1980) studies cited in *What Works* found evidence favoring strategies incorporating more instructional or evaluative comments. For Austin (1976), who compared correct-

---

Research Finding
Well-designed homework assignments relate directly to classwork and extend students' learning beyond the classroom. Homework is most useful when teachers carefully prepare the assignment, thoroughly explain it, and give prompt comments and criticism when the work is completed.

Comment
To make the most of what students learn from doing homework, teachers need to give the same care to preparing homework assignments as they give to classroom instruction. When teachers prepare written instructions and discuss homework assignments with students, they find their students take the homework more seriously than if the assignments are simply announced. Students are more willing to do homework when they believe it is useful, when teachers treat it as an integral part of instruction, when it is evaluated by the teacher, and when it counts as a part of the grade.

Assignments that require students to think, and are therefore more interesting, foster their desire to learn both in and out of school. Such activities include explaining what is seen or read in class; comparing, relating, and experimenting with ideas; and analyzing principles.

Effective homework assignments do not just supplement the classroom lesson; they also teach students to be independent learners. Homework gives students experience in following directions, making judgments and comparisons, raising additional questions for study, and developing responsibility and self-discipline.

References
Austin, J. (1976). "Do Comments on Mathematics Homework Affect Student Achievement?" *School Science and Mathematics*, Vol. 76, No. 2, pp. 159–164.
Coulter, F. (1980). "Secondary School Homework: Cooperative Research Study Report No. 7." ERIC Document No. ED 209200.
Dick, D. (1980). "An Experimental Study of the Effects of Required Homework Review Versus Review on Request Upon Achievement." ERIC Document No. ED 194320.
Featherstone, H. (February 1985). "Homework." *The Harvard Education Letter*.
Walberg, H. J. (April 1985). "Homework's Powerful Effects on Learning." *Educational Leadership*. Vol. 42, No. 7, pp. 76–79.

FIGURE 11.2 "What Works" on Homework Quality

ness feedback with correctness feedback plus instructional feedback plus encouraging remarks, the effect held in only five of nine classes. For Dick (1980), who looked at reviewing all homework versus only problems requested by students, the effect was nonsignificant ($F < 1$). In addition, this review found two other studies relevant to the feedback issue. One of these studies (Baxter, 1973) found a minuscule *negative* effect for instructional comments on homework when compared with simple correctness feedback. The other study found a nonsignificant difference between four feedback strategies (Stewart & White, 1976).

In sum, then, although the guidelines that *What Works* gives for useful and effective homework generally are sensible, they are not based on research outcomes. To date, the relevant research indicates only that well-designed homework is more likely to be completed than homework that is not well-designed and that feedback on homework assignments has little effect on achievement. The effects of other aspects of well-designed homework have gone untested, as have its effects on nonacademic-related outcomes.

Kappa Delta Pi

Kappa Delta Pi, the international honor society in education, publishes a series of booklets on classroom practices. One booklet, by Timothy Keith (1986), discusses homework. Keith's work includes a review of the homework research literature. It is not surprising, then, that the issues Keith focuses on are time spent or homework, grade level, subject matter, quality, individualization, parent involvement, and feedback. Figure 11.3 presents excerpts from Keith's work on each of these topics.

Keith's general recommendations regarding the amount of time students should spend on homework reflect the research finding that homework is more efficacious at higher grades. However, the results of this review are somewhat at odds with his specific time recommendations, especially for upper-level elementary school and junior high school students. Considering the generally small effects of homework on achievement in fourth through sixth grade, an upper range of 90 minutes of homework a night seems excessive. Likewise, the data indicate that students in seventh through ninth grade doing 15 minutes to one hour of homework perform as well as students that spend one to two hours. Bear in mind as well that the estimates of time spent on homework were generally provided by the students themselves and are therefore more likely to be overestimates than underestimates. In general, then, my recommendation is that Keith's lower ranges should actually serve as guidelines for the average amount of homework teachers should assign at each grade level.

If homework has no noticeable effect on achievement in elementary school grades, why assign any at all? Keith's comments on grade level and parent involvement hint at what I think is the primary rationale. In earlier

Time

...Much will depend on the individual community, the individual school teacher, and even the individual student. Nevertheless, the following time ranges, geared toward the average student, should be workable for many situations.
- Ten to 45 minutes per night in grades one to three
- Forty-five to 90 minutes per night in grades 4 to 6
- One to two hours per night for grades 7 through 9
- Ninety minutes to 2½ hours per night for grades 10 through 12 (p. 17)

Grade Level

...Types of homework assiged should change, at least in proportion, as children grow older. If the types of homework are considered a hierarchy, from practice at the lowest level to creative at the highest, it seems apparent that, in general, the proportion of higher level homework should increase with grade level (p. 14).

Subject Matter

Math and spelling, for example, lend themselves to practice assignments, especially in the early grades, while a class in literature would seem to lend itself to preparation and creative homework. But again, there is much room for variation, depending on the purpose, the particular topic being covered, and the grade level of the students (p. 17).

Quality

The purposes of the assignment should be clear, to the teacher and to the students, as should the notion of how the students should profit and what they should learn from the assignment. The tasks assigned should be relevant to what the children are learning in school, and the assignment type should be appropriate for the purposes, the grade, and the subject matter. Finally, there should be some review or reinforcement of assignments so that homework is not a dead end. If the tasks assigned as homework have a worthwhile purpose in the first place, they should certainly be worth following up in class (p. 19).

It is often wise to start a homework assignment in class in order to make sure students understand the assignment and are getting off on the right foot. This practice will be especially important for less able students or when students in the class are completing different assignments (p. 20).

Individualization

In many cases, homework may offer an opportunity to provide some differential, or individualized, instruction. This does not mean that every child in the class needs a different homework assignment every night. On the other hand, it is quite possible to vary the difficulty level, and at times even the assignment type, for those students in the class who seem unlikely to benefit from the assignment as given (p. 20).

Parent Involvement

The wisest course would seem to be to keep parental involvement to a minimum (Rosemond, 1984). Parents should provide a quiet place for their children to study, even if only the kitchen table. They should provide the structure and the encouragement to help the child complete the assignment, and they should convey that they feel the completion of homework (and learning in general) is important....

Parents should also be available to help with an occasional question if they feel comfortable in this role, and should be available to review completed assignments if there is time (Rosemond, 1984) (p. 22).

Again, while extensive involvement may be helpful on occasion, minimal involvement in actual homework should be the rule; parents should be encouraged to remember that it is their *child's* homework, not theirs.... As with any rule, there are exceptions. And the parental involvement rule should probably be relaxed with elementary students (p. 23).

Feedback
Once students have completed homework, their work should be evaluated in some way. This generally means collecting, evaluating, and returning their assignments.... Although not every assignment must be graded, it is good to remember that homework that is graded or commented on seems to produce higher achievement than homework that is ungraded (Paschal et al., 1984). Thus graded homework should be the norm.... Comments, particularly *positive* comments, on students' papers will also produce better learning (cf. Austin, 1976; Page, 1958; Paschal, 1984), as well as demonstrating that you think homework is important (p. 28).

FIGURE 11.3.   Excerpts from Keith (1986) on Issues in Homework. From *Homework* (pp. 14–28) by T. Z. Keith, West Lafayette, Ind.: Kappa Delta Pi.

grades, students can be given homework assignments meant not so much to foster achievement as to promote good attitudes and good study habits, to dispel the notion that learning occurs only in school, and to allow parents the opportunity to express to their children how much they value education. In order for such effects to occur, it seems crucial that assignments be short and simple. Of course, there is as yet no research evidence to support or refute whether the recommended homework actually has the intended effects.

With regard to subject matter, Keith points out the subtle differences in content that may lie behind the finding that homework is differentially effective for different subjects. He suggests that math and spelling lend themselves to practice assignments. The present review found that subjects and topics amenable to practice-type assignments also show the strongest relation between homework and achievement. Based on this reasoning, I suggested that homework may be most effective for the learning of simple tasks. Therefore, I recommend that if the purpose of homework is to foster achievement it should focus primarily on skills that require practice or that are simple enough to be self-taught. If the purpose of homework is to generate interest in a topic, it should be more challenging, requiring the use of higher-order thinking skills and the integration of different domains of knowledge and experience. Because learning any subject matter requires both simple and complex processes, the content area is largely irrelevant.

Instead, teachers should choose different types of assignments based on what they hope the homework will accomplish.

The main message of homework research regarding both grade level and content is clear. Teachers should not assign homework to young children with the expectation that it will noticeably enhance achievement. Nor should they expect students to be capable of teaching themselves complex skills at home. Instead, teachers might assign short and simple homework to younger students, hoping it will foster positive, long-term, education-related behaviors and attitudes. Simple assignments should be given to older students to improve achievement, and complex assignments should be given to generate interest in the subject matter.

Keith's recommendations regarding quality mirror those made in the booklet *What Works*. Again, the suggestions make good sense, although they lack a research base. Keith also neglects to mention the value of distributing the topical content of homework across multiple assignments. From my review, it is clear that teachers should not exclusively assign material on the day it is addressed in class. Instead, homework should be used to familiarize students with topics yet to appear in class discussions and to reinforce material from past lessons. Research indicates that this strategy is an integral part of quality homework assignments.

Although Keith's recommendation concerning individualization seems innocuous, teachers should not expect great benefits to accrue from the practice. Keith cites the Bradley (1967) study as evidence favoring individualization. Bradley's study reported a significant main effect supporting individualization, but it also found an interaction indicating large positive effects of individualization in two schools and small negative effects in two schools. Bradley also found that individualized homework took significantly more time for teachers to prepare and check.

My sense is that individualized homework for students in the same class will rarely prove more effective than well-constructed group assignments. This statement is based on the assumption that most classrooms have relatively homogeneous student bodies. To the extent that learning skills are not homogeneous, individualization might take on some added value. In earlier grades, assignments should be short and simple enough that they pose no great difficulty to any student, though the time required to complete them may vary. In higher grades, tracking normally produces homogeneous groups of students, but the groups may differ, on average. In such cases, different homework assignments for various classes are certainly called for. Furthermore, if teachers teach, for example, one average class and one accelerated class, they might consider having the brightest students in the average class do parts of the homework assigned to the accelerated group.

I find myself in complete agreement with Keith's suggestions concerning parent involvement. Research examining whether there are positive effects to formally casting parents in the role of teacher is inconclusive. Considering the claimed positive and negative effects, it may be best for teachers not to promote too much direct involvement by parents. However, it makes good sense to have parents play a supportive role in the homework process. Indeed, some facilitation from parents is probably necessary for successful learning through homework. Teachers should encourage parents to take part in supportive but indirect ways.

Finally, Keith's recommendations and those of many others concerning evaluation of homework are not based on research findings. My review found no studies of the impact of grading or evaluative comments per se on the effectiveness of homework. The existing research indicates that different strategies for providing feedback differ little in their influence on homework. Realistically, it seems that students might not take assignments seriously or might not complete them at all if they are not going to be monitored, either through grading or some penalty for failure to turn the work in. The evidence suggests, however, that intermittent grading and comments is no less effective than providing continuous feedback. I suggest, therefore, that the practice of grading homework be kept to a minimum, especially if the assignment's purpose is to foster positive attitudes toward the subject matter. Grading might provide external reasons for doing homework that detract from students' appreciation of the intrinsic value of the exercise.

This does not mean that some homework assignments should go unmonitored. All homework should be collected, and teachers should use it in the diagnosis of learning difficulties. If a teacher notices a student falling behind in class, homework assignments can be carefully scrutinized to determine where the difficulty lies. When errors or misunderstandings on homework are found, the teacher should more assiduously go over the student's other assignments. Problems that the teacher finds should be communicated directly to the student. In a sense, then, homework can help teachers individualize instruction. I see no more reason to treat each homework assignment as if it were a test than I see reason to grade students for their performance on each class lesson.

In sum, I generally agree with Keith's homework guidelines, with four exceptions. First, his ranges for appropriate amounts of time spent on homework may be too long. I suggest that his lower range serve as an average. Second, I would be more explicit about the different purposes of homework for students at different grade levels. Third, Keith omits the distribution of content across assignments as a key element of quality homework. Fourth, he endorses the use of grading and evaluative comments on homework assignments. I am more equivocal. I view homework more as a diagnostic device than as an opportunity to test. Furthermore, the grading of homework may severely limit its ability to foster in students positive attitudes toward the material it covers.

Phi Delta Kappa

The Phi Delta Kappa Educational Foundation publishes a series of booklets called "fastbacks" that are meant to promote a better understanding of the nature of schooling. One fastback is on homework. Its authors, David England and Joannis Flatley (1985), base their recommendations partly on research and partly on conversations about homework that they had with parents, principals, teachers, and students. England and Flatley's suggestions are summarized in a section of their fastback entitled "Homework Do's and Don'ts." These are reproduced in Figure 11.4.

England and Flatley focus primarily on the interpersonal aspects of homework—what should be expected of the different participants in the process and how expectations need to be communicated. These nicely complement the more substantive recommendations contained in Keith (1986). Perhaps the most noteworthy aspect of England and Flatley's discussion is its skepticism about the value of too much compulsory homework. They write:

> Then, too, kids need time to be kids—which is more than a kid's argument .... Just getting kids to do homework becomes recurring ground for battle in many homes. In the background we hear chants of "Teach them discipline!" and "They must learn life is demanding!" We would submit that taking a cold shower teaches discipline, too; and, compared to doing homework until 11:00 p.m. three or four nights a week, it would probably do more to keep kids awake in school. As for learning that life is demanding, perhaps being in

---

The following homework do's and don'ts provide a quick summary of the points covered in the preceding narrative. Our lists are selective but not mutually exclusive. We have tried to limit our admonitions to those few we feel would really matter if heeded.

For Principals

1. *Do not* believe everything you hear about a teacher's homework practices.
2. *Do not* expect all teachers to be equally enthusiastic about a schoolwide homework policy.
3. *Do not* expect a schoolwide homework policy to please all parents.
4. *Do not* expect teachers with the heaviest instructional loads to assign as much homework as those with the lightest loads.
5. *Do* check out all rumors that come your way about teachers' homework practices.
6. *Do* put the teachers you least expect to be pleased by a schoolwide homework policy on the committee that formulates it.
7. *Do* involve parents in the development of schoolwide homework policies.
8. *Do* everything possible to assist teachers with managing homework paper loads, including use of school aides and parent volunteers.

For Teachers

1. *Do not* ever give homework as punishment.
2. *Do not* make up spur-of-the-moment homework assignments.

3. *Do not* assume that because there are no questions asked about a homework assignment students have no questions about the assignment.
4. *Do not* expect students (even your best students) always to have their homework assignments completed.
5. *Do* understand that not all types of homework assignments are equally valuable for all types of students.
6. *Do* explain the specific purpose of every homework assignment.
7. *Do* listen to what students say about their experiences in completing your homework assignments.
8. *Do* acknowledge and be thankful for efforts students make to complete their homework.

For Parents

1. *Do* make sure your child really needs help before offering to help with homework.
2. *Do* help you child see a purpose or some value in homework assignments.
3. *Do* encourage your children to complete assignments after absences from school.
4. *Do* suggest an alternative to watching TV on nights when no homework is assigned, such as sharing a magazine article, enjoying a game together, or going to an exhibit or concert.
5. *Do not* try to help with homework if you are confused and really cannot figure out what is expected.
6. *Do not* hesitate to have your child explain legitimate reasons for nights when homework simply cannot be completed.
7. *Do not* place yourself in an adversarial role between your child and teachers over homework issues until all other alternatives are exhausted.
8. *Do not* feel your child always has to be doing "something productive." (There are few things sadder than a burned-out 14-year-old.)

For Students

1. *Do* ask your parents for help with your homework only when you really need help.
2. *Do* ask the teacher for help before or after class if you are confused about a homework assignment.
3. *Do* explain to teachers legitimate reasons that sometimes make it impossible to complete some homework assignments.
4. *Do* make every effort to complete homework assignments when they are very important for a particular class.
5. *Do not* expect that your parents will be able to help with all your homework. (Parents forget things they have learned, and some of what is taught in school today is foreign to adults.)
6. *Do not* ask teachers to help with any homework assignment you really can complete independently.
7. *Do not* confuse *excuses* for incomplete homework assignments with legitimate *reasons*.
8. *Do not* think doing your homework "most of the time" will be satisfactory for those classes where homework counts the most. (In such classes, even a 75% completion rate may not be enough.)

FIGURE 11.4. England and Flatley's (1985) "Homework Do's and Don'ts" From *Homework—and Why* (pp. 36–38) by D. A. England and J. K. Flatley, 1985, Bloomington, Ind.: Phi Delta Kappa.

school seven hours a day is demanding enough. And if it is not, having the school day encroach on what might otherwise be family time may not be the solution (pp. 11–12).

England and Flatley are not against homework, but they do see problems in its implementation. One of their major concerns, which is not addressed in the discussion of Keith's work, is captured nicely in their fourth admonition to teachers: "Do not expect students (even your best students) always to have their homework assignments completed." This raises two questions: Should homework be mandatory, and if so, what should be the consequence for failure to complete assignments?

The one contemporary study of compulsory versus voluntary homework (Taylor, 1971) found no significant difference between the two types, but this small study is no basis for drawing firm conclusions. I believe that most homework should be compulsory. The kinds of difficulties that England and Flatley describe should not arise if assignments are kept to a reasonable length. Voluntary homework should also be assigned occasionally. It might be reserved for assignments that students will find most interesting, because voluntary assignments are probably most valuable for producing intrinsic motivation.

Consistent with the feedback policy outlined above, I recommend that formal sanctions be associated with uncompleted homework assignments only in serious cases of neglect. Again, missing assignments should be viewed as diagnostic and treated in the context of the student's overall learning performance. Although some positive or negative incentive may be necessary, it should be kept to a minimum, again so as not to interfere with what should be the obvious intrinsic merits of completing assignments. It seems doctrinaire to reduce the grade of an otherwise "straight A" student for assignments not completed. Likewise, missing assignments of poor performing students are more likely symptom than cause.

OTHER SOURCES OF POLICY GUIDELINES

The three policy guides examined above include the major issues that need to be addressed when a district, school, or classroom decides to develop a policy on homework. The national organization guides, however, are by no means exhaustive. They were chosen primarily because they are general and visible. It is beyond the scope of this book to go into the specifics of how policies ought to be developed and what they should contain, because much of this material would vary from school to school. In addition, excellent sources of information, several of which are listed below, already exist.

The Pennsylvania Department of Education (1984) published a resource folder entitled *Homework Policies and Guidelines*. It takes the position that for homework to be effective a clearly written policy is necessary. The resource folder contains guidelines for preparing homework policies, suggestions about factors that should be considered for inclusion in policies, and most important, examples of district policies. The examples range from quite brief to remarkably detailed.

The Connecticut Department of Education (1984) published a manual on policy development and administrative procedures entitled *Attendance, Homework, and Promotion and Retention*. The manual is composed from policies and procedures submitted by 96 Connecticut school districts. A panel of school administrators and teachers then isolated key policy elements and identified good examples of policies and procedures. The manual contains many sample policies but does not evaluate their content.

Similar though less ambitious manuals have been developed by state agencies in Indiana, Kentucky, and Minnesota. I am certain that other states have also undertaken the task of helping school districts develop homework policies.

Finally, examples of homework policies are obtainable from school districts and even from individual schools. From the correspondence I received while conducting this review, it was obvious that many schools and districts take great pride in the care and thoroughness with which their policies have been constructed.

GUIDELINES BASED ON THE PRESENT REVIEW

It is advisable that homework policies exist at the district, school, and classroom levels. The issues addressed at each level are generally different, though some overlap.

At the district level, the detail of a policy need not be great, but the policy should address the general purposes of homework. A policy should at least contain a succinct statement indicating that homework is a cost-effective instructional technique. It should have a positive effect on student achievement. It may also have some unique benefits for the general character development of children. Finally, homework may serve as a vital link between schools, families, and the broader community.

It is also important that district policies address three substantive issues. These guides would be meant to prevent the wide variations in practices from one school to another that so often cause trouble for administrators and teachers. However, the recommendations should be broad enough that schools have ample flexibility to respond to local conditions.

First, districts ought to take a stand on whether the assigning of homework is to be mandatory or voluntary. My recommendation is that districts adopt a policy that requires some homework to be assigned at all grade levels but recognizes that a mixture of both mandatory and voluntary assignments may be most beneficial to students.

Second, districts should prescribe general ranges for the frequency and duration of assignments. These ought to reflect the grade-level differences mentioned above, but they should also be influenced by community factors. Such guidelines for a nationally representative district might be:

- Grades 1 to 3—one to three mandatory assignments a week, each lasting no more than 15 minutes
- Grades 4 to 6—two to four mandatory assignments a week, each lasting between 15 and 45 minutes
- Grades 7 to 9—three to five mandatory assignments a week, each lasting between 45 and 75 minutes
- Grades 10 to 12—four to five mandatory assignments a week, each lasting between 75 and 120 minutes
- All grade levels—additional voluntary assignments presented at the discretion of the teacher

Third, district policies need to acknowledge that homework should serve different purposes at varying grades. For younger students, homework should be used to foster positive attitudes toward school and better academic-related behaviors and character traits, not to improve subject matter achievement measurably. As students grow older, the function of homework should gradually change toward facilitating the acquisition of knowledge in specific topics.

A school homework policy might further specify the time ranges for different grade levels and subjects. This is especially important in schools where different subjects are taught by different teachers. A scheme must be adopted so that each teacher knows (a) what days of the week are available to him or her for homework assignments and (b) how much of the students' total daily homework time can be allocated to that subject.

School policies should also contain guidelines that describe the roles of administrators in the homework process. Included in the administrative guidelines should be (a) communicating the district and school policy to parents, (b) monitoring the implementation of the policy, and (c) coordinating the scheduling of homework among different teachers, if needed.

Whether guidelines for teachers should be included in school-wide homework policies is a decision probably best made at each school. Some teachers might view such policies as unnecessary intrusions on their professional judgment. Others might perceive them as opportunities to learn from the experience of other teachers and to foster a strong community spirit in the school.

I recommend that school-wide policies relating to the role of the teacher focus primarily on the design of high-quality assignments. Among these recommendations would be that teachers must clearly state (a) how the assignment is related to the topic under study, (b) the purpose of the assignment, (c) how the assignment might best be carried out, and (d) what the student needs to do to demonstrate that the assignment has been completed. It is also important that teachers ensure that students have available the necessary resources to carry out an assignment.

Finally, teachers need to adopt a policy governing homework in their classes. Based on the research reviewed in this book, a nationally representative classroom might adopt the following classroom policies:

- Assignments will generally be the same for all students in the class or learning group. Although some individualization may occur, it will be the exception rather than the rule.
- Students are expected to complete all mandatory homework assignments. Failure to do so will necessitate remedial activities.
- Individualization and choice in homework will be obtained through the provision of voluntary assignments of high interest to students.
- The teacher will not formally evaluate or grade each homework assignment. While it would be ideal for all assignments to be carefully scrutinized, time constraints might not make this possible. Teachers should at least scan students' work to get a sense of whether they have taken the assignment seriously. If homework indicates a student does not understand the concepts or has not mastered the skills, it should be used to help guide interactive instruction between the teacher and the student.
- Homework assignments will disperse content so that topics will appear in assignments before and after they are covered in class.
- Homework will not be used to teach complex skills and material. If the purpose of homework is to enhance achievement, it will generally focus on the learning of simple skills and material. More complex tasks (e.g., writing compositions or research reports) can be valuable homework assignments but should generally require the integration of skills already possessed by the students.
- Parents will rarely be asked to assist in homework in a formal instructional role. Instead, their help will be recruited to ensure that the home environment facilitates student self-study.

These guidelines, along with others, should be explicitly communicated to students and parents. "Do's and Don't" lists like those suggested by England and Flatley (1985) are a useful format for conveying homework rules and roles.

As I have already stated in numerous contexts, the general guidelines I offer are not applicable to all classrooms. They need to be adapted to meet local conditions. They also must be supplemented with recommendations concerning other aspects of homework—for example, the role of group and long-term projects. What they are, simply, is a set of general suggestions concerning aspects of policy that can be informed by the cumulative empirical research. Figure 11.5 summarizes these recommendations.

For Districts

Homework is a cost-effective instructional technique. It can have positive effects on achievement and character development and can serve as a vital link between the school and family.

Homework should have different purposes at different grades. For younger students, it should foster positive attitudes, habits, and character traits. For older students, it should facilitate knowledge acquisition in specific topics.

Homework should be required at all grade levels, but a mixture of mandatory and voluntary homework is most beneficial.

The frequency and duration of mandatory assignments should be:
1. Grades 1 to 3—one to three assignments a week, each lasting no more than 15 minutes
2. Grades 4 to 6—two to four assignments, each lasting 15 to 45 minutes
3. Grades 7 to 9—three to five assignments, each lasting 45 to 75 minutes
4. Grades 10 to 12—four to five assignments, each lasting 75 to 120 minutes

For Schools

The frequency and duration of homework assignments should be further specified to reflect local school and community circumstances.

In schools where different subjects are taught by different teachers, teachers should know:
1. What days of the week are available to them for assignments
2. How much daily homework time should be spent on their subject

Administrators should:
1. Communicate the district and school homework policies to parents
2. Monitor the implementation of the policy
3. Coordinate the scheduling of homework among different subjects, if needed

Teachers should state clearly:
1. How the assignment is related to the topic under study
2. The purpose of the assignment
3. How the assignment might best be carried out
4. What the student needs to do to demonstrate that the assignment has been completed

For Teachers

All students in a class will be responsible for the same assignments, with only rare exceptions.

Homework will include mandatory assignments. Failure to turn in mandatory assignments will necessitate remedial activities.

Homework will also include voluntary assignments meant to meet the needs of individual students or groups of students.

All homework assignments will *not* be formally evaluated. They will be used to locate problems in student progress and to individualize instruction.

Topics will appear in assignments before and after they are covered in class, not just on the day they are discussed.

Homework will not be used to teach complex skills. It will generally focus on simple skills and material or on the integration of skills already possessed by the student.

Parents will rarely be asked to play a formal instructional role in homework. Instead, they should be asked to create a home environment that facilitates student self-study.

FIGURE 11.5. Summary of Homework Policy Guidelines

12

The Future of Homework Research

My recommendations concerning the future of homework research should come as no surprise. They are based directly on the methodological weaknesses and conceptual omissions of past investigations. Therefore, I will state succinctly the improvements I think are called for and discuss briefly how they can best be obtained.

OVERCOMING METHODOLOGICAL WEAKNESSES

The most important element in improving homework research involves *increasing the frequency with which students are randomly assigned to treatment conditions*. For studies involving small numbers of elementary school classes, random assignment should be accomplished within classes. Two content areas can be chosen for study. One group of students can be assigned homework treatment X in subject A and treatment Y in subject B. The other group of students can simultaneously receive Y in A, and X in B. The design can then be reversed for a second unit within each subject area. If time permits, the reversal process can be repeated multiple times.

When a single class studies multiple subjects, this design is simple and elegant. It not only controls for threats to validity associated with intact-group comparisons, but also protects against bias if the experimenter is the teacher, since students in the different conditions are exposed to the same class lessons. It is easy to carry out and creates no more ethical problems than administering different treatments to different intact classes. Why it has been used so infrequently in past research is a mystery.

When classes study only a single subject area, as is typically the case in high school, experimenters should examine whether "computer-assigned" class placement has in fact produced equivalent groups. If possible, experimenters should document the algorithm used to assign students to classes to verify randomization. They should attempt to identify students who have asked for class changes and determine if some characteristic systematically distinguishes them from others. Experimental treatments should be assigned to classes randomly, and the treatment should be administered as soon as possible in the school term.

Pretests should be used to demonstrate the equivalence of groups and as additional factors in data analysis. This procedure is especially important when random assignment has not been carried out. Then, a priori matching of students and the dropping of students who have no match are essential. *Counterbalancing of treatments across groups* also helps rule out many rival explanations for results, if the results are consistent over the experimental replications. These two design features are extremely cost-effective. Numerous valuable pretest measures are routinely collected by schools, and most schools that permit homework research to be conducted will also allow researchers access to these data. Any homework study that spans two class units can employ a counterbalanced design.

Homework studies should be conducted using *larger samples of students and classrooms*. This design feature is not as easily realized as those described above. A large portion of homework research is done to fulfill doctoral degree requirements, and these studies are generally conducted with limited funds. Scarce funds mean limited designs and correspondingly restricted inferences.

Related to larger samples of students and classrooms is the need to *employ the classroom as the unit of analysis*. Even when treatments are instituted within classes, it is most appropriate to use the class as the unit and treat the groups of students as either repeated measures or factors nested within classes. In past studies, students have been used as the data unit partly out of ignorance of statistical principles and partly because of the high premium placed on obtaining significant results. Most studies are conducted on such small numbers of classes that legitimate analyses would have unacceptably low statistical power.

Researchers who cannot obtain large samples and who feel compelled to use the student as the data unit ought to recognize these limitations in their interpretation. More important, they should present *detailed descriptions of the data*. Raw data should be included when possible. For example, dissertations can put raw data in an appendix, and authors of journal articles can make data available on request. At a minimum, student and classroom means and standard deviations for every level of the variables used in the primary statistical analyses should be presented. Detailed reporting can often be accomplished with surprisingly little additional manuscript space. The greater detail goes a long way toward allowing future reviewers to integrate the findings of numerous small but related investigations systematically. In fact, detailed data reporting is important for large-scale studies as well.

FILLING CONCEPTUAL GAPS

As Figure 10.2 demonstrates, the list of homework topics that have never been researched is long. Most critical for future investigations is *the inclusion of nonachievement-related outcome measures*. Better study habits, greater self-discipline and self-direction, better time organization, and more inquisitiveness and independent problem-solving have all been offered as important positive outcomes of homework. Yet none has appeared in homework research. Cheating on homework is also unstudied. Finally, the effects of homework on parents have never been gauged in an experimental investigation. We have no data testing a causal relation between homework and parental appreciation of or involvement in school. The belief that homework causes parentally induced pressure to perform well and confusion of instructional techniques also rests on informal observation.

The likely reason for omission of these measures is the added costs associated with collecting them. Achievement measures are plentiful and are administered as a routine part of schooling. On the other hand, measures of study habits and inquisitiveness, for example, are more difficult to find, probably less reliable and valid, and would require taking class time to administer. It is also likely that researchers shy away from nonacademic measures because homework's effect on these more personal characteristics is more subtle. Added home study should translate directly into higher scores on the associated class test. However, a few weeks of short homework assignments may have only a minute effect on a student's self-directedness, a character trait that is built up over many years and influenced by an enormous variety of events.

Another issue for future research, also related to the subtlety of homework's effects, is the need for *longer treatment durations*. Homework policies influence students' learning throughout their years of schooling. Yet the typical homework treatment in research lasts about 10 weeks. Again, however, the use of this desirable design feature runs up against pragmatic considerations. Degree requirements must be met, research reports published, and policy decisions made. Each of these constraints affects the quality of the data that homework research can produce.

Of the remaining influences on the homework process that have gone unresearched, I would list the *inclusion of home-related factors* as most critical for understanding homework's effects. Parent involvement should be researched not only as an outcome of homework, as it was conceptualized above, but also as a mediating variable that influences the effect of homework on the child. Past research in this area has been woefully inadequate. Equally important, the home environment needs to be systematically studied. Parameters of the physical setting, especially as they relate to social class, have begun to be examined in descriptive studies like those briefly mentioned in Chapter 9. Teachers, however, need a much better understanding of how home environments affect students' ability to study. This will permit them to tailor homework assignments to have realistic goals.

Finally, the *parameters of a well-designed homework assignment* need some empirical validation. Most policy guidelines contain admonitions that homework be clearly explained and well integrated into class lessons and that students be made aware of the value of doing assignments. The importance of these procedures seems obvious, but the literature suggests that in practice they may not be routinely followed. Some demonstration of their effects is needed.

SUMMARY

Future homework research needs to employ sounder methodology. More frequent use of random assignment, pretesting, and counterbalancing are three design improvements that can be realized without much additional cost. Similarly, use of the appropriate unit of analysis and more detailed data reporting are well within the capabilities of even the most constrained homework researcher. Other improvements will come at greater expense. These include larger samples of students and classrooms and longer treatment durations.

Future homework research also needs to incorporate a wider variety of outcome measures. Nonacademic effects on students and effects on parents are cited too often as homework rationales for these effects to be neglected in research. Home factors—that aspect of the homework process that gives it its distinct character—also deserve more rigorous examination.

There has never been a large-scale experimental study of the homework process. Perhaps it is time such a study was carried out. Certainly, the effects of homework will continue to be a frequent topic for small-scale investigations. This is not necessarily bad if researchers with constrained samples and time frames do not allow restricted resources to narrow their thinking. In the area of homework, imaginative and well-conducted small studies can still make large contributions.

References

Abramowitz, N. (1937). Homework in the foreign language class. *High Points, 19*, 72–74.

Allison, D. E., & Gray, R. F. (1970). A study of the interaction of anxiety and assigned homework on the academic achievement of elementary school children. *Conseiller Canadien, 4*(2), 135–139.

Ames, S. (1983). *An Experimental Study of the Effects of Required Homework Versus No Homework on Student Achievement.* Unpublished research project, Wright State University, Dayton, Ohio.

Anderson, W. E. (1946). An attempt through the use of experimental techniques to determine the effect of home assignments upon scholastic success. *Journal of Educational Research, 40*(2), 141–143.

Anthony, C. P. (1977). *An experimental study of the effects of different amounts of homework upon student achievement in Algebra I, Algebra II, and Algebra III.* Unpublished doctoral dissertation, Rutgers University, 1977.

Asp, E., & Levine, V. (1985). *The social context of home environment and achievement at school.* Paper presented at the annual meeting of the American Educational Research Association, Chicago.

Austin, J. D. (1976). Do comments on mathematics homework affect student achievement? *School Science and Mathematics, 76*(2), 159–164.

Austin, J. D. (1979). Homework research in mathematics. *School Science and Mathematics, 79*, 115–121.

Austin, J. D., & Austin, K. A. (1974). Homework grading procedures in junior high mathematics classes. *School Science and Mathematics, 74*(4), 269–272.

Bailey, B. W. (1981). *A multivariate study of the allocation of student time to school and homework.* Unpublished doctoral dissertation, Teachers College, Columbia University.

Bangert, R. L., Kulik, J. A., & Kulik, C.-L. C. (1981). *Individualized systems of instruction in secondary schools.* Unpublished manuscript, University of Michigan, Ann Arbor.

Baughman, D., & Pruitt, W. (1963). Supplemental study for enrichment vs. supplemental study for reinforcement of academic achievement. *Bulletin of the National Association of Secondary School Principals, 47,* 154–157.

Baxter, M. (1973). *Prediction of error and error type in computation of sixth-grade mathematics students.* Unpublished doctoral dissertation, Pennsylvania State University.

Bird, T. (1983). *Homework Versus No Homework in High School French Classes.* Unpublished research project, Wright State University, Dayton, Ohio.

Blackwell, W. B. (1979). *An analysis of the Dial-a-Teacher Assistance Program (Dataline).* Paper presented at the National Urban Education Conference, Detroit.

Bradley, R. M. (1967). *An experimental study of individualized versus blanket-type homework assignments in elementary school mathematics.* Unpublished doctoral dissertation, Temple University.

Brink, W. G. (1937). *Direct study activities in secondary schools.* New York: Doubleday.

Brooks, E. C. (1916). The value of home study under parental supervision. *Elementary School Journal, 17,* 187–194.

Brouillet, F. B., Rasp, A., & Ensign, G. B. (1982) *Washington High School and beyond.* Olympia, WA: Department of Public Instruction.

Burningham, R. (1963). *Pupil and parent reactions to types of homework.* Unpublished master's thesis, University of Utah, Salt Lake City.

Butcher, J. E. (1975). *Comparison of the effects of distributed and massed problem assignments on the homework of grade nine algebra students.* Unpublished doctoral dissertation, Rutgers University.

Camp, J. S. (1973). *The effects of distributed practice upon learning and retention in introductory algebra.* Unpublished doctoral dissertation, Teachers College, Columbia University.

Carlberg, C., & Kavale, K. (1980). The efficacy of special versus regular class placement for exceptional children: A meta-analysis. *Journal of Special Education, 14,* 295–309.

Carmichael, J. A. (1933). [Master's thesis, University of Southern California.] (See also Crawford, C. C., & Carmichael, J. A. (1937). The value of home study. *Elementary School Journal, 38*(3), 194–200.)

Carroll, C. D., & Brown, G. H. (1985). *Time spent on studying dropped, partially recovered between 1972 and 1982.* U.S. Department of Education, National Center for Education Statistics.

Chandler, J., Argyris, D., Barnes, W. S., Goodman, I. F., & Snow, C. E. (1983). *Parents as teachers: Observations of low-income parents and children in a homework-like task.* ERIC Document Reproduction Service No. ED 231 812.

Cohen, J. (1977). *Statistical power analysis for the behavioral sciences* (rev. ed.). New York: Academic Press.

Connecticut Department of Education. (1984). *Attendance, homework, promotion, and retention.* Hartford, CN: Author.

Cook, T. D., & Campbell, D. T. (1979). *Quasi-experimentation: Design and analysis issues for field settings.* Chicago: Rand McNally.

Cooke, D. H., & Brown, G. B., Jr. (1935). Home study has many angles. *Journal of Education, 118*(15), 409–410.

Cooke, D. H., & King, L. (1939). Should children study at home? *American School*

Board Journal, 98(2), 49–50.

Cooper, H. M. (1984). *The integrative research review: A systematic approach.* Beverly Hills, CA: Sage.

Cooper, H. M. (1986a). Literature-searching strategies of integrative research reviewers. *Knowledge: Creation, diffusion, utilization, 8,* 372–383.

Cooper, H. M. (1986b). On the social psychology of using research reviews: The case of desegregation and black achievement. In R. Feldman (Ed.), *The social psychology of education.* Cambridge, England: Cambridge University Press.

Cooper, H. M. (1986c). *Moving beyond meta-analysis.* Paper presented at the National Committee on Statistics Conference on the Future of Meta-Analysis, Hedgesville, WV.

Cooper, H., & Rosenthal, R. (1980). Statistical versus traditional procedures for summarizing research findings. *Psychological Bulletin, 87,* 442–449.

Coulter, F. (1979). Homework: A neglected research area. *British Educational Research Journal, 5*(1), 21–33.

Coulter, F. (1980). *Secondary school homework. Cooperative research Study Report No. 7* (Research report). Perth, Australia: University of Western Australia. (ERIC Document Reproduction Service No. ED 209 200).

Dadas, J. E. (1976). *A study of the effects of assigning spiral exploratory homework upon achievement in and attitude towards mathematics.* Unpublished doctoral dissertation, New York University.

Deci, E. L., & Ryan, R. M. (1985). *Intrinsic motivation and self-determination in human behavior.* New York: Plenum.

Denham, C., & Lieberman, A. (1980). *Time to learn.* Washington, DC: National Institute of Education.

Dick, D. (1980). *An experimental study of the effects of required homework review versus review on request on achievement.* Bowling Green, KY.: Western Kentucky University. (ERIC Document Reproduction Service No. ED 194 320).

DiNapoli, P. J. (1937). *Homework.* New York: Teachers College, Columbia University.

Doane, B. S. (1972). *The effects of homework and locus-of-control on arithmetic skills achievement in fourth-grade students.* Unpublished doctoral dissertation, New York University.

Eash, M. (1983). Educational research productivity of institutions of higher education. *American Educational Research Journal, 20,* 5–12.

Edmonton Public Schools. (1985). *Student-Parent-Staff Survey: 1985.* Edmonton, Canada: Edmonton Public Schools.

Education Commission of the States (ECS). (1977). *Analysis of supplemental background questions on homework and TV.* Denver, CO: Education Commission of the States.

England, D. A., & Flatley, J. K. (1985). *Homework—and why.* Bloomington, IN: Phi Delta Kappa.

Epps, M. (1966). *Homework.* U.S. Department of Health, Education, and Welfare, Office of Education.

Epstein, J. L. (1983). *Homework practices, achievements, and behaviors of elementary school students.* Baltimore: Johns Hopkins University. (ERIC Document Reproduction Service No. ED 250 351).

Epstein, J. L. (1986). *Toward an integrated theory of school and family corrections.* Report No. 3, Center for Research on Elementary and Middle Schools, Johns

Hopkins University, Baltimore.

Epstein, J. L. (1987a). Parent involvement: What research says to administrators. *Education in Urban Society*, *19*, 119–136.

Epstein, J. L. (1987b). What principals should know about parent involvement. *Principal*, *66*, 6–9.

Fetler, M. (1984). Television viewing and school achievement. *Journal of Communication*, *34*(2), 104–118.

Fink, S., & Nalven, F. B. (1972). Increasing homework motivation. *Education*, *92*, 31–33.

Foran, T. G., & Weber, M. M. (1939). An experimental study of the relation of homework to achievement in arithmetic. *Mathematics Teacher*, *32*, 212–214.

Fort Worth Independent School District. (1983). *Homework practices in FWISD*. Fort Worth, TX: Fort Worth Independent School District.

Foyle, H. C. (1984). *The effects of preparation and practice homework on student achievement in tenth-grade American history*. Unpublished doctoral dissertation, Kansas State University, Manhattan, KS.

Fredrick, W. C., & Walberg, H. J. (1980). Learning as a function of time. *Journal of Educational Research*, *73*, 183–194.

Frick, T., & Simmel, M. I. (1978). Observer agreement and reliabilities of classroom observational measures. *Review of Educational Research*, *48*, 157–184.

Friesen, C. D. (1975). *The effect of exploratory and review homework exercises upon achievement, retention, and attitude in a first-year algebra course*. Unpublished doctoral dissertation, University of Nebraska at Lincoln.

Friesen, C. D. (1978). *The results of surveys, questionnaires, and polls regarding homework*. ERIC Document Reproduction Service No. ED 159 174.

Friesen, C. D. (1979). *The results of homework versus no-homework research studies*. ERIC Document Reproduction Service No. ED 167 508.

Gallup, A. M. (1985). The seventeenth annual Gallup poll of the public's attitudes toward the public schools. Reprinted from *Phi Delta Kappan*, *67*, 35–47.

Gay, Jr., A. A. (1985). *Homework hotline survey: Results and conclusions*. Unpublished research report, Norfork, Virginia, Public School District.

Glass, G., McGaw, B., & Smith, M. (1981). *Meta-analysis in social research*. Beverly Hills, CA: Sage.

Goldstein, A. (1960). Does homework help? A review of research. *Elementary School Journal*, *1*, 212–224.

Grant, E. E. (1971). *An experimental study of the effects of compulsory arithmetic homework assignments on the arithmetic achievement of fifth-grade pupils*. Unpublished doctoral dissertation, University of the Pacific.

Gray, R. F., & Allison, D. E. (1971). An experimental study of the relationship of homework to pupil success in computation with fractions. *School Science and Mathematics*, *71*(4), 339–346.

Great Britain Board of Education. (1937). *Homework*. London: His Majesty's Stationary Office.

Hagan, H. (1927). The value of homework as compared with supervised study. *Second Yearbook, Chicago Principal's Club*, pp. 147–149.

Harding, R. C. (1979). *The relationship of teacher attitudes toward homework and the academic achievement of primary grade students*. Unpublished doctoral dissertation, Lehigh University.

Harris, V. W. (1972). *Effects of peer tutoring, homework, and consequences upon the academic performance of elementary school children.* Unpublished doctoral dissertation, University of Kansas.

Hedges, L. V., & Olkin, I. (1985). *Statistical methods for meta-analysis.* Orlando, FL: Academic Press.

Heintz, P. (1975). *High school peer tutoring (homework helpers) program* (Evaluation Report No. 09–59615). New York: NYC Board of Education.

Hinckley, R. H., et al. (1979). *Student home environment, educational achievement, and compensatory education.* Technical Report 4 from the Study of Sustaining Effects of Compensatory Education on Basic Skills. Santa Monica, CA: Decima Research.

Hines, S. (1982). *Student Achievement with and without Homework.* Unpublished research project, Wright State University, Dayton, OH.

Hines, V. A. (1957). Homework and achievement in plane geometry. *Mathematics Teacher, 50*(1), 27–29.

Holtzman, W. H. (1969). Study. In *Encyclopedia of Educational Research* (4th ed.). New York: Free Press, pp. 1389–1394.

Huddleson, S. (1983). *Homework versus no homework in high school English classes.* Unpublished research project, Wright State University, Dayton, OH.

Hudson, J. A. (1965). *A pilot study of the influence of homework in seventh grade mathematics and attitudes toward homework in the Fayetteville public schools.* Unpublished doctoral dissertation, University of Arkansas.

Hume-Cummings, P. (1985). *Homework versus no homework.* Unpublished research project, Wright State University, Dayton, OH.

Jacobs, J. N., et al. (1965). *An evaluation of programmed instruction for teaching facts and concepts* (Final Report, April 1964–August 1965). ERIC Document Reproduction Service No. ED 130 650.

James, J. (1986). *Mean first quarter GPA by self-reported amount of homework.* Seattle, WA: Seattle Public Schools.

Johnson, D. W., Maruyama, G., Johnson, R., Nelson, D., & Skon, L. (1981). Effects of cooperative, competitive, and individualistic goal structures on achievement: A meta-analysis. *Psychological Bulletin, 89,* 47–62.

Johnson, L. M. (1931). *Directed supervised study versus home study in sixth grade history.* Unpublished master's thesis, Loyola University.

Joiner, L. M. (1970). *Final report of the evaluation of the 1969–1970 homework-helper program.* New York: Teaching & Learning Research Corp.

Jongsma, E. (1985). Homework: Is it worthwhile? *The Reading Teacher, 38,* pp. 702–704.

Keith, T. Z. (1982). Time spent on homework and high school grades: A large-sample path analysis. *Journal of Educational Psychology, 74,* 248–253.

Keith, T. Z. (1986). *Homework.* West Lafayette, IN: Kappa Delta Pi.

Keith, T. Z. (1987). Children and homework. In A. Thomas & J. Grimes (Eds.), *Children's needs: Psychological perspectives.* Washington DC: National Association of School Psychologists.

Keith, T., Reimers, T., Fehrman, P., Pottenbaum, S., & Aubey, L. (1986). Parental involvement, homework, and TV time: Direct and indirect effects on high school achievement. *Journal of Educational Psychology, 78,* 373–380.

Knorr, C. L. (1981). *A synthesis of homework research and related literature.* ERIC

Document Reproduction Service No. ED 199 933.

Koch, E. A., Jr (1965). Homework in arithmetic. *The Arithmetic Teacher*, *12*(1), 9–13.

Kohr, R. L. (1979). The relationship of homework and television viewing to cognitive and noncognitive student outcomes. Pennsylvania Educational Quality Assessment Program. (ERIC Document Reproduction Service No. ED 175 441).

Kulik, C.-L. C., & Kulik, J. A. (1981). *Effects of ability grouping on secondary school students*. Unpublished manuscript, University of Michigan, Ann Arbor.

Kulik, C.-L. C., Shwalb, B. J., & Kulik, J. A. (1982). Programmed instruction in secondary school: a meta-evaluation. *Journal of Educational Research*, *75*, 133–138.

LaConte, R. T. (1981). *Homework as a learning experience: What research says to the teacher*. ERIC Document Reproduction Service No. ED 217 022.

Laing, R. A. (1970). *Relative effects of massed and distributed scheduling of topics on homework assignments of eighth-grade mathematics students*. Unpublished doctoral dissertation, Ohio State University.

Langdon, G., & Stout, I. W. (1969). *Homework*. New York: John Day (Interordered 6/20).

Lash, S. W. E. (1971). *A comparison of three types of homework assistance for high school geometry*. Unpublished doctoral dissertation, Temple University.

Lee, J. F., & Pruitt, K. W. (1979). Homework assignments: Classroom games or teaching tools? *Clearinghouse*, *53*, 31–35.

Leichter, H. J. (Ed.). (1974). *The family as educator*. New York: Teachers College Press.

Leichter, H. J. (1985). Families as educators. In M. D. Fantini & R. L. Sinclair (Eds.), *Education in school and nonschool settings*. Chicago: University of Chicago Press.

Leonard, M. H. (1965). *An experimental study of homework at the intermediate-grade level*. Unpublished doctoral dissertation, Fordham University.

Levenstein, P. (1983). Implications of the transition period for early intervention. In R. M. Golinkoff (Ed.), *The transition from prelinguistic to linguistic communication*. Hillsdale, NJ: Erlbaum.

Los Angeles Unified School District. (1984). *Three surveys of staff and parent opinions about the Los Angeles Unified School District instructional program* (Publication No. 455). Los Angeles: Los Angeles Unified School District.

Los Angeles Unified School District. (1985). *Three surveys of staff and parent opinions about the Los Angeles Unified School District instructional program* (Publication No. 472). Los Angeles: Los Angeles Unified School District.

Luiten, J., Ames, W., & Aerson, G. (1980). A meta-analysis of advance organizers on learning and retention. *American Educational Research Journal*, *17*, 211–218.

McDermott, R. P., Goldman, S. V., & Varenne, H. (1984). When school goes home: Some problems in the organization of homework. *Teachers College Record*, *85*, 391–409.

McGill, J. V. (1948). *Comparative value of assigned homework and supervised study: An experimental study of the two methods of preparation as used by students of the social studies at the high-school level*. Unpublished doctoral dissertation, New York University.

Maertens, N. W. (1967). *An analysis of the effect of arithmetic homework upon the arithmetic achievement of third-grade pupils.* Unpublished doctoral dissertation, University of Minnesota.

Maertens, N. W., & Johnston, J. (1972). Effects of arithmetic homework upon the attitudes and achievement of fourth, fifth, and sixth grade pupils. *School Science and Mathematics,* 72(2), 117–126.

Marshall, P. M. (1983). *Homework and social facilitation theory in teaching elementary school mathematics.* Unpublished doctoral dissertation, Stanford University.

Montgomery, C. F. (1933). *An evaluation of required home study in junior high school arithmetic and English.* Unpublished master's thesis, University of West Virginia, Morgantown.

Nadis, M. L. (1965). *A status study of homework practices and attitudes of Detroit ninth grade social studies teachers and ninth grade students including a pilot experimental study of two ninth grade social studies classes.* Unpublished doctoral dissertation, Wayne State University.

National Assessment of Educational Progress. (1977). *Analysis of supplemental background questions on homework and TV.* ERIC Document Reproduction Service No. ED 159 055.

National Center for Education Statistics. (1984). *High school course grade standards.* ERIC Document Reproduction Service No. ED 252 570.

National Center for Education Statistics. (1985). *Time spent on homework dropped, partially recovered between 1972 and 1982.* Washington, DC: Department of Education.

National Commission on Excellence in Education. (1983). *A nation at risk: The imperative for educational reform.* Washington, DC: U.S. Department of Education.

Natriello, G., & McDill, E. L. (1986). Performance standards, student effort on homework, and academic achievement. *Sociology of Education,* 59, 18–31.

North Carolina Department of Public Instruction. (1983). *Special research studies, 1983–1984.* Raleigh, NC: North Carolina Department of Public Instruction.

North Carolina Department of Public Instruction. (1985). *Special research studies, 1984–1985.* Raleigh, NC: North Carolina Department of Public Instruction.

O'Connor, W. L. (1985). *Two methods of grading homework and their effects upon student achievement.* Unpublished master's thesis, University of Texas, Austin.

Otto, H. J. (1941). Elementary education. In *Encyclopedia of educational research* (1st ed.). New York: Free Press, pp. 444–445.

Otto, H. J. (1950). Elementary education. In *Encyclopedia of educational research* (2nd ed.). New York: Free Press, pp. 380–381.

Otto, W. (1985). Homework: A meta-analysis. *Journal of Reading,* 28, 764–766.

Parrish, D. C. (1976). *An investigation of the effects of required drill homework versus no homework on attitudes toward and achievement in mathematics.* Unpublished doctoral dissertation, University of Houston.

Paschal, R. A., Weinstein, T., & Walberg, H. J. (1984). The effects of homework on learning: A quantitative synthesis. *Journal of Educational Research,* 78(2), 97–104.

Paulson, J. (1983). *A Study of Homework.* Unpublished research project, Wright State University, Dayton, Ohio.

Paulukaitis, K. R., & Kirkpatrick, S. W. (1986). *Reading homework: Structured versus nonstructured*. Unpublished manuscript.

Pennsylvania Department of Education. (1984). *Homework policies and guidelines*. Harrisburg, PA: Pennsylvania Department of Education.

Perry, W. G. (1974). *The effects of selected homework procedures on the achievement of second semester high school shorthand students*. Unpublished doctoral dissertation, University of North Dakota.

Peterson, J. C. (1969). *Effects of exploratory homework exercises upon achievement in eighth-grade mathematics*. Unpublished doctoral dissertation, Ohio State University.

Pflaum, S. W., Walberg, H. J., Karegianes, M. L., & Rasher, S. (1980). Reading instruction: A quantitative synthesis. *Educational Researcher, 9*, 12–18.

Rankin, P. T. (1967). *The relationship between parent behavior and achievement in inner city elementary school children*. Paper presented at the annual meeting of the American Educational Research Association, New York, NY.

Raphael, D., & Wahlstrom, M. (1986). *Mathematics instruction and achievement in the York Region Board of Education: Grade 8 student achievement and attitudes*. Ontario, Canada: Educational Evaluation Center, Ontario Institute for Studies in Education.

Redfield, D. L., & Rousseau, E. W. (1981). A meta-analysis of experimental research on teacher questioning behavior. *Review of Educational Research, 51*, 237–245.

Rhode Island Department of Education. (1978). *Rhode Island statewide assessment program*. Rhode Island: Rhode Island Department of Education.

Rickards, J. P. (1982). Homework. In *Encyclopedia of Educational Research* (5th ed., 2nd vol.). New York: Free Press, pp. 831–834.

Rosenstengel, W. E., & Turner, C. (1936). Supervised school study versus home study. *American School Board Journal, 92*(4), 42.

Rosenthal, G. C. (1974). *A study of some of the ways that homework is used in a school system and an evaluation of its possible value*. Unpublished specialist thesis, Western Michigan University.

Rosenthal, R. (1964). The effects of the experimenter on the results of psychological research. In B. A. Maher (Ed.), *Progress in experimental personality research* (vol. 1). New York: Academic Press, pp. 79–114.

Rosenthal, R. (1984). *Meta-analytic procedures for social research*. Beverly Hills, CA: Sage.

Rutter, M., Maughan, B., Mortimer, P., & Oustan, J. (1979). *Fifteen thousand hours: Secondary schools and their effects on children*. Cambridge, MA: Harvard University Press.

Statistical Analysis System. (1985). *SAS user's guide: Statistics version 5 edition*. Cary, NC: SAS Institute.

Schain, R. L. (1954). Another homework experiment in the social studies. *High Points, 36*(2), 5–12.

Schneider, S. (1953). An experiment on the value of homework. *High Points, 35*(4), 18–19.

Schroeder, H. A. (1960). *Homework versus no-homework in elementary algebra*. Unpublished master's thesis, Mankato State College, Mankato, MN.

Schunert, J. (1951). The association of mathematical achievement with certain factors resident in the teacher, in the teaching, in the pupil, and in the school. *Journal of Experimental Education, 19*, 219–238.

Seattle Public Schools. (1986). *Fall 1985 "High School and Beyond" Survey Participants—Grade 9*. Seattle, WA: Seattle Public Schools.

Singh, J. M. (1969). *An investigation of the effect of individualized enrichment homework upon academic achievement with children in the fourth, fifth, and sixth grades*. Unpublished doctoral dissertation, Arizona State University.

Singh, J. M. (1970). *An investigation of the effect of individualized enrichment homework upon the academic achievement of children in the fourth, fifth, and sixth grade*. Paper presented at the International Reading Association, Anaheim, CA.

Small, D. E., Holtan, B. D., & Davis, E. J. (1967). A study of two methods of checking homework in a high school geometry class. *The Mathematics Teacher, 60*, 149–152.

Steiner, M. A. (1934). Value of home-study assignments. *School and Society, 40*(1019), 20–24.

Stennett, R. G., Earl, L. M., & Rachar, B. (1985). *Program monitoring: An attempt to apply the methodology of the second international study of mathematics* (Research Report No. 85-06). London, Ontario: Board of Education.

Stennett, R. G., & Rachar, B. (1985). *Grade nine general level mathematics monitoring: Overview* (Research Report No. 85-05). London, Ontario: Board of Education.

Stewart, L. C., & White, M. A. (1976). Teacher comments, letter grades, and student performance: What do we really know? *Journal of Educational Psychology, 68*, 488–500.

Strang, R. M. (1955). Guided study and homework. *What Research Says to the Teacher*. Washington DC: National Education Association.

Strang, R. M. (1960). Homework and guided study. In *Encyclopedia of educational research* (3rd ed.). New York: Free Press, pp. 675–680.

Strang, R. M. (1968). Guided study and homework. In *What Research Says to the Teacher*. Washington DC: National Education Association.

Strang, R. M. (1975). Guided study and homework. *What Research Says to the Teacher*. Washington DC: National Education Association.

Strother, D. B. (1984). Homework: Too much, just right, or not enough? *Phi Delta Kappan, 65*, pp. 423–426.

Sutcliffe, A., & Canham, J. W. (1937). *Experiments in homework and physical education*. London: J. Murray, Albermarle Street.

Talmage, H., & Rasher, S. P. (1979). *A study of the effects of three dimensions of instructional time on academic achievement*. Paper presented at the annual meeting of the American Educational Research Association, San Francisco. (ERIC Document Reproduction Service No. ED 173 327).

Tarbuck, G. (1984). *The relationship of school achievement to time spent doing homework among selected tenth and twelfth grade students in the U.S.* Unpublished doctoral dissertation, University of Akron.

Taylor, H. D. (1971). *A comparative study of compulsory homework versus non-compulsory homework in Algebra I and Geometry I at Hillsdale High School*. Unpublished doctoral dissertation, University of Northern Colorado.

Teahan, E. G. (1935). Required home study is unwise. *American School Board Journal, 91*(5), 41.

Teddlie, C., & Stringfield, S. (1986). A differential analysis of effectiveness in middle and low socioeconomic status schools. *Journal of Classroom Interaction,*

20(2), 38–44.

Ten Brinke, D. P. (1964). *Homework: An experimental evaluation of the effect on achievement in mathematics in grades seven and eight.* Unpublished doctoral dissertation, University of Minnesota.

Tupesis, J. A. (1972). *Mathematics learning as a consequence of the learner's involvement in interaction problem-solving tasks.* Unpublished doctoral dissertation, University of Wisconsin.

U.S. Department of Education. (1986). *What works.* Washington, DC.

U.S. Department of Health, Education, and Welfare. (1969). *Homework helper program New York City: It works.* Washington, DC: Department of Health, Education, and Welfare.

Urwiller, S. L. (1971). *A comparative study of achievement, retention, and attitude toward mathematics between students using spiral homework assignments and students using traditional homework assignments in second-year algebra.* Unpublished doctoral dissertation, University of Nebraska—Lincoln.

Vincent, H. D. (1937). An experimental test of the value of homework in grades five and six. *The National Elementary Principal, 16*(5), 199–203.

Walberg, H. J. (1986). Syntheses of research on teaching. In M. C. Wittrock (Ed.), *Handbook of research on teaching* (3rd ed.). New York: Macmillan, pp. 214–229.

Walberg, H. J., Fraser, B. J., & Welch, W. W. (1986). A test of a model of educational productivity among senior high school students. *Journal of Educational Research, 79*(3), 133–139.

Walberg, H. J., Pascarella, E., Haertel, G. D., Junker, L. K., & Boulanger, F. D. (1982). Probing a model of educational productivity in high school science with National Assessment samples. *Journal of Educational Psychology, 74*, 295–307.

Walberg, H. J., & Shanahan, T. (1983). High school effects on individual students. *Educational Researcher, 12*(7), 4–9.

Ward, B., Mead, N. A., & Searls, D. T. (1983). *The relationship of students' academic achievement to television watching, leisure time, reading, and homework.* Princeton, NJ: Educational Testing Service.

Webb, E. J., Campbell, D. T., Schwartz, R. D., Sechrest, L., & Grove, J. B. (1981). *Nonreactive measures in the social sciences.* Boston: Houghton Mifflin.

Whelan, J. A. (1965). *An analysis of the effect of systematic homework in two fourth-grade subjects.* Unpublished doctoral dissertation, University of Connecticut.

Wildman, P. R. (1968). Homework pressures. *Peabody Journal of Education, 45*, 202–204.

Wilkinson, S. S. (1980). *The relationship of teacher praise and student achievement: A meta-analysis.* Unpublished doctoral dissertation, University of Florida, Gainsville.

Williams, P. A., Haertel, E. H., Haertel, G. D., & Walberg, H. J. (1982). The impact of leisure-time television on school learning. *American Educational Research Journal, 19*, 19–50.

Willson, V. L., & Putnam, R. R. (1982). A meta-analysis of pretest sensitization effects in experimental design. *American Educational Research Journal, 19*, 249–258.

Winston-Salem Public School. (1985). *California Achievement Test summary for ninth grade.* Winston-Salem, NC: Winston-Salem Public School.

Wolf, R. M. (1979). Achievement in the United States. In H. J. Walberg (Ed.), *Educational environments and effects*. California: McCutcheon.

Young, A., & Kehoe, J. (1982). *Homework policy*. Rochester, NY: Board of Education.

Zajonc, R. B. (1965). Social facilitation. *Science, 149*, 269–274.

Ziebell, D. G. (1968). *A comparative study of the effect of assigned homework for biology students on achievement test results of sophomores in a private school*. Unpublished manuscript, Wisconsin State University in Oshkosh.

Index